Reaching the City

Other Books in the EMS Series

No. 1   *Scripture and Strategy: The Use of the Bible in Postmodern Church and Mission*, David Hesselgrave

No. 2   *Christianity and the Religions: A Biblical Theology of World Religions*, Edward Rommen and Harold Netland

No. 3   *Spiritual Power and Missions: Raising the Issues*, Edward Rommen

No. 4   *Missiology and the Social Sciences: Contributions, Cautions, and the Conclusions*, Edward Rommen and Gary Corwin

No. 5   *The Holy Spirit and Mission Dynamics*, Douglas McConnell

No. 6   *Reaching the Resistant: Barriers and Bridges for Mission*, Dudley Woodberry

No. 7   *Teaching Them Obedience in All Things: Equipping for the 21st Century*, Edgar Elliston

No. 8   *Working Together With God to Shape the New Millennium: Opportunities and Limitations*, Kenneth Mulholland and Gary Corwin

No. 9   *Caring for the Harvest Force in the New Millennium*, Tom Steffen and Douglas Pennoyer

No. 10 *Between Past and Future: Evangelical Mission Entering the Twenty-first Century*, Jonathan Bonk

No. 11 *Christian Witness in Pluralistic Contexts in the Twenty-first Century*, Enoch Wan

No. 12 *The Centrality of Christ in Contemporary Missions*, Mike Barnett and Michael Pocock

No. 13 *Contextualization and Syncretism: Navigating Cultural Currents*, Gailyn Van Rheenen

No. 14 *Business as Mission: From Impoverished to Empowered*, Tom Steffen and Mike Barnett

No. 15 *Missions in Contexts of Violence*, Keith Eitel

No. 16 *Effective Engagement in Short-Term Missions: Doing it Right!* Robert J. Priest

No. 17 *Missions from the Majority World: Progress, Challenges, and Case Studies*, Enoch Wan and Michael Pocock

No. 18 *Serving Jesus with Integrity: Ethics and Accountability in Mission*, Dwight P. Baker and Douglas Hayward

No. 19 *Reflecting God's Glory Together: Diversity in Evangelical Mission*, A. Scott Moreau and Beth Snodderly

About EMS

www.emsweb.org

The Evangelical Missiological Society is a professional organization with more than 450 members comprised of missiologists, mission administrators, teachers, pastors with strategic missiological interests, and students of missiology. EMS exists to advance the cause of world evangelization. We do this through study and evaluation of mission concepts and strategies from a biblical perspective with a view to commending sound mission theory and practice to churches, mission agencies, and schools of missionary training around the world. We hold an annual national conference, and regional meetings are held throughout the United States and Canada.

Evangelical Missiological Society Series
no. 20

Reaching the City
Reflections on Urban Mission
for the Twenty-first Century

Gary Fujino
Timothy R. Sisk
Tereso C. Casiño

Editors

Available at missionbooks.org

Reaching the City: Reflections on Urban Mission for the Twenty-first Century
Copyright © 2012 by Evangelical Missiological Society

All Rights Reserved. No part of this book may be reproduced, stored in a retrieval system, or transmitted in any form or by any means—electronic, mechanical, photocopy, recording, or otherwise—without prior written permission from the publisher, except brief quotations used in connection with reviews in magazines or newspapers. For permission, email permissions@wclbooks.com. For corrections, email editor@wclbooks.com.

Unless otherwise noted, Scriptures are taken from the Holy Bible, New International Version®, NIV®. Copyright © 1973, 1978, 1984, 2011 by Biblica, Inc.™ (Some quotations used are from the 1984 edition of the NIV.) Used by permission of Zondervan. All rights reserved worldwide. www.zondervan.com. The "NIV" and "New International Version" are trademarks registered in the United States Patent and Trademark Office by Biblica, Inc.™

Scripture quotations marked (ESV) are from The Holy Bible, English Standard Version® (ESV)® Copyright © 2001 by Crossway, a publishing ministry of Good News Publishers. All rights reserved. ESV Text Edition: 2007.

Scripture quotations marked (NLT) are from the Holy Bible, New Living Translation copyright © 1996, 2004, 2007 by Tyndale House Foundation. Used by permission of Tyndale House Publishers Inc., Carol Stream, Illinois 60188. All right reserved. New Living, NLT, and the New Living Transla-tion logo are registered trademarks of Tyndale House Publishers.

Scripture quotations marked (KJV) are from the King James Version.

Published by William Carey Publishing (formerly William Carey Library)
10 W. Dry Creek Cir | Littleton, CO 80120 | www.missionbooks.org
William Carey Publishing is a ministry of Frontier Ventures
Pasadena, CA | www.frontierventures.org

Francesca Gacho, editor | Cheryl Warner, copyeditor
Hugh Pindur, interior designer | Mike Riester, cover designer
Rose Lee-Norman, indexer

Printed Worldwide
27 26 25 24 23   2 3 4 5 6   IN
IBSNs: 978-1-64508-496-9 (paperback), 978-0-87808-928-4 (epub)

Library of Congress Cataloging-in-Publication Data

Reaching the city : reflections on urban mission for the twenty-first century / edited by Tereso C. Casiño, Gary Fujino, and Timothy R. Sisk.

  p. cm.
  Includes index.
  ISBN 978-1-64508-496-9

1. City missions. I. Casiño, Tereso C. II. Fujino, Gary. III. Sisk, Timothy R.

BV2653.R43 2012
266.009173'2--dc23   2012023623

Contents

Introduction xi

Contributors xvii

Section 1: Today's Emerging Megacities in Global Perspective

The Strategic Nature of Urban Ministry 1
    Alan McMahan

The Next Frontier: The Implications for Missions of Global Urbanization
in the Twenty-first Century.. 19
    Bob Garrett

Emerging Global Mega-Regions and Globalization:
Missiological Implications 35
    Gary Fujino and John Cheong

Section 2: Historical and Theological Perspectives on the City

Basil of Caesarea: An Early Christian Model of Urban Mission 59
    Edward L. Smither

Jacques Ellul's Contribution to an Evangelical Theology of the City 77
    Stephen Strauss

Section 3: Theological Education and Training for Ministry in Today's Cities

Riots in the City: Replacing Nineteenth-century Urban Training Models
with Relevant "Urbanized" Training Models for the Twenty-first Century....... 97
    Larry W. Caldwell and Enoch Wan

"Let Those in the City Get Out": Making a Way of Escape 119
    Larry Poston

Section 4: Contemporary Case Studies on Today's Cities

Examining Evangelical Concentrations and International Migrations
in the US and Canada: A Call for More and
Better Urban Research 139
    J. D. Payne

Extreme Makeover: Church Addition
(Church Mergers as an Opportunity for Urban Missions) 159
    Derek Chinn

From Niche to Parish: A Qualitative Study of Congregations
Engaging Transitional Neighborhoods 181
    Kathryn Lewis Mowry

Immigrant Communities in America—Objects of Mission or Missional Agents?
The Case of the Church of Pentecost (Ghana) in Urban America 199
    Birgit Herppich

Appropriating Faith within the City:
An Examination of Urban Youth Ministry in Immigrant Churches 219
    Janice A. McLean

A New Day Dawning in the Old Country? Twenty-first-century Urban Trends
in Germany and Their Implications for Urban Church Planting 233
    Stephen Beck

Islam in Urban America:
Developing Strategy to Reach Diaspora Muslims through the Local Church. . . .253
    Mark Hausfeld

Index. 273

Scripture Index 283

Figures

Figure 2.1	Urbanization of the world's more-developed and less-developed societies	25
Figure 2.2	Urbanization of world populations by 2030	26
Figure 3.1	Table showing the relationship between the UN 2007 report and Harvie Conn's waves of urbanization	42
Figure 3.2	Chart showing the accessibilities to hierarchies of scale in globalized networks that transcend space-time	52
Figure 6.1	The Continuum: From "Traditional Missiology" to "Diaspora Missiology" in four aspects	112
Figure 6.2	The Continuum: From "Traditional Missions" to "Diaspora Missions" in two aspects	113
Figure 8.1	Progress of the gospel by people group	145
Figure 8.2	US metropolitan areas of 5 percent or less evangelical	147
Figure 8.3	Selected Canadian metro areas where the evangelical church to population ratio is greater than 1:2000	148
Figure 8.4	Numbers of international migrants in the United States and Canada, 2010	149
Figure 8.5	Top places of origin for international students in the US, 2009–2010	151
Figure 8.6	Refugees and asylum-seekers in the United States and Canada as of 2009 (UNHCR 2009)	151
Figure 8.7	Refugee arrivals in the United States by country of nationality, 2009 (Martin 2009, 3)	152
Figure 8.8	Unreached People Groups in Canada and the United States, Joshua Project, Global Research	153
Figure 10.1	Motivational Themes I: Anxiety themes	190

Figure 10.2	Motivational Themes II: Trusting in Resurrection	191
Figure 10.3	Decision points about acceptable degree of displacement	196
Figure 11.1	Top 20 metropolitan areas in the US, immigrant populations by numbers	205
Figure 11.2	African-born population in the United States (Grieco & Trevelyan 2010)	206
Figure 11.3	African-born in the United States (US Census, ACS 2010)	206
Figure 11.4	Membership of the Church of Pentecost in urban America	209
Figure 11.5	The Church of Pentecost, U.S.A., Inc. membership in 2009	210

Introduction

It was 1987 and the theme verse for the triennial Urbana Student Missions Conference was from Jonah 4:11, "Should I not be concerned about that great city?" Ajith Fernando wonderfully exposited the four chapters of the book of Jonah over four mornings. Billy Graham challenged, "Are you a follower of Jesus Christ?" Helen Roseveare queried whether we had the mind of Christ: "Do the people we meet matter to us as much as they matter to God?" And Tony Campolo gave a rousing charge for students to go overseas as missionaries, to which 14,000 of the more than 18,000 attendees stood in response to this "altar call." Perhaps most significant, however, were the keynote addresses given by Raymond Bakke and Harvie Conn on mission in the city, the theme of Urbana 1987:

> [T]he great mission surge of the past decades is missing one of the greatest migrations in history, the migration of rural peasants to the city. By the year A.D. 2000, the world will have 5,000 cities with a population of one million people or more. This compares with 300 such cities today. Most of the 1.5 billion babies expected to be born in the next 12 to 14 years will grow up as city dwellers. The mission field is moving to the city, and Christians need to respond to the opportunity.[1]

This was perhaps the first large-scale, organized evangelical foray into urban mission. It was also an era when seminal works by Ray Bakke, Harvie Conn, Manuel Ortiz, Roger Greenway, Timothy Monsma, and a host of others were being published as evangelicals began to engage and strategize to reach their cities for Christ.

---

1   See Richard Hertel and Phyllis Hertel, *Missionary Monthly* 95:2, (February 1, 1988), 12.

Fast forward twenty years. The prescience of these great pioneer thinkers has been proven correct. In July of 2007, the United Nations Population Fund reported that more than half of the world's inhabitants of 6.6 billion souls now reside in cities. Thoraya Ahmed Obaid, then Executive Director of the UN Population Fund, urged:

> We must abandon a mindset that resists urbanization and act now to begin a concerted global effort to help cities unleash their potential to spur economic growth and solve social problems. This wave of urbanization is without precedent. The changes are too large and too fast to allow planners and policymakers simply to react: In Africa and Asia, the number of people living in cities increases by approximately 1 million, on average, each week. Leaders need to be proactive and take far-sighted action to fully exploit the opportunities that urbanization offers.[2]

With the world population totaling more than 7 billion in 2012, that global urban resident statistic has increased accordingly, and so has the need to engage the cities of our world. If the former executive director of a United Nations organization senses urgency over the pace of urban growth in our world and how to deal with it, should we not also be concerned as laypersons, pastors, missionaries, educators, and mission executives?

In 2012, *Christianity Today* featured a five-part series on "This Is Our City," how resident urban Christians across the US are seeking to transcend cultural Christianity by serving their cities and local communities. God's admonition to Jonah of his divine concern for the city is being incarnated in his people in urban areas in the United States and across the world as well.

We stand on the shoulders of evangelical giants from the 1970s and 1980s who thought, wrote, and practiced urban mission. Since that time others have stood up and engaged and written on how to reach the city, among them Viv Gregg, John Dawson, Stuart Murray, and Andrew Davey. But there still remains a contemporary paucity of research and writing on how missional urban Christians are engaging their cities around the world today.

---

2 See Noel McKeegan, "Over half the world now live in cities according to UN report," *Gizmag*, http://www.gizmag.com/go/7613/ (accessed May 21, 2012, 23:44); See also The World Bank Group, "More than half the world is now urban, UN report says," *The World Bank,* http://web.worldbank.org/WBSITE/EXTERNAL/NEWS/0,,contentMDK:21405637~pagePK:64257043~piPK:437376~theSitePK:4607,00.html.

This volume seeks, as its goal, to address anew the cry of Jonah 4:11 with new research and new perspectives and strategies to reach our cities for Christ. At the same time, as *this* generation of evangelicals, we rely on the timeless, inspired Word of God, and our contributors explicate and suggest many helpful biblical and theological insights, as well as missiological and practical implications for engaging the twenty-first-century city.

In section one, **Today's Emerging Megacities in Global Perspective**, the authors take a holistic view of "new" cities on the rise at the dawn of a new millennium. *Alan McMahan* begins this section by identifying ten realities and their corresponding opportunities. McMahan establishes that urban ministry offers so much opportunity with efficiency and power to advance the Great Commission and the Great Commandment. The synergy of these realities and opportunities results in a "multiplicational dynamic" that maximizes the potential and strategic nature of urban mission. With the new demographic phenomenon of exponential urbanization, *Bob Garrett* argues that the primary strategy of missions must move its focus from unreached people groups to that of the burgeoning megacities of the world. *Gary Fujino and John Cheong* survey the expansive growth of globalization and mega-regions. Based on their examination of a variety of biblical, historical, demographic, anthropological, and sociological aspects, they conclude with some missiological implications for future urban ministry practitioners and strategists.

Historical and Theological Perspectives on the City are featured in section two, where *Edward Smither* examines the approach to urban ministry by the fourth-century church father, Basil of Caesarea. Basil's strategies and theology are discussed in order to draw possible applications for modern urban ministry practitioners. The sociological and theological insights concerning the city contained in the writings of Jacques Ellul are comprehensive and profound. *Stephen Strauss* summarizes and critiques Ellul's thoughts and reflects on his contribution to a theology of the city for the twenty-first century.

Section three, **Theological Education and Training for Ministry in Today's Cities**, explores the crucial aspect of how we are to raise up the next generation to reach the cities we live in now. *Larry Caldwell and Enoch Wan* attempt to give some preliminary answers to the type of urban ministry training in the twenty-first century, which is relevant to both the Majority World and North American urban settings. Written primarily for seminaries and theological institutions of all sorts, the authors offer practical steps to "urbanizing" course offerings and curricula based on the framework of diaspora missiology. In contrast, *Larry Poston* offers a radical philosophy of "recovery and discipleship" by bringing people out of the cities. The primary purpose is to provide opportunities to certain categories of new Christians from urban areas to live in a "sufficiently distant" place so they can reacquaint and reengage with the "Cultural Mandate" of Genesis 1 and 2.

Finally, a host of helpful case studies coming out of research in both North America and overseas comprises section four, **Contemporary Case Studies on Today's Cities.**

By revealing the scarcity of urban research conducted by evangelicals, *J. D. Payne* opens this section with the challenge that we often know more about unreached people groups on the other side of the world than we do about unreached people groups in North America. His chapter is a call for concentrated and collaborated research by evangelicals of the urban contexts of the United States and Canada. *Derek Chinn* and *Kathryn Mowry* both write about transitional neighborhoods. Chinn focuses on the fresh idea of church mergers as a way to transform and revive a Christian witness in the inner cities of North America through the joining of congregations from different socioeconomic, racial, and age backgrounds. He approaches his study via contemporary case studies and personal, practical experience, focusing on the redemptive and reconciling nature of mergers. Mowry uses ethnographic interviews and participant observation to develop "thick description" to uncover patterns of North American churches in transitional neighborhoods. Using the Church of Pentecost based in Ghana and its exponential growth in the United States, *Birgit Herppich* illustrates how a sizable percentage of diaspora communities should be considered as *coagents* of mission rather than "objects" of missionary work. These communities establish vibrant congregations and serve as effective agents of mission to migrants in North America because of their common struggles, challenges, and experience of marginalization. *Janice McLean* compares church ministries to second generation West Indian youth in two world-class cities, New York and London. McLean focuses on how faith is appropriated by young people in these urban contexts, examining such fundamentals as calling, discipleship, characteristics, and challenges to youth ministry in the city. *Stephen Beck* takes a bird's-eye view of the current urban configuration of Germany's megacities, reviewing key church planting studies on ministry in that country's urban contexts. Beck then shares a recent case study of an urban German church multiplication movement that occurred in one of these megacity regions. Finally, *Mark Hausfeld* argues that a diaspora Muslim in America would have a greater opportunity to accept Christ than while living in his or her home country. Using a missional helix process that the South Asian Friendship Center observes in the West Rogers Park neighborhood in Chicago, Hausfeld demonstrates how theological foundation, historical perspective, and cultural analysis can impact strategic formation that results in a missions outreach among diaspora Muslims in America.

As coeditors for this twentieth edition of the Evangelical Missiological Society monograph series, *Reaching the City: Reflections on Urban Mission for the Twenty-first Century*, it is our hope that the richness and breadth of the papers presented here will inspire and continue to birth a new generation of writers and researchers, strategists and educators, as well as practitioners who will engage and influence mission for our cities today.

A quarter of a century ago after Urbana '87, when Ray Bakke was famously quoted as saying, "While Scripture began in a garden, it ends in a city," the pressing and expanding trend of urbanization on a global level continues to encroach upon this generation of city-dwelling evangelicals. Should we not also be concerned?

Gary Fujino
Timothy R. Sisk
Tereso C. Casiño
Editors

Contributors

Editors

Gary Fujino is the Japanese diaspora strategist for the International Mission Board, SBC. With his wife and four children, they have been urban church planting missionaries in Tokyo, Japan since 1996. Gary is also a visiting professor of world missions at Dallas Theological Seminary.

Timothy R. Sisk is professor and chair of the Department of World Missions at Moody Bible Institute. Previously, he and his wife, Donna, served as missionaries for fourteen years doing church planting and theological education in Japan and Bolivia.

Tereso C. Casiño is professor of missiology and intercultural studies at the School of Divinity of Gardner-Webb University in Boiling Springs, North Carolina, and serves as chair of North America Diaspora Educators' Forum-Global Diaspora Network. He has been involved in training multi-generational leaders from multicultural, intercontinental, and cross-denominational backgrounds for more than two decades.

Authors

Stephen Beck is married to Susan, and together they have four daughters. Stephen planted and pastored churches in the Philadelphia, USA, and Toronto, Canada areas. Currently, he lives in Germany, where he is a professor of practical theology at the Giessen School of Theology and European director of the City Mentoring Program for Church Planters as well as the European Institute for Church Planting & Church Growth. Since 2011, Stephen and a number of his students have been planting a multicultural, multisite, multidenominational church in Frankfurt, Germany, called Mosaik: Kirche für alle Nationen.

Larry W. Caldwell recently completed twenty years teaching missions and Bible interpretation at Asian Theological Seminary in Manila, Philippines. He has now relocated to the USA and is director of missionary training and strategy development for Converge Worldwide (formerly Baptist General Conference), as well as visiting professor of intercultural studies at Sioux Falls Seminary, Sioux Falls, SD. He continues to teach at seminaries worldwide as well as researching and writing on missions.

John Cheong previously served in church planting ministries in Southeast Asia in the 1980s and 1990s and in evangelism of international students and Muslims in the Chicagoland area in the past decade. He is currently a full-time professor of mission and intercultural studies in a Southeast Asian seminary and adjunct professor of intercultural studies at Lincoln Seminary in Illinois.

Derek Chinn is director of the Doctor of Ministry Program and Distance Education at Multnomah Biblical Seminary, Multnomah University. He is also a teaching elder at a multiracial church that formed by merging two congregations together. He and his family make their home in Portland, OR.

Bob Garrett currently holds the Piper Chair of Missions at Dallas Baptist University, where he directs the MA in Global Leadership degree and leads the Global Missions Center. Formerly, he taught missions for ten years at Southwestern Baptist Theological Seminary in Fort Worth, and served for fifteen years as a Baptist missionary in Buenos Aires, Argentina, serving as a theological educator, pastor, cell group ministry coordinator, and denominational leader.

Mark Hausfeld is married to Lynda and has three grown children. He is the international director for Global Initiative: Reaching Muslim Peoples (Assemblies of God World Missions) and associate professor of urban and Islamic studies at the Assemblies of God Theological Seminary. Prior to his present ministry, his family and he served in Central Asia for over fifteen years and before that pastored the church Lynda and he started in the city of Chicago's Southwest Side for ten years.

Birgit Herppich is a doctoral candidate at Fuller School of Intercultural Studies. She worked for eight years in Ghana with WEC International facilitating the establishment of the Children's Ministry Department of the Evangelical Church of Ghana as well as serving in leadership training and as language and cultural adviser for new missionaries. After returning to Germany she has continued working with WEC.

Janice A. McLean is a faculty member of City Seminary of New York and co-director of the Andrew Walls Gallery and Research Center. While at City Seminary, she has overseen the Global New York Church Project, funded by support from the Louisville Institute. Janice is an editor, with Mark Gornik and William Burrows, of *Understanding World Christianity: The Vision and Work of Andrew Walls*.

Alan McMahan is associate professor of intercultural studies at Biola University and serves as the department chair for the undergraduate program. He is also editor of the *Great Commission Research Journal*.

Kathryn Mowry is associate professor of intercultural studies and Christian education at Trevecca Nazarene University in Nashville, TN. Her ministry experiences include pastoral work in multicultural congregations in Los Angeles and pastoral training and church development in Russia.

J. D. Payne serves as the pastor for church multiplication with The Church at Brook Hills in Birmingham, Alabama. Before moving to Birmingham, he served for ten years with the North American Mission Board of the Southern Baptist Convention and as an associate professor of Church Planting and Evangelism in the Billy Graham School of Missions and Evangelism at The Southern Baptist Theological Seminary in Louisville, Kentucky, where he directed the Center for North American Missions and Church Planting.

Larry Poston is chair of the department of religion and professor of religion at Nyack College in Nyack, New York. He and his wife served with Greater Europe Mission and lived for several years in Saffle, Sweden, where Larry taught at the Nordic Bible Institute. He is the author of *Islamic Da'wah in the West: Muslim Missionary Activity and the Dynamics of Conversion to Islam* and *The Changing Face of Islam in America*, as well as numerous articles.

Edward Smither is married to Shawn and together they parent Brennan, Emma, and Eve. Currently a professor of intercultural studies at Columbia International University, he served for fourteen years in intercultural ministry in France, North Africa, and the United States. His books include *Augustine as Mentor* and *Brazilian Evangelical Missions in the Arab World*, and he served as translator of *Early Christianity in North Africa*.

Stephen Strauss lived and ministered for nineteen years in Ethiopia (primarily at the Evangelical Theological College and Ethiopian Graduate School of Theology) and was USA director for SIM (Serving in Mission) for eight years. He is currently the department chair and professor of mission and intercultural studies at Dallas Theological Seminary.

Enoch Wan is a research professor of intercultural studies and director of the Doctor of Missiology Program at Western Seminary. He also serves as president of the Evangelical Missiological Society (EMS) and is the founder/editor of the multilingual electronic journal, *Global Missiology* (www.GlobalMissiology.org).

Section 1: Today's Emerging Megacities in Global Perspective

The Strategic Nature of Urban Ministry

Alan McMahan
alan.mcmahan@biola.edu

White evangelicals in the last half-century have, for the most part, viewed the city with suspicion, distrust, and criticism. Vilified as a cesspool of violence, moral decay, and poverty, the urban center was largely vacated by post-World War II white evangelicals as they fled on the newly constructed superhighways to the relative comfort, security, and homogeneity of the suburbs.

In time, theology complied with this shift, and the white, evangelical worldview either erected justifications for demonizing urban living[1] or simply neglected the city altogether. Seminaries and Bible colleges, looking for less expensive land and more compatible audiences, often followed. Missionaries and pastors were recruited from suburban churches and sent to rural and suburban contexts abroad to work with receptive peoples and newly established churches.

As a result of these trends, the evangelical community has lost a strategic advantage in the worldwide expansion of the church and the mission it carries on. This paper will reflect on the strategic nature of urban ministry for the twenty-first century and issue a call for action. With limited resources and yet an ever-expanding challenge, the evangelical church will do well to consider the convergence of multiple opportunities that make urban ministry a point of high leverage in the task of global evangelization. In the pages that follow, ten strategic realities and the corresponding opportunities for mission will be explored.

---

1 See Jacques Ellul, *The Meaning of the City* (Grand Rapids, MI: William B. Eerdmans Publishing Co., 1970) for an example of this demonization.

Though most of us may quickly dismiss the negative stereotype of the city as described above, perhaps we have thought less about how the city may offer strategic leverage in the years to come. The following ten realities may help us in that regard.

Reality #1:
Cities Are Where the People Are

The year of 2008 marked a turning point in world history. For the first time in human history, more than 50 percent of the world's population lived in cities. The forces that propelled the world's population to achieve this milestone will continue to drive it toward even faster rates of urbanization in the years to come. Between 2007 and 2050 the world's population is expected to increase by 2.5 billion to a total 9.2 billion. All of this growth will be absorbed by the world's urban population, mostly in the undeveloped world. The global urban population is expected to double in size by 2050, adding 3.1 billion to reach a total of 6.4 billion, and accounting for 70 percent of the total number of people on earth.

Clearly, the rapidly expanding mission fields of the future will be centered in urban contexts in the developing world. That is where the people will be en masse. That is where the needs and opportunities will be the greatest. A strategic point of mission investment needs to be focused on these large population groups for whom Christ died. Mission agencies that previously achieved success in evangelizing the remote corners of the earth will need to retool to reach the majority of the people who now live in the crossroads.

Reality #2:
High Density Creates Opportunity

As urbanization continues at an unprecedented rate, cities are not only getting larger, but they are also becoming denser. This rising population density is inevitable as more and more people compete for scarce resources, and entrepreneurs see the opportunity to make more money with high-occupancy buildings. While in 1925 there was only one city whose population exceeded more than 10 million (Chandler 1987) in 2009 there were twenty-five cities with populations higher than that (Brinkoff 2005). By the middle of the twenty-first century, the world's total urban population will be the size of the entire world's population in 2004 ("World Urbanization Prospects" 2008, 3).

With urban compression, several changes take place in the social patterns of the city. Louis Wirth (1938) argued that a large number of people collecting in the same space increases the likelihood that one will encounter a larger number of people of diverse backgrounds. The dissimilarity among these masses of people is displayed as higher variation in racial, cultural, economic, and class types.

Jonathan Freedman (1975) put forth a density-intensity hypothesis arguing that urban compression has the effect of amplifying a person's normal behavioral responses to a particular situation. Negatively a person's dysfunctions may become more intense in an urban context, while positively a person's good qualities may be drawn out more intensely, too. Therefore, lonely people become lonelier, and creative people become more creative, etc.

While Wirth's understanding of urban compression emphasized the negative effects of the city and the power of dissimilarity to divide people and place them in conflict with each other, Claude Fischer (1984) recognized that high-density environments often give rise to a multitude of new groups who emphasize similarity. The critical mass created by urban compression generates groups that may be less based on ethnicity or region of origin and more centered on special interests and personal preferences. Where else could one find a group interested in eighteenth-century Slovakian literature or a society for poisonous snake lovers (Krupat 1985, 55). Given enough people, even the most idiosyncratic of virtues will find a home and a group of people to support it.

The city, therefore, introduces the individual to a host of people unlike us and other groups of people very much like us. The close and frequent encounters with people of other backgrounds and beliefs may challenge the individual to retreat to the safety of the cultural ghetto or seek an affiliation with those who share a common interest. This renegotiation of the social contract can lead to new freedoms and receptivity, as mentioned below.

Urban compression then creates the opportunity to realign affiliations and relationships while increasing the exchange of ideas. These two factors and many others make high-density environments a strategic point of leverage for doing missions where the good news can be proclaimed with greater efficiency and effectiveness in a rapidly shifting world.

Reality #3:
The City Brings Freedom

As described above, the increasing heterogeneity one encounters in a large urban city tends to break down the cohesion of the social unit and erode any consensus around a moral code. Family and village values no longer control behavior; gossip, which is the village version of enforcement, no longer has the power to curb deviance from the norms. Human interaction becomes segmented so that one knows another only in a single context (i.e., just as with the supermarket clerk that you never see anywhere else) rather than as "a whole person" where one's life intersects with another in multiple roles and contexts. High density ensures that these people frequently rub shoulders with each other and adopt patterns of behavior that allow them to cope with "a world of strangers" (Krupat 1985, 50–63).

While negatively these realities can lead to loneliness, exploitation, and despair, positively they can loosen the ties (and the bondage) to traditional ways of thinking and increase the likelihood that these individuals will be freer to consider new ideas. Instead of the pressure to conform to traditionalism, they are now free to consider new ideas and new ways of doing things. Though this threatens to undermine one's faith commitment, more often than not the new freedom that people experience becomes an opportunity of engagement if the gospel can be presented in terms that make sense and meet needs.

Reality #4:
Cities Are Filled with Receptive People

Often it is assumed that the city is a place that is hardened to the gospel and resistant to outside influences. This association may be due to the fact that urbanites are often perceived to be disinterested in or even rude to strangers. In my own ministry experiences in New York and other large cities, I have found this tough exterior to be merely a veneer of disinterest which functions as a protective covering to help shield out the overstimulation typical of the city or to protect against those who would seek to take advantage of others. In most encounters, however, this tough exterior quickly gives way to friendly engagement and a willingness to help if one can establish rapport.

However, being friendly is still quite different from being open to the gospel. Despite our expectations of the urban environment, is it really true that urbanization can induce receptivity?

It has long been recognized that receptivity among people fluctuates widely given a host of environmental and internal conditions. Indeed, the parable of the sower[2] indicates that Jesus himself recognized this fact and instructed his disciples accordingly. Donald McGavran in his magnum opus, Understanding Church Growth, identified a number of factors as early as 1970 that influence the receptivity of people to the gospel and other new ways of thinking. McGavran noticed that new settlements, returning travelers, conquest, nationalism, freedom from control, and acculturation were all associated with an increased level of receptivity (McGavran 1970, 216–227). George Hunter expanded on this list to identify thirteen indicators of receptivity that are important in changing the receptivity of a population toward the gospel (Hunter 1987, 76–89). Several of these factors are especially significant to the urban context. Population mobility, major culture change, and the opportunity to join new groups or make new affiliations that are not "controlled" by traditional culture all work together to create an open attitude toward new things. Likewise, churches that can meet the felt needs of both newcomers and old-timers, or minister to people who are experiencing personal dissatisfaction with themselves or their new context, as well as those who are going through major life transitions that urbanization brings, will often discover receptive people.

Unfortunately, receptivity theory also suggests that people do not remain open or receptive forever. While some people, especially newcomers, may become receptive upon moving to the city, others may become more resistant. Overstimulation from so many competing truth claims can cause some to become more aggressive in shutting out unwanted influences. In these cases, the city produces the opposite effect.

Nevertheless, it is significant that early Christianity grew rapidly in the cities. Paul concentrated his church planting efforts there as he found spiritually hungry people. In the same manner, modern church planting efforts are finding increasing success in meeting the unique needs of urbanites as they look for new meaning and a spiritual home that may not be typical of their roots.

---

2   Matthew 13:1–23; Mark 4:1–20; and Luke 8:1–15.

Reality #5:
The Nations Are Moving to the City

Today there are approximately 200 million international migrants, according to the Population Division of the United Nations ("Migration in an Interconnected World," 2005, 1). This figure is about as large as the population of Brazil, and it is twice as large as it was in 1980. If the migrant population continues to increase at the rate it has in the last five years, by the year 2050, the number of international migrants will be as high as 405 million (Koser and Laczko 2010, 3). Approximately half of these migrants are women, many of whom are traveling independently as heads of households, representing a new trend in migration patterns. Furthermore, the ethnic and cultural diversity of these migrants is higher than ever. As a general pattern, the flow of immigration is from the southern hemisphere to the northern hemisphere and from rural areas to the city.

The United States was the leading migration destination in 2005 with a total of 38 million international migrants (about 20 percent of the worldwide total), followed by Russia with 12 million and Germany with 10 million ("International Migration Report" 2009, xv). From 1995 to 2000 a full 75 percent of the population growth in the US came from migration ("Migration in an Interconnected World" 2005, 85). The disproportionate migration to Western nations is seen in the fact that one out of three international migrants live in Western Europe and one out of four live in North America ("International Migration Report" 2009, 1).

Upon their arrival in the destination country, the vast majority of migrants first live in the city. For many, this will be their home, where they will put down their roots and raise their families. For others, cities represent a place to get their feet under them and adapt to their new world before they move on to a less densely populated area where others from their nationality await. Thus, cities represent "ports of entry" for newcomers. As a point of comparison, Miami represented the city with the most foreign-born of any city in North America with 59 percent, followed by Toronto at 44 percent and Vancouver at 37 percent ("Miami Tops Foreign Born Cities" 2004). New York City is estimated to be home to 170 nationalities that speak approximately 800 languages (Roberts 2010) while Los Angeles is estimated to be home to 140 nationalities speaking 224 different languages (City Basics 2010).

In terms of mission strategy, these population trends are staggering. Clearly, urban contexts offer a way to serve multiple ethnicities and people groups with a level of efficiency not possible anywhere else. From a single location, representatives from the nations of the earth can be engaged with the good news, and given the receptivity factors already discussed, they are likely to be more open to hearing it. Furthermore some Christian workers are finding it easier to participate in all aspects of culture with immigrant peoples in US cities than they would find in the originating cultures of these people. For example, Chris Clayman's efforts in interacting with the people of West Africa were more successful in New York City than they were when he was a missionary in West Africa (Clayman, personal communication, March 17, 2011).

Urban compression combined with geographical relocation and the need for immigrants to build new affiliations and relationships converge to create receptivity to new ideas that is uncommon in many other contexts. While the diversity and pluralism of the city can be difficult for the newcomer to navigate, it nevertheless breaks down traditional ways of thinking and provides opportunity for the gospel witness.

In order to respond to this opportunity, churches, mission agencies, and NGOs will need to retool their efforts in order to make them function well in the relatively unfamiliar multicultural territory of the city. A clear understanding of how to grow both monocultural and multicultural churches will be necessary, recognizing that both types of churches are needed to effectively reach different kinds of people. Monocultural churches offer the fewest number of cultural barriers for newcomers to overcome and therefore may be more tolerated by first-generation immigrants. Multicultural churches, on the other hand, better display the ways the gospel breaks down cultural barriers to create a new oneness in Christ and may provide a more attractive environment for second-generation, bicultural young people.

Reality #6:
The City Is Going to the World

Typically, it is believed that migration is a one-way road as people move from less developed, less safe, and less prosperous areas to arrive in "a land of opportunity" where they can improve their standard of living, the prospects for their children, and their future. Especially given the difficulty of legal migration and the costs and inherent dangers of illegal crossings (i.e., exploitation by unscrupulous smugglers, arrest by law enforcement agents, or physical dangers), it is commonly assumed that migration is a one-time act. The reality is much different.

Migrants often cross back and forth across national boundaries several times in their lifetime. So common is the pattern that some sociologists prefer to use the term "human mobility" as opposed to "migration," which implies a more static movement in one direction. Other terms include "repatriation" and "circular migration" to describe the phenomenon of returning to the homeland on multiple trips. Of course, some migrants cross borders for seasonal work, international trade (legal and illegal), health care reasons, or just to keep up social relationships with friends and family. In these cases, they may not intend to stay long term in the destination country but only as it meets a temporary need.

Even for those who do intend to stay long term in the destination country, contact with the homeland is rarely lost. This truth is well illustrated on any trip into an urban immigrant community where one can observe a host of businesses that cater to helping immigrants make phone calls to the home country, wire money, or obtain the "proper" papers to get a driver's license or government benefits. Most intend to eventually bring other family members or friends to the new destination, while many intend to return back home to retire on their newly acquired wealth. In one study it was discovered that 68 percent of migrants arriving in the city had someone waiting to meet them; 96 percent of all housing help was from these individuals, not churches or government agencies (Choldin 1973, 167–168) the strong dependence on the primary group (usually extended family members) correlates to the inactivity of formal organizations such as churches in helping new migrants adjust to life in the city. The family serves a protective function for new migrants to an area—a form of social insurance and a smoother adaptation during the transitional phase of adjustment.

It is across these social networks that span international boundaries that ideas and resources flow. One of the most obvious of these commodities is money. In 2004, the official migrant remittances amounted to $226 billion, of which $145 billion went to developing countries in aid of extended family members and community development projects (International Migration Report 2006, xv). In our own research of Mixtecas (immigrants from the southernmost provinces of Mexico) in New York, we discovered that while many worked in the lowest paying jobs at less than half the minimum wage, they nevertheless were faithful in sending money home. The money they sent back was invested in village improvement projects, such as putting lights on a soccer field or putting in an Internet café. In doing so, their status went up in the local community, and they were frequently consulted for all manner of decisions. As they were able, they would return home from time to time and eventually seek to bring back a fianceé or spouse in order to start a family in the newly adopted country.

These international migration streams and the social networks they maintain serve as conduits to exchange knowledge, skills, and ideas as well as resources. While these networks may function as agents of globalization, they also often function as a means by which the gospel gets disseminated. This phenomenon is certainly not new as there are frequent examples of how refugees, exiles, and sojourners in the Old and New Testaments served often unwittingly as bearers of the good news. In fact, one could make the case that more success is achieved in global evangelization through the natural processes of migration than through all the purposeful efforts of mission agencies.

Churches and mission agencies could respond to this opportunity in two very helpful ways. First, there is a great need to link arms with immigrant churches and the communities they serve to meet the needs of newcomers by welcoming them and aiding them in their adjustment. Certainly the biblical support for taking care of the stranger and alien is abundant, as Israel was repeatedly reminded of its obligation to the nations. Secondly, all efforts should be made to equip and empower these migrants to take the gospel back to their homeland. The gospel, when communicated in this fashion, does not typically encounter the barriers common to ministries done by expatriates because it comes through a trusted source. Local Christian agencies in the home country could then be engaged to provide nurture and follow-up for converts as they come to faith. In this way the urban church extends its impact globally through those that they serve.

Reality #7:
The City as the Engine of Culture

For a long time, it has been recognized that trends and fashions seem to begin in the city and travel outward. Cities are the generators and communicators of new ways of doing things and new fads. However, Tim Keller, the successful pastor of Redeemer Presbyterian Church in New York City, takes this concept much further. Arguing out of a theology of the city, Keller declares that cities are part of God's plan and are God's invention to draw out the resources of creation and thus to build civilization (Keller 2002). This function goes beyond the temporal world, but it also describes the heavenly future and is part of God's purpose for humanity. As such, city building functions as a mandate or an ordinance on a par with marriage and work and is not simply a product of human effort or a sociological phenomenon.

According to Keller, cities function not only to provide refuge from the wilderness and give shelter to the weak, but they also function as cultural mining or development centers and as places to meet God (Keller 2002). Building off the insights described earlier by Wirth, Freedman, and Fischer, Keller argues that the city produces both diversity and a culture-forming intensity that uniquely work together to function as an engine of culture.

Clearly, high population density serves to accelerate and animate the exchange of ideas and skills from one group to another and to prevent the loss of new innovations (University College London 2009). Researchers found that complex skills passed from generation to generation could only be maintained when a critical level of interaction was maintained by shrinking the distance the communication has to travel; thus, when the frequency of "collisions" intensifies between one's world and that of his or her neighbor, the likelihood of knowledge exchange increases. The result is "a cultural explosion" that results in innovation and energy being produced as a by-product.

Cities then take these cultural products and magnify and broadcast them over a wide region. The bigger the city is, the more power it has to promote its ideas and styles and disseminate them throughout large population groups. Los Angeles, for example, is not only considered the fifth most powerful and influential city in the world (after only New York in the United States) (Revealed: Cities that Rule, 2010), but it is also considered to be the "Creative Capital of the World" where one out of six residents work in the creative arts industry (Otis College of Art and Design 2009, 1, 28). Other cities around the world are known for some other major talent, influence, or product. Throughout the regions in which they are located, as well as the world at large, these cities cast a long shadow of influence. He who rules the city, rules the world.

Reality #8:
The City at the Crossroads

As most air travelers know, to get to virtually anywhere on earth, you must travel through certain hub cities to change planes or pick up alternative forms of ground transportation. What is true for air travel is also true of freeway travel, railroad, shipping, communications, and even social mobility. By magnetically drawing resources to themselves, transforming them into new products, and then sending them back out to broader populations, they create intersections of people, ideas, and commodities. Like giant supercolliders, they smash particles together, releasing energy, innovation, and power.

Consider for a moment the claim by some that New York is the world's capital. New York is the home of the seven largest media conglomerates in the world; 78 cable networks; more Fortune 500 company headquarters than any other city; 6 of the top 10 consumer magazines; 6 international wire services; more museums, ballet, opera, and theater companies than any other city; 200 foreign language newspaper publishers; and over 100 foreign language media bureaus. The metropolis is also served by 3 major international airports, rail lines, highway systems, shipping ports, and communication hubs (NYC Latin Media and Entertainment Commission 2010).

In 2010, the journal *Foreign Policy*, in conjunction with the management consulting firm of A. T. Kearney and the Chicago Council on Global Affairs, ranked the most powerful, interconnected cities by measuring their cumulative scores in economics, politics, cultural, and infrastructure characteristics. Publishing their report as the "Global Cities Index," they list New York as number one, followed by London, Tokyo, Paris, Hong Kong, Chicago, Los Angeles, Singapore, Sydney, and Seoul in that order (Foreign Policy "Global Cities Index" 2010). To achieve top rankings, cities not only had to be large, but they also had to project power across their own borders to influence and integrate with global markets, human capital, and political realities.

This confluence of power, ideas, and economic might is measured by the "size of its capital markets, the flow of goods through its airports and ports, as well as other factors such as the number of embassies, think tanks, political organizations, and museums" (Foreign Policy, "Metropolis Now" 2010). Just as "all roads lead to Rome," certainly it is in the city that political power, influence, financial power, communications resources, transportation, fashion, and trade all converge to create a synergistic mix of influence like nowhere else on earth.

As strategic centers of regions and nations, cities then become high points of leverage to extend influence over vast areas. Evangelism and church planting efforts can be naturally buoyed by these rivers of communication that will produce fruit in faraway places.

Reality #9:
The City as a Place for Meeting Human Need

When many people think of the city, the images conjured up are negative. Urban poverty, visible as inner city slums, environmental problems, unregulated growth, social deviancy, crime, and exploitation, all stand out as prominent problems indicative of the worst of the human experience. The pristine beauty of the wilderness is by contrast esteemed, and the romanticized ideal of the noble savage is used to represent mankind as uncorrupted by modernism and urbanization.

Yet the reality is that as the world's population expands, cities play an increasingly vital role to sustain economic growth, reduce the negative impact on the environment, address the causes for poverty, and create long-term sustainability. As George Martine, et. al states:

> Urban development is essential—if not in itself sufficient—for economic and social development. No country has ever achieved significant economic growth in the modern age by retaining its population in rural areas. Most increments in national economic activity already take place in urban areas. These cities and towns account for a growing share of economic production because of their advantages in terms of proximity, concentration, and scale. In the context of globalized economic competition, these advantages can be heightened. Proximity and concentration make it easier and cheaper for cities to provide their citizens with basic social services, infrastructure, and amenities. The higher intensity of economic activity in cities can foster employment and income growth, the starting points for social welfare. (Martine, et al. 2008)

Proximity, efficiency, competition, and scale may all be features of the economic and social architecture of the city that helps meet human need. Yet it is especially in the city that the church has a unique role to play. As if it were on stage, the church's response to human need in the city is on display for the world to see. Indeed, "in most societies, the church's service and compassionate ministries provide the credibility for its message. Most people do not find believable, or worth considering, the message of the church that, as far as they know, 'just preaches'" (Hunter 1987,

133). Certain parts of the gospel message are better understood through the church's service than through proclamation.

Historically, urban ministries focused on meeting the needs of people have been part of the church's legacy. A. B. Simpson, founder of the Christian and Missionary Alliance in the early twentieth century, established soup kitchens, homes for unwed mothers, ministries to new immigrants, and other social services that connected the church's compassion ministries to the evangelistic preaching for which he was so passionate. John Wesley's ministries included setting up funds for poor people, homes for aged and infirmed widows, a school for poor children at Kingswood near Bristol, hospital visitation teams, micro-loan financing, and so on in order to serve people holistically (Hunter 1987, 132). Indeed, throughout the history of the church around the world, service to the marginalized, dispossessed, and poor accompanied the work of evangelism.

Cities remain a strategic point of engagement to meet needs and, in so doing, locate those who are receptive to the gospel of grace and hope. Such ministries easily cross cultural and social barriers and add credibility to the church's message.

Reality #10:
The City as the Place for Reinvention

The nine realities covered so far speak of opportunities the city affords for proclaiming the gospel in ways that are strategic and influential. However, this last reality perhaps speaks more to our own need rather than to that of the needs of others. In fact, it might be true that the evangelical church needs the city as much as the city needs us.

Many scholars now agree that white evangelical theology in the US over the last fifty years has become more suited for rural or suburban living than urban. It now finds itself ill equipped to handle the complexity and sophistication that urban contexts invariably present. A traditional faith that grows out of homogeneous village and family values has difficulty confronting the pluralism and diversity of the city. Beliefs once taken for granted are now tested with competing truth claims with the unfortunate result that many Christians either fall away from the faith or retreat back into the safety of an insular community. Moreover, a rural faith often lacks a doctrinal orientation that insists the church work beyond its own walls to serve the community at large. Roger Greenway in his book, *Discipling the City*, comments,

> Rural religion tends to present the gospel in terms that leave vast areas of human life untouched and unchallenged. Strange as it may seem, this weakness has been reinforced by countless city pulpits, especially in conservative church circles where rural attitudes continue to dominate urban congregations and popular pulpiteers keep their members socially tranquilized through rural-oriented preaching and teaching. As a consequence, one of the greatest weaknesses of some large city churches is that, so far as social consciousness is concerned, they are still living in their rural past. (Greenway 1997, 43)

The problem is further exacerbated by the fact that few pastors receive training in seminary to deal with urban complexities. They are not equipped with the tools to properly exegete the context nor handle pluralistic challenges. An evangelical reluctance to engage in the city emerges from a Greek-mindedness,[3] class captivity, professionalization of the priesthood, a self-defense posture, and a misunderstood mandate that leaves out compassion ministries (Ellison 1997, 97–102). The result of these orientations is that the white evangelical church is incapacitated in carrying out its mission in the urban places of our world and, as a result, is in danger of being left behind.

To counter these trends, the white evangelical church needs to assume a new learning posture and see the city as a mission field that can teach them something vital about themselves. Clearly the history of missions shows that in the act of reaching out beyond the walls of the church to serve the lost and the marginalized, there is healing and health that comes to those who serve. Perspectives are renewed, energies are quickened, and an anesthetized faith reawakens to the joy of new life. It is in this context that new religious awakenings are born that have the power to sweep through the world. Indeed, the church needs the city as much or more than the city needs the church.

Synergy and Multiplication

Any one of the previous ten realities should provide enough reason to consider the city a strategic place from which to advance the Great Commission and the Great

---

[3] Greek-mindedness means that the good news is considered to be one-dimensional, addressing the needs of the soul without addressing the physical and practical needs of the body.

Commandment. Few ministry contexts afford so much opportunity to impact the world for Christ with an efficiency and a power as that of urban ministry.

The ultimate truth, of course, is that each of these realities is connected to the others to augment and further amplify their effect. The result is a dynamic of multiplication that further intensifies the opportunity and strategic nature of urban mission. Generating a kind of synergy among them, they build upon themselves to create a high point of leverage from which one could move the world. May God give us the humility and courage to leave our comfort zones to once again enter the world of challenge and unpredictability, and through that be changed ourselves.

References

BBC News. (2004, July 15). Miami tops foreign born cities. Retrieved from http://news.bbc.co.uk/2/hi/americas/3898795.stm.

Brinkhoff, T. (2005, October 1). The principal agglomerations of the world. Retrieved from http://www.citypopulation.de.

Chandler, T. (1987). *Four thousand years of urban growth: An historical census.* Lewistown, NY: St. David's University Press.

Choldin, H. M. (1973). Kinship networks in the migration process. *International Migration Review* 7 (22), 163–75.

City Basics. (2010, April 13). Retrieved from http://www.lacity.org/index.htm#

Clayman, Chris. (2011, March 17). Personal correspondence.

CNN. (2010, April 10). "Revealed: Cities that Rule the World." CNN. Retrieved from http://www.cnn.com/2010/BUSINESS/04/10/cities.dominate.world/index.html.

Ellison, C. (1997). Addressing felt needs of urban dwellers. In H. M. Conn (Ed.), *Planting and growing urban churches: From dream to reality* (94–110). Grand Rapids, MI: Baker Book House.

Ellul, J. (1970). *The meaning of the city.* Grand Rapids, MI: William B. Eerdmans Publishing Company.

Fischer, C. (1984). *The urban experience* (2nd ed.). New York: Harcourt Brace Jovanovich.

Freedman, J. L. (1975). *Crowding and behaviour.* San Francisco, CA: W. H. Freeman and Company.

Greenway, R. S. (Ed.). (1997). *Discipling the city: A comprehensive approach to urban ministry.* Grand Rapids: Baker Book House.

Foreign Policy. (n.d.). The Global cities index 2010. *Foreign Policy.* Retrieved from http://www.foreignpolicy.com/node/373401.

_____. (2010, August 11). Metropolis now: Images of the world's top global cities." *Foreign Policy.* Retrieved from http://www.foreignpolicy.com/articles/2010/08/11/the_global_cities_index_2010.

Hunter, G. G., III. (1987). *To spread the power: Church growth in the Wesleyan spirit.* Nashville: Abingdon Press.

Keller, T. (2002, July). A biblical theology of the city." *Evangelicals Now.* Retrieved from http://www.e-n.org.uk/p-1869-A-biblical-theology-of-the-city.htm.

Koser, K,. & Laczko, F. (Eds.). (2010). International Organization for Migration. The future of migration: Building capacities for change. World Migration Report 2010. Geneva, Switzerland. Retrieved from http://www.jcp.ge/iom/pdf/WMR_2010_ENGLISH.pdf.

Krupat, E. (1985). *People in cities: The urban environment and its effects.* New York: Cambridge University Press.

Martine, G., McGranahan, G., Montgomery, M. & Fernandez-Castilla, R. (Eds.). (2008). *The new global frontier: Urbanization, poverty and environment in the 21st century.* London: Earthscan.

McGavran, D. (1970). *Understanding church growth.* Grand Rapids, MI: William B. Eerdmans Publishing Company.

NYC Latin Media and Entertainment Commission. "About New York City." Retrieved from http://www.nyc.gov/html/lmec/html/about/nycapital.shtml.

Otis College of Art and Design. (2009, November). Report on the Creative Economy of the Los Angeles Region. Retrieved from http://www.otis.edu/creative_economy/download/2009_Creative_Economy_Report.pdf.

Roberts, S. (2010, April 28). Listening to (and saving) the world's languages. *The New York Times.* Retrieved from http://www.nytimes.com/2010/04/29/nyregion/2910st.html?pagewanted=all.

The Global Commission on International Migration. (2005). "Migration in an Interconnected World: New Directions for Action." Report of the Global Commission on International Migration. Switzerland: SRO-Kundig, 2005. Retrieved from http://www.queensu.ca/samp/migrationresources/reports/gcim-complete-report-2005.pdf.

United Nations, Department of Economic and Social Affairs. (2009). International migration report 2006: A global assessment. Retrieved from http://www.un.org/esa/population/publications/2006_MigrationRep/report.htm.

United Nations, World Urbanization Prospects, 2007 revision. Department of Economic and Social Affairs. Retrieved from http://www.un.org/esa/population/publications/wup2007/2007WUP_Highlights_web.pdf.

University College London. (2009, June 4). High population density triggers cultural explosions. *ScienceDaily*. Retrieved from http://www.sciencedaily.com/releases/2009/06/090604144324.htm.

Wirth, L. (1938). Urbanism as a way of life. *American Journal of Sociology* 44, 1–24.

The Next Frontier: The Implications for Missions of Global Urbanization in the Twenty-first Century

Bob Garrett
bobg@dbu.edu

The New Macedonia for the twenty-first century must shift from the focus on unreached people groups that characterized the last twenty-five years of the twentieth century. Global demography defines the unprecedented urbanization in Asia as a new frontier for missions. While the challenge to reach the unreached peoples of the world has yet to be completed and must still play a role in strategic priorities, the Unreached People Groups (UPG) emphasis can legitimately today be replaced with a new priority. The fact that burgeoning mega-cities and new metropolises are popping up like mushrooms in underdeveloped nations constitutes an emerging next frontier that should rank as the top priority for deploying new missionaries and crafting strategies for sending agencies. These rapidly growing cities are primarily among unreached populations. These populations are in transition from rural to urban, and so they are open to the gospel since they are redefining so many aspects of their lifestyle and worldview. Therefore, these new urban centers are potentially a harvest field—and if there is a rapid enough response of missionaries who get in on the ground floor as these new cities are growing, the coming years could see one of the greatest movements of people coming to Christ in all of history.

Frontier Missions Today

In 1974 at the Lausanne Congress on World Evangelization, Ralph Winter read a paper called "The New Macedonia" (Winter 1999). In that watershed essay Dr. Winter suggested a new way of looking at the unfinished task of world evangelization. His argument was that missionaries and all Western Christians were too bound to the twentieth-century concept of "nationalism" which had defined the nation-state as a fundamental entity in establishing identity, government, and culture. In the nineteenth and twentieth centuries the maps of missions organizations analyzed progress by how many of these countries they could enter. Winter suggested that in the New Testament the Greek word *ethnos* meant a people group bound together by a common language, kinship structures, habits and customs, and worldview, and that identity in this ethnolinguistic group was determinative for the identity of its members whether they shared citizenship in the same nation-state or not. While there are a few references in the New Testament where *ethnos* can very well refer to the machinery of government, Winter's point is well-taken. In fact, in the majority of New Testament contexts *ethnos* seems to refer to a group sense of identity as found in families, clans, villages, and cities. There is no reason to read modern concepts of nation-state back into the biblical text.

Ralph Winter's insight was influenced by his experience in Guatemala, where he worked with mountain people whose aboriginal tongue and customs were quite different from the Spanish-speaking neighbors he worked with in the barrios of Guatemala City. So Winter considers his gospel conversations with Peace Corps workers from the US to be "E1 evangelism" to near neighbors, and his preaching in Spanish in the barrio churches to be "E2 evangelism" across greater cultural/linguistic distance. The trips to the highlands speaking about Christ through interpreters that the tribal peoples called blancos was "E3 evangelism" because the culture and language were remote.

Ralph Winter's insight into the predominant role of ethnicity in forging identity turned out to be prophetic for the last decades of the twentieth century. His focus on ethnolinguistic people groups prepared mission agencies for the realities of life after the Cold War. After the Berlin Wall fell in 1989, it suddenly became clear that the Soviet Union, which had appeared so ideologically monolithic before that President Ronald Reagan could dub it an "evil empire," had always been a patchwork quilt of rival ethnicities and peoples. The people group focus prepared evangelical missionaries to understand and engage these distinct peoples.

The simple concept that the focal point of all missionary efforts should be the people group, and that there needed to be a Bible, believers, and churches in every people group on earth, gave rise to statistics carefully collected in shared databases among missions agencies and the published representation of them in David Barrett's *World Christian Encyclopedia* (Barrett 2000). Also, the missionary fervor associated with the end of the millennium leading up to year 2000 spawned many groups who proposed to "win the world for Christ before the year 2000" (Barrett 1988). The concept of people groups provided the metrics for measuring progress, spawning the concept by Luis Bush of a 10/40 window. This has meant a significant shift in how and where missionaries are deployed and how they perceive their roles in coordinating strategies for gospel engagement of the unreached.

Without any doubt what Winter called a New Macedonia in 1974 has become missiological orthodoxy for the evangelical missionary force in 2011. The deliberations at the 2010 Lausanne Conference at Cape Town continued to reflect this focus. It remains to be said that the present author affirms the people group orientation as an indispensable tool for developing missionary strategy. A compelling case can be made that unreached peoples are "the mission field of the mission field." It is heartening to see that a chorus of voices has been raised recently that makes "gospel access" the watchword of determining strategic priorities. It is not just a matter of how many lost people there are in the world and where, but now we can measure who has and does not have access to hear the gospel. This concern is a reflection of the priorities of Paul in Romans 15:21 as he explains to the Roman church why in a region where there were new, developing, and only partly formed churches in the capital cities he could say that he "had no more room" and needed to go on to Spain where people had never once had a chance to hear. Providing access to the gospel to all peoples was a primary motivator for the Apostle Paul, and should continue to shape missions strategy today.

Perhaps a new emphasis on the demographic reality of urban growth need not be seen in conflict with the consensus among missiologists that unreached peoples represent a legitimate priority. The regions in which the growth of cities is most pronounced happen to coincide with the least reached areas of the 10/40 window. Therefore, we have seen in the last decades and will see in the coming decades a stunning growth of city populations among people groups who are largely non-Christian and untouched by the gospel.

Other Older Frontiers

The orientation toward ethnolinguistic peoples was not the first paradigm shift among missiologists. Without reviewing here the basic historical paradigms suggested by David Bosch (1991), it is helpful to see that historically time and again there have been key figures who have received from God a burden for those from "regions beyond." These intrepid missionary pioneers were those who "boldly go where no one has gone before." In the modern missionary movement, William Carey looked at the spiritual void in India and called fellow Christians to join him in his calling to "expect great things from God, attempt great things for God." Soon after in Africa, explorer David Livingstone traveled the length of the Zambezi River and discovered the realities of Central Africa. He described what others had called "the dark continent" to church audiences, proclaiming, "I have seen the smoke from the campfires of a thousand villages where the name of Christ has never been proclaimed" (Livingstone 1857). In China, Hudson Taylor stirred the more traditional missionaries, who stayed in compounds living in port cities on the coast, by the audacious suggestion that they could venture inland. Formerly it had only been possible for people of financial "means" to become missionaries, but Taylor succeeded in recruiting an army of middle-class Englishmen to do the job, founded the China Inland Mission, and initiated the "faith missions" movement. Many other examples of those who saw a "next frontier" could be named. The point is that whenever God's people engage in fulfilling the Great Commission they are always on the march, and the changing social and cultural realities of our world set a moving target for the efforts of missionary strategies.

The fact that another frontier can be seen on the horizon should not be taken to imply that the existing understanding of ethnolinguistic dynamics in isolating people groups and doing population segmentation are somehow no longer necessary. Now more than ever! However, it is necessary to post a lookout on the horizon for what God is bringing into his world in our time as the next big challenge.

The rapid growth in global population is redefining the task of world evangelization. The United Nations Population Division (March 2007) reports: "the world population will likely increase by 2.5 billion over the next forty-three years, passing from the current 6.7 billion to 9.2 billion in 2050. This increase is equivalent to the total size of the world population in 1950, and it will be absorbed mostly by the less developed regions, whose population is projected to rise from 5.4 billion in 2007 to 7.9 billion in 2050." Former CIA Director Michael Hayden declared that the most worrying trend is no longer terrorism, but demography, stating: "Today there are 6.7 billion people sharing the planet. By mid-century, the best estimates point to a world population of more than 9 billion. That's a 40–45 percent increase—striking enough—but most of that growth is almost certain to occur in countries that are least able to sustain it" (Friedman 2008, 29).

A Significant New Thing: Immigration Patterns

In reality, even those who are staunchly committed to identifying the lost by their ethnolinguistic identity are recognizing that one of the great ways to "engage" the groups within their own heartland is to start with immigrants who are living elsewhere, and while making adjustments to living in a new setting, may be more open to the gospel. As these immigrants living elsewhere convert, some of them will be excellent recruits to return to their homeland to share their newfound faith in Christ with their extended families and friends back home. More human beings have migrated from one place to another during our lifetime than in any other segment in history, a reality that has been discussed in other forums. A "diaspora missiology" looks at the patterns of dispersions of people groups and sees new opportunities to foster gospel witness along the relationship lines that bind displaced individuals with family and friends back in their homeland (Wan 2011). Rather than offering a different strategy, a diaspora missiology, which focuses on immigrant populations, complements a UPG focus, and has been subsumed as an essential part of developing a strategy for unreached peoples. In a way, it could be called the "almost next thing." There is at least one agency that is asking missionary personnel who newly engage an unreached people to incorporate a strategy to identify and to address the needs of significant immigrant populations who live far from their homeland, but who still identify with it and practice its culture in tiny colonies wherever they happen to live. Those from unreached peoples who live in more accessible places are prime candidates for evangelism. Once reached, they can then be discipled with reproducible methods so that they can carry the gospel back to their homeland. By some measures, learning to evangelize immigrants would deserve to be considered the next frontier, but at least in the missionary community this emphasis seems to have been readily incorporated into ongoing strategies. Certainly helping immigrants requires the same kind of population segmentation that is done when engaging these same populations in their home setting. Immigrant populations should be studied to construct a worldview understanding from ethnographic research, just as in working with their homeland counterparts.

The Next Frontier: Burgeoning Cities

In the USA, the movement toward rapid urbanization happened about a century ago. This movement of people from the countryside to the cities in the early 1900s brought farm boys streaming into the cities to look for work in the factories. The dislocation and adaptations required by city life made the newcomers open to new evangelistic strategies such as the YMCA and the Salvation Army. However, in the USA today the demographic movement is back toward the countryside as city dwellers and workers endure long commutes just so they can go to bed where they hear cows mooing at night.

In 1986 David Barrett published a study of the exponential growth in urbanization in the developing world (Barrett 1986). The global growth trends he described in some ways mimicked the urbanization pattern in the USA some one hundred years ago. However, the rapid growth of cities in Asia is beyond anything that humanity has ever seen before. Barrett's statistics projected that by the year 2010 there would be more urban dwellers than those living out in the countryside. In fact, he predicted that if current trends persist, by the year 2025 fully 76 percent of the global population will live in a city. His statistics make a telling point: as the cities go, so goes the world!

In China especially, but all across Central Asia and the Middle East, the rapid development of societies in transition, from rural peasants to factory and knowledge workers in the cities, has unleashed a population tsunami whose consequences will be far greater than most of us can imagine. At the dawn of what can be called "the urban millennium," city life is defining lifestyles for an ever-increasing percentage of humanity.

> In 2008, the world reaches an invisible but momentous milestone: For the first time in history, more than half its human population, 3.3 billion people, will be living in urban areas. By 2030, this is

expected to swell to almost 5 billion. Many of the new urbanites will be poor. Their future, the future of cities in developing countries, the future of humanity itself, all depend very much on decisions made now in preparation for this growth. (United Nations Population Fund)

While the world's urban population grew very rapidly (from 220 million to 2.8 billion) over the twentieth century, the next few decades will see an unprecedented scale of urban growth in the developing world. This will be particularly notable in Africa and Asia where the urban population will double between 2000 and 2030—that is, the accumulated urban growth of these two regions during the whole span of history will be duplicated in a single generation. By 2030, the towns and cities of the developing world will make up 81 percent of urban humanity (State of World Population 2007).

The following charts on global demography show the recent growth in urbanization in the developing world:

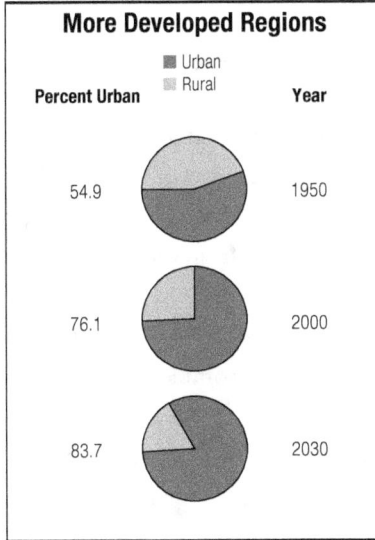 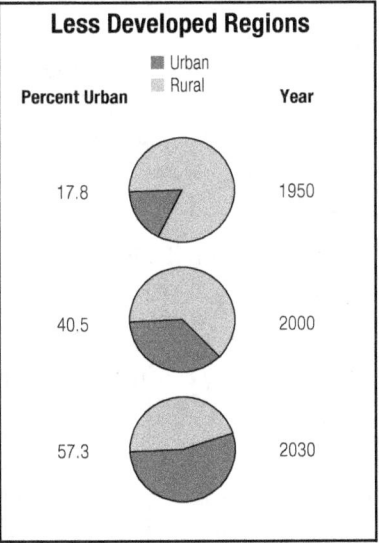

Figure 2.1 Urbanization of the world's more-developed and less-developed societies

Notice that at mid-century only 17.8% of the population of Third World societies lived in cities, but in the fifty years since 1950 that percentage has increased to over

40%. By the year 2030, almost 60% of Third World populations will live in cities. In just a few years the world will become predominantly urban—about eighty to eighty-five years after that happened in the United States.

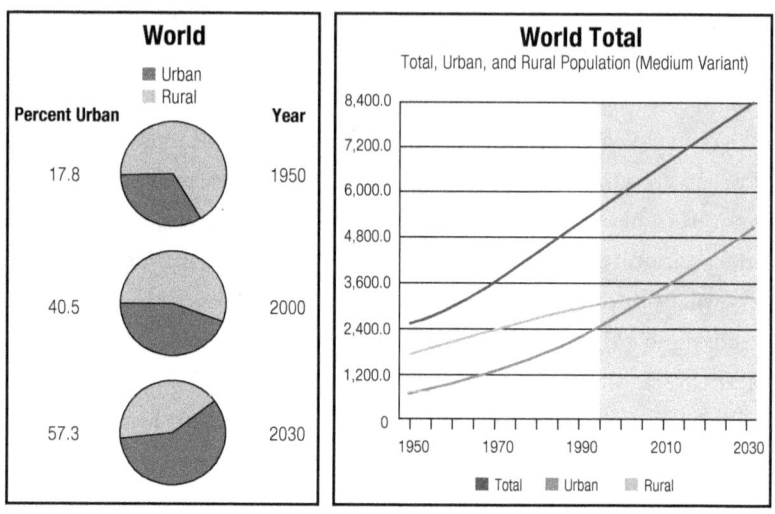

Figure 2.2 Urbanization of world populations by 2030

There is no better example of this than China in recent decades, where a remarkable rate of economic growth has been accompanied by a process of urbanization that is unprecedented in human history, both in scale and in speed. The proportion of the Chinese population living in urban areas increased from only 20% in 1980 to 27% in 1990, and reached 43% in 2005 (World Bank 2006). By the middle of this century, the country's urbanization rate has been forecast to reach 75% (Yusuf and Saich 2008). In the space of just a few decades, China will complete the urbanization process that lasted hundreds of years in the West.

The article "Urbanization in China in the 1990's" by Kim Wing Chan and Ying Hu points out that between the 1990 and 2000 census, the growth in urbanization far exceeded expectations. The census showed that China had reached 455.94 million or 36.09% of the total population, rather than the 30.89% that had been projected (Chan and Hu 2003).

In his most recent book, *Hot, Flat, and Crowded*, Thomas Friedman explains that there are over one hundred cities in China that have about 500,000 inhabitants today (small by Chinese standards), but that will have over 5 million within the next ten years (Friedman 2008). A missionary friend, who is an accomplished "China hand," commented that there is nothing exaggerated about this claim. In fact, he said, "You can go to the train station in any of these small cities at any time of day and on any day of the week to watch the trains coming in and going out. The trains come into the cities loaded to overflowing with passengers, but they return to the rural areas with less than one-third of capacity. It's almost eerie to think about. How do you put that many new people into your city every day?"

The McKinsey Global Institute released the most recent of its reports tracking the rapid growth of global urbanization in March 2011 (Dobbs et al. 2011). Their report declares: "The world is in the throes of a sweeping population shift from the countryside to the city. The global urban population is growing by 65 million annually, equivalent to adding seven new cities the size of Chicago a year. And for the first time in history, more than half of the world's population is now living in towns and cities." While the report is designed to assist corporate managers and economists who would strategically position business models to capture markets in this incredibly rapid urban growth, the information is equally relevant to crafters of missiological strategies. How can we prepare strategies for China's urban billion? In a study of the largest and wealthiest 600 cities in the world, 1.5 billion live in these cities today, but by 2025, 2 billion will live in them. Currently these 600 largest cities alone generated $30 trillion in GDP in 2007 (the McKinsey database tracks over 2,000 of the larger cities), but GDP from the top cities will more than double by 2025 to $64 trillion, which will represent 60 percent of the global GDP.

Most of us have an obsolete view of global demographics, and the pace of change is so dizzying that it will be hard to wrap our minds around demographic realities that no longer belong to futurologists. The McKinsey Report calls the rapid growth in urban population a "white space" in our global understanding. It says: "We live in an urban world. Half of the world's population already lives in cities, generating more than 80% of global GDP today." Furthermore we can anticipate that in the next fifteen years "the makeup of the group of the top 600 cities will change as the center of gravity of the urban world shifts south, and even more decisively, east. … By 2025, we expect 136 new cities to enter the top 600, all of them from the developing world and overwhelmingly (100 new cities) from China." In fact, "we expect the 216 Chinese cities in the top 600 cities of the world to contribute 30% of global growth between 2007 and 2025."

One unexpected factor in the McKinsey findings is that the largest growth will not be in the largest cities, but in numerous "middleweight" cities that presently are over 100,000 but will soon be over 1 million in population. The growth in city life is so rapid and will be so pervasive a force in dominating cultural transitions in the coming years that the report suggests a need to "shift focus from economies as a whole to cities within them, and beyond high-profile megacities to the most attractive middleweights, particularly in emerging markets." The thesis of this essay takes this cue from the business world and suggests that for missionary strategists, it is now necessary to shift from thinking about entire ethnicities and to focus upon the key cities among each ethnicity. Better yet, why not make the cities the primary focus and then do the population segmentation to see what ethnicities each contains?

A suggestion for further research might be that careful thought needs to be given to crafting specific strategic steps for engaging these cities ready to blossom with new population growth. Just as the goal of engaging new people groups has generated specific strategies, attention must now be turned to how best to engage lostness among the newly arrived in growing urban populations. Obviously many methods in current use will need to transition into the brave new urban world in which we find ourselves. However, more thought needs to be given to the specific character of city life as such. Strategic thought should be given to implementing similar strategies among clusters of cities which share commonalities like size, growth rate and pattern, similar ethnic profiles, and governing models.

Also, the databases used by missions strategists to measure the unfinished task of global evangelization are based on current population figures. How can these projections of teeming millions of new urban dwellers, who will be added to rapidly growing cities in the next years, be incorporated into the models used for strategy research?

Strategic Significance of Rapid Urbanization for Missions

The idea that urban ministry will be significant for twenty-first-century missions has been widely recognized. Patrick Johnstone suggests:

> The great cities of the world are the key challenge for mission in the twenty-first century. We ignore the cities to our peril. The great

cities of our world are the source of most of our wealth and misery, wisdom and depravity, innovations and sin. The engine for societal change is in the cities, but, if used wisely, it could be the dynamo for the growth of the Kingdom. ... The twenty-first century will be an urban world, just as the previous 20 centuries of Christianity have been a rural world. (Johnstone 1998, 240)

Johnstone further points out that cities have not been given the importance that corresponds to their global significance:

There has been a tendency for Western missionaries to miss the importance of the massive urbanization now taking place. Most of those migrating to the cities have been driven by economic necessity from their impoverished rural homes to a poverty often greater than that which they left. A vast, receptive, desperate, barely surviving people need help and the Christians are not there to offer hope with a vital spiritual message and a future as an alternative community. In the past, middle and upper classes were often targeted, and most of the churches were planted among these upwardly mobile people. The theory was that as these movers and shakers came to Jesus, the gospel would trickle down to the poorer people. It rarely happened. ... The urban poor are the most receptive, but also the most underevangelized. It is strategic to reach them, for the gospel has an uplifting effect. (Johnstone 1998, 244)

Johnstone would be representative of a chorus of voices calling Christians to ministry in the urban centers.

Missionaries have experience with similar rapid urbanization in Brazil through the last decades as its population was migrating from the campo into new cities in the interior. One of the things we learned in Brazil was that people who are in transition, who have moved to a new place, who are adjusting their lifestyles to new realities, are open to the gospel in a way that is almost impossible in a society where all is settled and continues on with a comfortable status quo. New cities teeming with new immigrants are prime candidates for harvest fields. Churches that are planted in the early days of these cities get in on the ground floor and become forces to be reckoned with in the civic life of those cities for decades to come.

In God's providence many of these new and growing cities are geographically positioned and can be "gateways" into the unreached peoples who surround them. The gateway factor for urban centers among unreached peoples has already been recognized by missions mobilizers who have asked for focused prayer for some of these gateway cities (Wagner et al. 2010). Planting the gospel in the city is seen as stage one of penetrating the unreached peoples who live in the countryside surrounding them.

Since it can be predicted with some accuracy which cities will be growing most rapidly and where they are located, why not position our missionary force to be ready to receive new immigrants from the rural areas into their new cities? What if the newly arrived urban dwellers find a new and growing indigenous local church that could help them to transition into urban life? The McKinsey Report again states: "The world's middleweights are growing so fast that 13 cities are likely to cross the ten million population and become megacities by 2025. We see all but one new megacity—Chicago—being in developing countries."

In a past generation that viewed the lost populations of the world in their nation-states, Kenneth Strachan developed saturation church planting strategies that led to a commitment to "disciple a whole nation." In the last quarter-century missionary strategy has shifted its focus on the unreached people group as the defining reality for how to engage these populations. Subsequently, there has again been considerable reflection on how to craft strategy to create a church planting movement that will cover an entire people. Such strategic thinking is best seen in the works of David Garrison, *Church Planting Movements* (Garrison 2003) and Steve Smith and Ying Kai, *T4T: A Discipleship Re-Revolution* (Smith and Kai 2011). It is now time again to retool and to consider how best to adapt these statements of missiological "best practice" for urban contexts.

Can you imagine a more strategic place to plant your life and your ministry than in one of these growing cities where peoples who have never heard the gospel are moving? When new urban dwellers arrive, they find that their lives have been uprooted and suffer greatly as they learn to live in the city rather than back on the subsistence farms from which they came. They need a new organizing center for the values and behaviors required by their new urban environment. Can you conceive of a place where you could have more influence in the way that the world is growing than to bring the salt and the light of the gospel into the civic life that is only now taking shape in these new and growing cities? Can you imagine a way to create a legacy that will transcend your own lifetime better than by making sure that the gospel is introduced as a leavening agent into the lives of many people, just when the new civic life of these potentially significant communities is being kneaded out before it gets baked?

Conclusion

I now tell my students that if they want to be strategic with their lives, they should go to contexts that are not so gospel-rich and where people lack access to hear the gospel. Secondly, I tell those who are serving in traditional mission fields like Latin America (where I served) that there is still very much to be done there—especially in many societies where evangelicals do not count for more than 2–3 percent of the population. Nevertheless, their lives could be even more significant if they were to engage an unreached people where there is little or no evidence of gospel presence among their entire society.

Thirdly, I tell my students that if they want to bring unreached peoples to Christ and to plant churches that will have an impact on newly forming urban societies for generations to come, then they should seriously consider planting their lives as gospel tellers and church planters in strategic cities in East and Central Asia. In such places their witness will influence a population that is open to hear the good news, and their efforts there could just be the tipping point that would deeply change the worldview and life structures of the newly emerging cities of the world, and these cities may just become the cultural trendsetters worldwide for the twenty-second century.

During most of the Modern Missionary Movement through the nineteenth and twentieth centuries, missions strategy has focused on the nation-state as the key determining factor for culture and worldview, as evidenced in the approach of Kenneth Scott Latourette, *History of the Expansion of Christianity.* During the last twenty-five years of the twentieth century, unreached people groups were discovered as an alternative way of understanding the ethnic identities and worldview realities for the world's lost peoples. These unreached people groups were no longer somewhere in "regions beyond," but identifiable ethnic groups, each meriting a focused strategy that studied their own cultural realities. However, by the mid-twenty-first century, managing urban culture and learning to surf the social contours of the world's great cities will become the predominant way of understanding how most human beings forge their own personal sense of identity. Therefore, the new demographic phenomenon of exponential urbanization (especially in Asia) deserves to be called the "Next Frontier" for our strategic efforts in world evangelization.

References

Barrett, D. B. (1988). *700 plans to evangelize the world* (AD 2000 series). Birmingham, AL: New Hope.

_____. (1986). *World class cities and world evangelization*. Birmingham, AL: New Hope.

_____, Kurian, G. T., & Johnson, T. M. (2001). *World Christian encyclopedia: A comparative survey of churches and religions in the modern world* (2nd ed., Vols. 1–2). New York: Oxford University Press.

Bosch, D. J. (1991). *Transforming mission: Paradigm shifts in theology of mission*. Maryknoll, NY: Orbis Books.

Chan, K. W., & Hu, Y. (2003). Urbanization in China in the 1990's. *China Report* 3(2), 49–71. Available online http://www.iussp.org/Activities/wgc-urb/kamwingchan.pdf.

Conn, H. (1997). *Planting and growing urban churches: From dream to reality*. Ada, MI: Baker Academic.

Dobbs, R., Smit, S., Remes, J., Manyika, J., Roxburgh, C., & Restrepo, A. (2011). Urban world: Mapping the economic power of cities. McKinsey Global Institute. Retrieved from http://www.mckinsey.com/insights/mgi/research/urbanization/urban_world.

Friedman, T. L. (2008). *Hot, flat, and crowded: Why we need a green revolution and how it can renew America*. New York, NY: Farrar, Straus and Giroux.

Garrison, D. (2003). *Church planting movements: How God is redeeming a lost world*. Monument, CO: WIGTake Resources.

Greenway, R., & Monsma, T. (2000). *Cities: Missions' new frontier* (2nd ed.). Ada, MI: Baker Academic.

Gugler, J. (Ed.). (1996). *Urban transformation of the developing world*. Oxford University Press, USA.

Johnstone, P. (1998). *The church is bigger than you think: The unfinished business of world evangelisation*. WEC International.

Leautier, F. (2006). *Cities in a globalizing world: Governance, performance, and sustainability*. Washington, DC: World Bank.

Livingstone, D. (1857). *Missionary travels and researches in South Africa*. Leffmann Press.

Nachtigall, P. (2008). *Faith in the future: Christianity's interface with globalization*. Anderson, IN: Warner Press.

Smith, S., & Kai, Y. (2011). *T4T: A discipleship re-revolution*. Monument, CO: WIGTake Resources.

The World Watch Institute. (2007). *State of the world 2007: Our urban future: A Worldwatch Institute report on progress toward a sustainable society*. New York: W. W. Norton.

Wagner, P., Peters, S., & Wilson, M. (2010). *Praying through the 100 gateway cities of the 10/40 window* (2nd ed.). Seattle, WA: YWAM Publishing.

Wan, E. (2011). *Diaspora missiology: Theory, methodology, and practice*. Portland, OR: Institute of Diaspora Studies.

Winter, R. D. (1999). *Perspectives on the world Christian movement : A reader* (3rd ed.). Pasadena, CA: William Carey Library.

Wu, F. (2006). *Globalization and the Chinese city*. Routledge Contemporary China Series, 7. London & New York: Taylor & Francis Group.

Yusuf, S., & Saich, T. (2008). *China urbanizes: Consequences, strategies, and policies*. Washington, DC: The World Bank.

Emerging Global Mega-Regions and Globalization: Missiological Implications

Gary Fujino and John Cheong
fujig@aol.com
eaglexian@gmail.com

What does new research on emerging global cities and mega-regions mean for mission? Over a decade after his death, Harvie Conn's prescient view of the city is still relevant to this question that "attention is turning *from the city as place to the city (and to urbanization) as process*. Other dimensions—religious, institutional, social, cultural, behavioral—must also be examined" (Conn 2000, 992, emphasis added).[1] Globalization is one of these "other dimensions." Thus, globalization in its many forms must be examined in its multifaceted interconnectedness and symbiotic relationship to urbanization, "the process through which urban settlements grow and develop" (Davey 2002, 20). This article aims to examine urbanization and globalization, their theories, possible outcomes, and their relationship to one another missiologically. In various sections throughout, we will discuss missiological implications and will conclude with suggestions for further research.

---

1   Ray Bakke saw this earlier but defined "city as process" differently than Conn, "the magnifier function of cities, spinning out urban values, products and lifestyles into a world linked by media, even in rural and small-town places" (Bakke 1997, 12).

Biblical Perspectives on Global Urban Mission

The first mention of a "city" in the Bible is not with Babel, but earlier when Cain built a city for his son, Enoch (Gen 4:17). The word for "city" found in this context is the most common term in the Tanakh and was also later used for Babel, which became a symbol of humanity's prideful rebellion against God: "Come, let us build ourselves a city, with a tower that reaches to the heavens, so that we may make a name for ourselves" (Gen 11:4). Yahweh's intervention in confusing Babel's languages not only scattered the peoples, but also halted the construction of the *city* itself (11:8, cf. 11:5). Later Old Testament cities such as Jericho, Gibeon, Ai, Nineveh, and Babylon were also symbols of defiance against Israel and her God. Elsewhere, while Babylon and Rome are described as geographical entities in both the Old and New Testaments, they also represent sprawling world empires or symbolic spiritual entities raised up against God's kingdom and reign, and his people.

In the OT, Jerusalem or "Zion" was envisioned as a centripetal force to draw the Gentiles to God's temple (Isa 2; 56; 60). Visions of the city as a place for redemption and justice are also seen in Joshua, Judges, and Chronicles, where cities of refuge were to ensure justice for the manslayer. During the Babylonian exile, both Daniel (4:27) and Jeremiah (29:7) emphasized the paradoxical importance of praying for and seeking the good or *shalom* of the captor's city. Also, the Psalms often focus on seeking the good of the holy city, Jerusalem (Ps 9; 51; 69; 122; 132).

In the NT, cities become prominent in God's mission as a *place* for his presence and kingdom witness. For example, Joppa, Antioch, Jerusalem, Pisidian Antioch, Corinth, Athens, and Ephesus were key connectors for the Apostles' missionary journeys. In Acts and the Epistles, their witness was not confined to urban centers, but included larger geographical *regions* surrounding them such as Galatia/Phyrgia, Macedonia, and Asia, where the Apostles deployed from regional cities into the wider surrounding areas (Allen 1962). It is noteworthy that Jesus' first command to Saul on the Damascus road was "Arise, and *go into the city*, and it shall be told thee what thou must do" (Acts 9:6 KJV, emphasis added). This was perhaps a harbinger for the extent of Paul's ministry that ultimately led him to Rome, the capital and symbol of the Roman Empire itself. Lastly, the imagery of the seven cities in Revelation 2–3, Babylon's destruction in chapter 18, and the heavenly city's descent in Revelation 21–22 highlight the city as strategic and spiritual, central to God's eschatological plan.

The following implications are drawn from the biblical data concerning mission and the city:

1. Like Babel and Rome, cities may become monuments to human achievement or to Yahweh himself. At the same time, they are sometimes regarded as resistant, defiant enemies of God.
2. God cares for the city (Jer 29:7; Jonah 4:11; Luke 13:34) and is present even among great iniquities and opposition (Zeph 3:5; Acts 18:10).
3. More than "city-states," cities in Scripture are sometimes representative of empires and kingdoms that wield global influence, whether positively or negatively.
4. Mission itself arose from and is directed toward residents of a given urban locale.
5. Divine judgment falls upon urban structures that become unfaithful to God such as Nineveh (Nah 3:7; Zeph 2:13), Jerusalem (Jer 32:28-32; Luke 21:20–22), and Laodicea (Rev 3:14–22). However, such judgments are not always categorical since God also asks his people to work for the city's sake, as he promises that his presence will abide there (Ps 132:13–14). On occasion, judgment on the city is even withdrawn (Jonah 3:10) or reconsidered (Gen 18: 23–32).
6. In history's consummation, humankind will live with God in the heavenly city, Jerusalem (Rev 21).

Historical Underpinnings for Mission in the City

Here we utilize Harvie Conn's four "waves" of urbanization as a framework to examine cities and mission throughout history. "In the first wave, the city as the symbol of civilization shifted from its place as a religious shrine to a city-state to a military and socio-political center. And in the midst of the Greco-Roman world that was its climax, the church was born" (Conn 2000, 992).

The early church arose during the Roman Empire's peak, which had multiple urban centers at its disposal. A century after the Edict of Milan (AD 313), urban Christianity so permeated the Empire that "the church's urban orientation had transformed the Latin term paganus, originally meaning rural dweller, into the word used to describe the unbeliever" (ibid.). In the next phase, occurring mainly in Europe,

> God and gold introduced the second great urban wave as it did the third. Cities found new identities as permanent marketplaces; commerce became urbanization's new partner. ... By 1500 the continent numbered 154 cities each with at least 10,000 inhabitants. By 1800 there were 364 such cities. ... Interrupting this time of urban transition came the Reformation. Fifty of the sixty-five imperial cities subject to the emperor officially recognized the Reformation either permanently or periodically. ... Ultimately the Reformation remained a parenthesis. It had hoped the city would be the urban exhibition of God's righteousness in Christ. But it could not stop the growing Renaissance emphasis on the secularization of the city. (Ibid., 992–93)

The third great wave arose during the age of global colonization fueled by the Industrial Revolution:

> The city turned for its symbol from the temple, the castle, and the marketplace to the factory. Europe's colonial expansion and 'new world discoveries' prefaced that revolution with previews of future urban patterns. ... Greed bypassed the indigenous cities of Africa, Asia, and Latin America to found colonial port cities as collection points for gathered wealth and natural resources. European racism harvested Africa's "black gold" of slaves from those same ports. Christian missions used those urban paths opened by colonialism, promoting a growing pattern of 'civilizing and Christianizing. ... By 1900, the number of urban Christians totaled 159,600,000. But they were located largely in the cities of Europe and North America. (Ibid., 993)

Notwithstanding the Europeanization of cities in Africa, Asia, and Latin America, these "indigenous cities" were made over into the image of the "civilizing and Christianizing" colonizers. This implicates "future urban" patterns where an indigenous form of "urbanization" was substituted in these places for something more essentially European or North American in nature. Such exchanges created their own problems since a Western urban model was imposed upon non-Western, less urbanized contexts.

The end of World War II marks the fourth wave, where "the number of city dwellers in 1985 was twice as great as the entire population of the world in 1800" (Abu-Lughod cited by Conn 2000, 993). Indeed, "a unique feature of this urban wave is the trend toward ever-larger urban agglomerations" (Conn 2000, 993). Conn views the rise of Christian mission being intimately linked to the ascent of the city in history. This trend continues as over half of the world's population now resides in urban centers (UN Habitat 2008).

This brief overview of the Scriptures and world history shows that urbanization and globalization have existed in varying degrees historically. Yet, what we encounter today is unmatched in its scale, scope, interconnectedness, and speed (Whiteman 2006, 61). Thus, in tackling key questions regarding the city, globalization's role will later be examined.

The Changing Nature of Global Cities: The Emergence of Mega-regions

Over ten years ago, Conn and Ortiz noted that "urban mission studies in recent decades have not moved as quickly as larger scholarship concerns into considering the city as process" (2001, 167).[2] However, recent major research has underscored some of the issues above. Particularly noteworthy are the United Nations reports: *State of the World's Cities (2008–2009): Harmonious Cities* and the United Nations Population Fund report on *State of World Population (2007): Unleashing the Potential of Urban Growth*. From a Christian standpoint, *The Status of Global Mission, 2011, in the Context of the 20th and 21st Centuries* (Barrett 2011, 29) and the focus by Lausanne III on "God's Global Urban Mission" at Cape Town 2010 are also key data sources on the changing nature of the city in our world today. A summary of some key findings are listed on the next page.

---

2   In doing so, Conn and Ortiz (2001, 167) highlighted gaps still needing to be addressed today: (1) A lack of "interface between Christian mission and the social sciences most useful in analyzing the city." (2) Studies which are "disproportionate geographically, ecclesiastically and topically." (3) The need for more cross-cultural studies. "Outside the Anglo-Saxon world both macro-level and micro-level research on urban mission is much more limited." (4) More interdisciplinary studies linking fields of study to that of urban mission, such as "neighborhood, role relationships, societal structures and networks" (ibid.).

The United Nations 2007 Urban Agglomerations (2008)[3] says that:

1. World population is expected to be 70% urban in 2050.
2. Latin America and the Caribbean have an exceptionally high level of urbanization (78%), higher than that of Europe. Africa and Asia, in contrast, remain mostly rural, with 38% and 41% respectively, of their populations living in urban areas.
3. Despite its low level of urbanization, in 2007 Asia was home to about half of the urban population in the world. Europe had the second highest share, at 16%.
4. The world rural population is expected to reach a maximum of 3.5 billion in 2018 or 2019 and to decline slowly thereafter, to reach 2.8 billion in 2050.
5. The world urban population is highly concentrated in a few countries. In 2007, three quarters of the 3.3 billion urban-dwellers on Earth lived in 25 countries. China, India, and the United States of America accounted for 35% of the world urban population.
6. Most countries have small urban populations.
7. China and India are projected to account together for about a third of the increase in the urban population in the coming decades.
8. In a few developed countries, the urban population will decrease.[4]
9. The rural population is even more highly concentrated in a few countries than the urban population.[5]
10. The 3.3 billion urban-dwellers in 2007 were distributed unevenly among urban settlements of different sizes. Over half of the world urban population (52%) lived in cities or towns with fewer than half a million inhabitants.

---

3 Data taken directly from http://www.un.org/esa/population/publications/wup2007/2007_urban_agglomerations_chart.pdf. The wording for the list is copied *verbatim*. Some sentences have been abbreviated, combined or truncated but the original words have been kept. One exception has been to convert the term, "per cent," in the original, to a symbol (%). Footnoted parts of this list are from the same original source and are left in their same original wording.

4 Despite the projected increases in the level of urbanization, overall population decline in several countries will lead to a reduction in the number of urban-dwellers. Those with the largest drops include Japan (a reduction of four million), the Republic of Korea (four million), the Russian Federation (seven million) and Ukraine (four million).

5 In 2007, eighteen countries accounted for 75% of the rural population and all but three (Japan, the Russian Federation, and the United States) are located in Africa or Asia. India has the largest rural population (828 million), followed by China (767 million). Together, they account for 47% of the world rural population.

11. Mega-cities are urban agglomerations with at least 10 million inhabitants. There are today 19 mega-cities on Earth and their number is expected to increase to 27 in 2025.[6]
12. Large urban agglomerations are not necessarily experiencing fast population growth.[7]
13. Eleven of these mega-cities are capitals of their countries.

A later UN report (2008) concluded that emerging cities of the third millennium should become "harmonious cities," which are spatially, socially, and environmentally "in harmony."[8] It urges nation-states to create plans for their own "harmonious cities":

> A society cannot claim to be harmonious if large sections of its population are deprived of basic needs while other sections live in opulence. A city cannot be harmonious if some groups concentrate resources and opportunities while others remain impoverished and marginalized. Harmony in cities cannot be achieved if the price of urban living is paid by the environment. Reconciling contradictory and complementary elements is critical to creating harmony within cities. A harmonious city promotes unity within diversity. Harmony within cities hinges not only on prosperity and its attendant benefits, but on two pillars that make harmony possible: equity and sustainability. Harmony is both an ancient social ideal as well as a modern concept.

A third United Nations study by the UN Population Fund, State of World Population (2007): Unleashing the Potential of Urban Growth, is similar in content to the 2007 Urban Agglomerations report and the 2008 State of the World's Cities (2008–2009) report. For this article, two key topics from the State of World Population report are directly relevant and compare favorably to Conn's waves of urbanization (see Figure 3.1).

---

6   The proportion of people living in megacities is small. In 2007, 9% of the world urban population resided in megacities, and by 2025 that share is expected to rise to almost 10%. In relation to the entire world population, megacities account today for 4% of the population, meaning that just one in twenty-five people on Earth live in megacities.

7   Among the nineteen megacities in 2007, seven megacities are expected to have annual population growth in the period 2005–2010 below 1% and just 3 above 2%.

8   From State of the World's Cities (2008–2009): Harmonious Cities. The section on globalization below will highlight some of these new realities of "harmony" and "dissonance" within the city.

The first topic regards "the second wave of urbanization" (UN Population Fund 2007, 7). The State of World Population (2007) report's second wave is equivalent to Conn's fourth wave of urbanization. Some characteristics include it being prominent mainly in developing countries, where it is "new" to these nations since urbanization is recent to them only within the past half century. The effects of this second wave in the Majority World today are unprecedented because of its scale and rapid movement upon populations in the hundreds of millions. Consequently the UN report emphasizes "equity" and "harmony" as urbanization develops in these places.

Traits	UN Report (2007)	Harvie Conn's waves of urbanization
Urbanization in developing countries	Second wave	Fourth wave
Industrial Revolution (Europe)	First wave	Third wave

Figure 3.1 Table showing the relationship between the UN 2007 report and Harvie Conn's waves of urbanization

The second important finding from the 2007 study is that "the growth of new religious movements is primarily an urban phenomenon" (ibid., 26). Here, fundamentalism and religious revivalism have surged as cities in Asia, Africa, Latin America, and the Muslim world have rapidly urbanized. Additionally, "increased urbanization, coupled with slow economic development and globalization, has helped to increase religious diversity as part of the multiplication of subcultures in cities. Rather than revivals of a tradition, the new religious movements can be seen as adaptations of religion to new circumstances" (ibid.). These UN findings also provide new insights on the status of urban Christianity.

According to David Barrett, the projected number of urban dwellers globally will surpass 3.6 billion by mid-2011, with the addition of 121,000 "new non-Christian urban dwellers per day," and 1.8 billion "urban Christians" among the total population (Barrett 2001, 29). While some definitions[9] may be disputed,

---

9   Barrett, Kurian, and Johnson define "urban dwellers" as "[t]he population living in urban areas usually including cities and towns with over 5,000 inhabitants" (*World Christian Encyclopedia*, 2nd ed., 2001, 676). "Christian" is defined as "One who believes in, or professes or confesses Jesus Christ as

Barrett's statistics indicate that approximately half of all urbanites globally are "adherent(s) of Christianity." The "challenge to the church," says Andrew Davey, is that "the world is now an urban place ... [t]heological challenges of the urban process today are those that have confronted Christians whenever the faith has been taken into unfamiliar patterns of social life" (Davey 2002, 7–8). Conn also saw this reality before his death, when he predicted that "the growth of the cities in non-Christian or anti-Christian countries, combined with the erosion of the church in the northern hemisphere, is multiplying the non-Christian urban population" (Conn 2000, 993). Thus, the missiological question (paraphrasing Conn) is: How might an unchanging faith confront an unfamiliar, radically changed world? The recent Lausanne III convocation gives insight here.

At Lausanne III, "God's Global Urban Mission" was highlighted in discussions on how to reach the world's cities. In "Creating Contextual Churches," Tim Keller presented his own Redeemer Presbyterian Church in New York City as a case study, calling for planting and renewing churches, which are contextualized to the city. For Keller, such churches must (Keller 2010):

1. Be extremely culturally sensitive. "We will be judged by the surrounding culture and will always hear about racial and cultural insensitivity. Churches in the city almost always have to be multi-cultural."
2. Be able to help people to integrate faith and work. "People go to cities to get work. You have to celebrate and affirm them in what they do." For example, for creating an entrepreneurship network, we will have to show them the gospel basis for business initiatives.
3. Know that urban people tend to like change and diversity and prefer things on the "cutting edge." Outside the city, citizens tend to prefer stability, order, etc. "To be an urban church leader you have to be comfortable with disorder and with change."
4. Know that "evangelism in the city is complicated." "You can't possibly give the same gospel presentation to everyone in a city."
5. "Make your church famous for compassion and caring about issues of justice in the city" (along with doing evangelism). "Your neighbors should say, I don't agree with them in everything, but I don't know what we would do without them."

Lord and Savior, or is assumed to believe in Jesus Christ; an adherent of Christianity" (ibid., 655).

6. Know that "in cities, artists are like an ethnic group. If you want to have a city-friendly church, you have to bring in artists and give them a voice. Take what they do very seriously."
7. Know that "things happen in cities through relationships. The worst thing you can do to an urban leader is pull them out of their context/networks to study in another place."
8. "Have a city-reaching movement, which happens when Christians grow at a faster rate than the population of the city itself."

In another Lausanne III case study, Jose da Silva, coordinator of URBANUS partnership in Montreal, Canada, shared of his ministry among the African diaspora there (da Silva 2010). First, in Africa itself there is a "demographic explosion" with cities expanding at a rapid rate and churches there were unprepared for such growth. But as some migrated to Canada, fierce residue from their ethnic conflicts was imported to their adoptive countries, primarily in the larger cities. Internecine strife continues to erupt in areas where these specific ethnic groups reside and cross paths. However, Montreal churches were unprepared to handle these dislocated, transnational refugees from war-torn areas such as Rwanda, Burundi, and Darfur. Ironically, many from different tribes in the same country frequent the same church in the same city, but are unable to integrate. Da Silva lists five key reasons why this occurs:

1. The church is silent when confronted with the genocide problem.
2. The church is silent when confronted with the ethnic problem.
3. The church has found a way to ignore the problem.
4. The church "sometimes tried to get around the problem."
5. In their homeland, congregants were in churches that opposed one another: they are not well received in these same denominations in the same cities.

Because of this, many new refugees are at a loss. In some cases, church leadership in the immigrant's city has already taken sides. The complaint is that "everything is spiritualized" and people think "it's not our problem. It is the problem for the politicians to solve." Da Silva's suggestions or implications, which he says are "not ready made solutions," remind us that:

1. We do not take sides.
2. We proclaim equality in Christ.
3. We integrate persons from different ethnic backgrounds into church leadership.
4. We biblically exegete/analyze passages and their ethnic and missiological implications.
5. We adopt and practice biblical hospitality toward strangers and aliens.

These two Lausanne III case studies of ministering through city churches in megacities underscore the complexities and challenges of ministry in a globalized context. We now discuss globalization and how its macrostructures, processes, and players underpin the phenomena and realities behind these case studies.

A Brief Overview of Globalization

One understanding of globally connected cities and the world is that such interconnections are driven by the world capitalist economy (Wallerstein 1974). Core centers such as the West, that are highly capitalist, relate to the periphery/non-West through this dominant mode. Capital, goods, and labor flow from a center-periphery relationship via the market system logic. This model is more consonant with the UN's first and Conn's third wave of urbanization.

Another understands globalization as one of the "consequences of modernity" (Giddens 1991, 21), "the intensification of world-wide social relations which link distant localities in such a way that local happenings are shaped by events occurring miles away and vice versa" (Giddens 1990, 64). It is a dialectical phenomenon—events at one pole of a distanciated relation produce divergent or even contrary occurrences at another" (Giddens 1991, 22). Consequently, social life is stretched across time and space (Giddens 1990, 16).

Space-time distanciation, however, implies "an 'action-reaction' relationship which does not fully capture the complexities of the global-local theme" (Robertson 1995, 27) (i.e., it is silent on the processes occurring between the local and global). Here, we consider Roland Robertson's definition of globalization where it refers

> both to the compression of the world and the intensification of consciousness of the world as a whole. The processes and actions to which the concept of globalization now refers have been proceeding, with some interruptions, for many centuries. (Robertson 1992, 8)

What occurs is the "interpenetration of the universalization of particularism and the particularization of universalism" (ibid., 100). It implicates localization and is termed "glocalization" (ibid., 26). Globalization is not merely "global" forces versus "local" places; cultural processes are always local and global at the same time (Tsing 2000, 338). The local is not the stopping point of global circulations, but where global flows are "consumed, incorporated, and resisted" (Pred and Waters, cited by Tsing 2000, 338).

Lastly, globalization may be understood as aspects of different forces that "offer new resources and new disciplines for the construction of imagined selves and imagined worlds" (Appadurai 1996, 3). These forces evoke a globality of contested "scapes" in which no single organizing principle rules. They are disjunctures among five dimensions of global cultural flows called ethnoscapes, mediascapes, technoscapes, finanscapes, and ideoscapes (ibid., 33). Each scape "is deeply subjunctive and profoundly unpredictable because each of these landscapes is subject to its own constraints and incentives ... at the same time as each acts as a constraint and a parameter for movements in the others" (ibid., 35).

There may be "a logical connection" of the scapes (Friedman 1994, 210) or "a deeper underlying unity" (Lewellen 2002, 98). These scapes may be better seen as social responses, not centering on one particular mode of experience nor individuals as these cultural experiences "are always partial and shifting" (Metcalf 2001, 180).

Implication: "Place" in ministry must move beyond traditional conceptions of local versus global since what is local is also global. The idea of local-global connectedness means that in every particularity of life today, global forces and their influences on the local should be accounted for. Informed by Appadurai's insights, identifying specific groups of people that flow along certain scapes yields context-rich insights on emotions that drive people to act in a globalized world. Identifying such places in megacities is key to evangelism. These scapes help us analyze where the flows of globalization organize themselves among specific demographics in the city, which opens up spaces for Christians to serve with focus.

Place and Locality in a Globalized World

"Globalization breaks assumptions about locality and place such as 'the nation-state' as the container of social process ... that if a process or condition is located in a national institution or in national territory, it must be national" (Sassen 2007, 3). This thinking is germane to the "city as process" as previously mentioned.

Similarly, where culture[10] was "thought of as a bounded entity that occupies a specific physical territory" (Inda and Rosaldo 2006, 12–13), globalization makes locality problematic—place can no longer be assumed to be "local" (as in geographical boundedness). Locality, once seen as fixed, and the symbols and practices of culture (e.g., birthplace, addresses, phone numbers, etc.) as ways of inscribing local identity were understood as consequences of that space, not its production (ibid., 179–180). When locality is deconstructed and culture de-territorialized, space is opened to examine creole cultures, transnational movements, and emerging diasporas (Tsing 2000).

Cultural production also occurs in the frames of daily life, the state, market, and movements where they are all involved in the "management of meaning and meaningful forms" (Hannerz 1996, 69–70), but with different motives and degrees of deliberateness. Three factors that directly affect the production of localities in globalization are the nation-state, diaspora flows, and media/virtual communities (Appadurai 1996, 198). Each varies depending on the country and people in relation to Appadurai's five scapes.

Culture, however, does not float freely; it reinserts itself into new and specific time-space contexts (Inda and Rosaldo 2006, 14). "[T]ranslocal culture is not without space ... but it involves an outward-looking sense of place" as opposed to "an inward-looking sense of space" in cultures closely linked to the land (Nederveen Pieterse 1995, 61). They are not two separate processes, but occur simultaneously—a double movement (Inda and Rosaldo 2006, 14).

Such flows highlight the permeable and fragile nature of the nation-state in relation to people, culture, information, goods, and institutions. Structural components formerly linked to the notion of society now also become de-territorialized. Nationally, globalization "compromises four critical aspects of the nation-state: its competence; its form; its autonomy; and ultimately its authority or legitimacy" (McGrew, cited by Tomlinson 1997, 173). The problem of space can be seen as insertions of the global into the national or local (Sassen 2007), or locality as primarily relational and contextual rather than as scalar or spatial (Appadurai 1996, 178).

Implication: Christians serving in megacities must evaluate the mélange of sights, sounds, and people, not assuming the world is becoming homogenous. Incarnational ministry in megacities should account for and work with urbanites

---

10   On culture, we use Hiebert's definition (1985, 30), "the more or less integrated systems of ideas, feelings" (*Anthropological insights for missionaries* by Paul G. Hiebert, Grand Rapids, MI: Baker, 1985).

to understand how they desire to utilize, contextualize. and ground these flows of culture. In a globalized world, we cannot return to a pristine, essentialized past due to the semi-permanence of locality and identity. A permanent ground of identity formation is for people to be reached and discipled in God's redemptive story; Christ is the ruler of all nations, in their lives and identity wherever they locate their home and identity among churches, house groups, or gatherings globally that are rooted in authentic fellowship (Fujino 2011).

The Nation-state and Mega-regions in a Globalized World

Early conceptions of the nation-state, its centralizing power to authorize meaning and order forms of social organization through its many apparatus of coercion promoting a vision of one people, one nation, one country within a bounded territory, essentialized culture and monolithic ideology called nationalism (Anderson 2006).[11] Conn's explication of the Industrial Revolution model and the city parallels this understanding.

However, in a globalized world, nationalism that was once contained in the territorial bottle of the nation-state's boundaries has now escaped, becoming diasporic (Appadurai Conn 1996, 161).[12] For example, economically, the role of megacities in globalization has become "so specialized that they can no longer be contained in the functions of [the national]. Global cities are strategic sites for the production of these specialized functions to run and coordinate the global economy" (Sassen 2007, 73).

Even as state power is penetrated by the global, it in turn is also internationalized. The state may (1) reposition itself in the global economic chain by upgrading itself to take advantage of internationalization or (2) influence the flows of globalization (e.g., special tax credits for multinational corporations (MNC) to locate, agglomerate into megacities) (Sassen 2007, 59, 65). Globalization thus "encourages macro-regionalism, which in turn, encourages micro-regionalism" (Nederveen 1995, 50). These are "sub-globalizations—movements with a regional rather than global

---

11   Nederveen (2002, 38) outlines three different paradigms of globalization's effect on the nation-state: (1) a strong discourse of borders, (2) a gradual erosion of borders due to increased modernization, or (3) ongoing mixing and hybridization resulting in neither the first two.
12   Examples include the shaping of national culture via the media or governmental institutions or activities of multinational corporations or the ambiguous handling of illegal immigrants (Sassen 2000, 225–226).

reach that are nevertheless instrumental in connecting the societies on which they impinge with the emerging global culture" (Berger 2004, 14). These sub or inner globalizations offer both benefits and dangers to nations within with respect to "the informal spaces that are created in between, in the interstices [that are] inhabited by diasporas, migrants, exiles, refugees, nomads" (Nederveen 1995, 50).

Types of the Globalized City

Geographically, borders and megacities are strategic settings to study globalization while phenomenologically, it is migrants and exiles (Sassen 2007). All are "circumstances that lend themselves to cross-cultural mixing and fertilization" (García Canclini 2005, xliii). The relationship between the local and global, national and local, nation-state and city all tend to crystallize in megacities, which are "dense and complex borderlands marked by the intersection of multiple spatiotemporal (dis) orders" (Sassen 2000, 221). Disorders such as de-territorialization decontextualizes, but also recontextualizes by materializing itself in "a worldwide grid of strategic places, uppermost among which are major international business and financial centers [creating] a new economic geography of centrality" (ibid., 225). Saskia Sassen calls this the global city while for Ulf Hannerz it is a world city.

Sassen's global cities are internationally linked nodes of globalization where major networks of finance, media, migrants, goods, and services join in varying combinations, which cluster and aggregate this symbiosis into a cycle of hyper-productivity and innovation that draw but also produce dynamic and new movements and structures of social orders in society (Sassen 2002). The "abundance of energetic processes that routinely travel" a transnational urban and national system also produces inequality between intranational and international cities (Sassen 2000, 225) as divisions of labor and expertise are produced in varying degrees according to the contextual demands of each global city and its inhabitants. This gap of inequality is one of the main themes of the UN report (2008). For example, the influx of overseas professionals and migrant workers disrupts "conventional hierarchies of scale" as these cross-border flows connect specific work locales with their home communities (ibid., 226). States, however, shape these interactions, not merely by resistances, but in a dialectic of national idiosyncrasies and global standards and demands (ibid., 227). Hierarchies are produced in these networks so that some (e.g., finance, media) dominate specific cities while others become second-tier. Such asymmetries that produce human, economic, and social inequalities are spaces for ministry.

For Hannerz, the world city is a place for economic and political transactions but also "transnational connections" since it orders these structures (Hannerz 1996, 12). They are "places in themselves and also nodes in networks; their cultural organization involves local as well as transnational relationships" (ibid., 128–129). These world cities have (1) transnational businesses filled with highly-educated, skilled, and mobile white-collar workers, (2) growing third-world populations that live inside such cities or serve these professionals within, (3) artistic/expressive workers bringing music, arts, and literature, and (4) tourists that ply these cities built on the multiplier effect of the previous three classes.

The forces for cultural creativity in world cities are the (1) concentration of talent, (2) international and legal supports, (3) workers' self-belief as the vanguards of change, (4) presence of diversity, (5) daily experiences of this "urban spectacle," and (6) a market that feeds on this experience (ibid., 136). These world cities are "doubly creolizing," exporting and importing images from one site to another in a continuous relationship at the top, but also creolizing immigrants from below into its image (ibid., 153–54). They are not "centers" (e.g., being at the origin of all things) but "places of exchange, the switchboards of culture" (ibid., 149). Resistance, however, may occur between one metropolis and another (e.g., Paris versus Tokyo), competing for money, status, or power (ibid., 169).

Implication: The globalized classes that inhabit megacities prompt an identification of specific needs of mega-regions to place workers in strategically influential places where globalization occurs most intensely. For example, globalization accelerates more advantages to groups with certain skills in high demand (e.g., smartphone developers, English speakers fluent in Chinese, etc.) or certain sectors of megacities that tap into specific needs of a globalized region.

Implication: In the twenty-first century, the church is challenged to engage the structural and larger societal aspects of the megacity such as increased flows of refugees and immigrants in the nation-state. Partnerships with organizations having a specialized global reach (e.g., Christian NGOs or denominations focusing on migrant ministry, ethnic/social inequalities) open up new avenues of ministry where neither the city nor the nation-state seem capable of administering the civil good.

Human Agency in Mega-regions

According to Robert Holton, two ways in which people participate in globalization are cross-border processes (e.g., trade, religion, diasporic relationships) or manipulation of "material or symbolic resources and repertoires" (e.g., media, foodstuff, law, or religious practices) (Holton 2005, 30). Hannerz (1996, 84) sees these elites in symbolic-analytic services work who manage "non-standardized manipulation of symbols—data, words, oral and visual representations [i.e.] the problem-identifiers, problem-solvers, strategic brokers." Consequently, there are human opportunities and constraints if people are set at the center of the phenomenon as one can "make or unmake globalization" (Holton 2008, 2).

The human dimension of globalization implicates the urban elite and non-elites. The former are mainly the "partially denationalized classes," many of whom are transnationals (Sassen 2007, 164). They bridge "the thick national environments within which most politics, economics, and civic life still functions and the global dynamics that are "denationalizing particular components of those national settings" (ibid., 170). Generally, they function in the context of weak national attachments and identities among global firms (ibid., 173). Their "work requires a physical infrastructure—the hyperspace of global business: state-of-the-art office buildings, residential districts, airports and hotels" (ibid., 176). For them, the points of departure and arrival are in flux so that stability of their identity becomes difficult (Appadurai 1996, 44).

Media and migrants are also penetrating features of globalization into the local/national arena as they create spaces of contestation on how to "annex the global into their own practices of the modern" (Appadurai 1996, 4). From these engagements flow many "transboundary issues" such as immigration, asylum, international women's agendas, and anti-globalization struggles. Even though local participation in these "localizations of global civil society" (e.g., politico-civic activities, activism in localized MNCs) (Sassen 2007, 184) may not entail international travel, they materialize in settings of sufficient proximal densities (i.e., in megacities) that they participate in translocal spaces (ibid., 183, 193). Others such as the diaspora and immigrants in local neighborhoods produce a "transnationalism in situ" (ibid., 184–85). We should note that though "both cosmopolitans and poor migrants erase the specificity of their cultural tracks, [they are] for different reasons: poor migrants need to fit in the worlds of others; cosmopolitans want more of the world to be theirs" (Tsing 2000, 343).

Implication: We cannot overlook human agency as an important driver of globalization (see below) as it implicates the glocal nature of people's actions in evangelism and discipleship in missions to play a vital role in shaping the desires, motivation, and outlook of people. When human feelings and motivations for travel and movement in a globalized world are considered, the need to study the affective dimensions of globalization arises.

Global Networks in Megacities and Mega-regions

Global networks of human actors are "the human face of globalization," linking people and institutions in a flow of shared interest (Holton 2008, 3, 81). For Holton, global networking (a) takes place across political and cultural boundaries, (b) creates intensive as well as spatially extensive interconnections between a range of institutions and actors, and (c) creates transnational processes, institutions, and ways of interpreting the world as a single space (ibid., 6). Holton's human dimension of networks complements Sassen's conception of networked global cities. How human networks mesh within the frames of global structures is shown below:

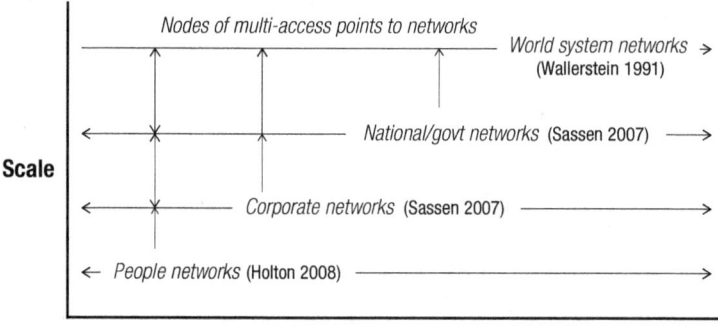

Figure 3.2 Chart showing the accessibilities to hierarchies of scale in globalized networks that transcend space-time

Global network activities are "associated either with functional types of activity, such as advocacy, knowledge acquisition and dissemination, policy-making and business; or with spheres of spatial operation such as empires or other transcontinental entities" (ibid., 77).

Holton (2008, 81) lists twelve network types: advocacy, business/trading/commercial, friendship, imperial, information, knowledge/intellectual, migrant, policy, professional, religious, terrorist, and women's networks. Certain networks include or exclude others. Networks also create a multiplier force for innovation, information exchange, and investment of time and energy. They usually begin by a single influential person with a connectivity charisma that draws people of similar ilk into webs of relationship that expand over space and sometimes endure over time for the purpose of transmitting this capital, enjoying a shared emotional energy and cultivating a reputation among its peers (ibid., 107–110). An outstanding example is John Stott and Billy Graham's friendship and co-signing of the Lausanne Covenant that spawned a network connecting like-minded evangelicals globally. Such networks are

> forms for multi-centered social organization that are distinct from two other major organizational types, namely markets and hierarchies. Networks are more enduring forms of social commitment and trust than markets but are more flexible and less centralized than hierarchies. (ibid., 4)

Networks do not operate in a social vacuum, may change over time (ibid., 65), and need to be studied contextually with each group of people. They also "typically exhibit non-randomness; that is clusters, asymmetries and complex cross-linkages [as] not all participating individual or grouping will have the same kind or number of connections with others"(Wellman, cited by Holton 2008, 53). However, connections may "wax and wane in intensity and may involve phases of conflict, or even breakdown, and this in turn may be connected to changes in the political and cultural context" (ibid., 151). Its usefulness, though, is to probe the interstices of globalization's structures.

Implication: People are not helpless in the currents of megacities or mega-regions as motivations and ideas for people to multiply their influence can occur by forming global networks. Because such networks work within but also transcend mega-regions, it is important to see that relationships with such persons open up global networking possibilities to multiply joint ventures or partnerships into larger synergistic forces that can overcome local or national limitations for mission.

Conclusion and Suggestions for Further Research

Some years ago, two leading evangelical scholars on urban ministry observed that:

> cities determine the destiny of nations, and their influence on the everyday affairs of individuals is incalculable. As cities grow in number, size and influence, it is incumbent on those responsible for leadership in world evangelization to focus attention on cities. Students and Christian colleges and seminaries will need to wrestle seriously with urban issues if they want to be ready for ministry in a largely urban world. (Greenway and Monsma 2000, xi)

This article has attempted to engage the first part of the charge coming from Greenway and Monsma, and that from Conn and Ortiz. The latter part of their advice, concerning Christian colleges, is being advanced but with only partial results. A new study shows that only twenty-five (9 percent) of 264 Christian colleges, seminaries, and universities surveyed in North America "offer any type of Urban Studies program, or in some cases, multiple types of programs" (Morgan forthcoming). We owe a debt of gratitude for the insights gained in the past from such sage Christian visionaries as Bakke, Conn, Ortiz, Greenway, and Monsma, who were influenced by Harvey Cox, Jacques Ellul, and a host of others. These scholars paved the way to today, leading us to the present study, and giving us a helpful peek at possible future ministry implications concerning globalization and the city.

We did this by examining global cities and mega-regions, integrating biblical, historical, demographic, anthropological, and sociological aspects (in particular the insights of Appadurai, Holton, Hannerz, and Sassen) to reveal missiological implications for understanding and exploring possibilities of innovative strategies for urban mission for the twenty-first century. Space delimits fuller explications of other potential multifaceted ministry applications that might arise from our brief survey. Nonetheless, we hope this article will further investigations into other areas, such as understanding the dynamics of flow in megacities, conducting case studies on diasporic urban congregations, investigating evangelism toward people with embedded or translocal identities, or the biblical basis for engaging megacities and their systems, and affective dimensions of globalization in today's people.

References

Allen, R. (1962). *Missionary methods: St. Paul's or ours?* Grand Rapids, MI: Eerdmans.

Appadurai, A. (1990). Disjunction and difference in the global cultural economy. In M. Featherstone (Ed.), *Global Culture* (295–310). Thousand Oaks, CA: Sage.

_____. (1996). *Modernity at large*. Minneapolis, MN: University of Minnesota Press.

Bakke, R. (1997). *A theology as big as the city*. Downers Grove, IL: InterVarsity Press.

Barrett, D. B., Kurian, G., & Johnson, T.M. (2001). *World Christian encyclopedia* (2nd ed.). Oxford: Oxford University Press.

Berger, P. L. (2004). The cultural dynamics of globalization. In P. L. Berger & S. P. Huntington, *Many Globalizations* (1–16). New York: Oxford University Press.

Conn, H. M. (2000). Urbanization. In A. S. Moreau, H. Netland, & C. Van Engen (Eds.), *Evangelical Dictionary of World Missions* (992–94). Grand Rapids, MI: Baker.

Conn, H. M., & Ortiz, M. (2001). *Urban ministry: The kingdom, the city and the people of God*. Downers Grove, IL: InterVarsity Press.

da Silva, J. (2010). African diaspora. Paper presented at the 2010 Lausanne Conference, October 2010, in Cape Town, South Africa.

Davey, A. (2002). *Urban Christianity and global order*. Peabody, MA: Hendrickson.

Friedman, J. (1994). *Cultural identity and global process*. Thousand Oaks, CA: Sage.

Fujino, G. (2010). "Glocal" Japanese self-identity: A missiological perspective on paradigmatic shifts in urban Tokyo. *International Journal of Frontier Missiology* 27 (4), 171–82.

García Canclini, N. (2005). *Hybrid cultures*. (C. L. Chiappari & S. L. López, Trans.). Minneapolis: University of Minnesota Press.

Giddens, A. (1990). *The Consequences of modernity*. Stanford, CA: Stanford University Press.

_____. (1991). *Modernity and self-identity*. Stanford, CA: Stanford University Press.

Greenway, R. S., & Monsma, T. M. (2000). *Cities: Missions' new frontier*. Grand Rapids, MI: Baker.

Hannerz, U. (1992). The global ecumene as a network of networks. In A. Kuper (Ed.), *Conceptualizing Society* (34–58). New York: Routledge.

_____. (1996). *Transnational connections*. New York: Routledge.

Holton, R. J. (2005). *Making globalization*. New York: Palgrave Macmillan.

⎯⎯⎯⎯⎯⎯⎯. (2008). *Global networks*. New York: Palgrave Macmillan.

Inda, J. X., & Rosaldo, R. (2006). Tracking global flows. In J. X. Inda & R. Rosaldo (Eds.), *The anthropology of globalization: A reader* (3–46). Malden, MA: Blackwell.

Johnson, T., Barrett, D.B., & Crossing, P.F. (2011). The status of global mission, 2011, in the context of the 20th and 21st Centuries. *International Bulletin of Missionary Research* 35 (1), 28–29.

Keller, T. (2010). Creating contextual churches. Paper presented at the 2010 Lausanne Conference, October 2010, in Cape Town, South Africa.

Lewellen, T. C. (2002). *The anthropology of globalization: Cultural anthropology enters the 21st Century*. Westport, CT: Bergin & Garvey.

Metcalf, P. (2001). Global "disjuncture" and the "sites" of anthropology. *Cultural Anthropology* 16 (2), 165–182.

Morgan, G. (2011). The "new" urban: Meeting the challenges of today's cities. Paper presented at the National Meeting of the Evangelical Missiological Society, Phoenix, AZ.

Nederveen, P. (1995). Globalization as hybridization. In M. Featherstone, S. Lash, & R. Robertson (Eds.), *Global Modernities* (45–68). Thousand Oaks, CA: Sage.

⎯⎯⎯⎯⎯⎯⎯. (2002). Fault lines of transnationalism: Borders matter. *Bulletin of the Royal Institute for Inter-faith Studies* 4(2), 33–48.

⎯⎯⎯⎯⎯⎯⎯. (2009). *Globalization and culture: Global mélange* (2nd ed.). Lanham, MD: Rowan and Littlefield.

Robertson, R. (1990). Mapping the global condition. In M. Featherstone (Ed.), *Global Culture* (15–30). Thousand Oaks, CA: Sage.

⎯⎯⎯⎯⎯⎯⎯. (1992). *Globalization: Social theory and global culture*. Thousand Oaks, CA: Sage.

⎯⎯⎯⎯⎯⎯⎯. (1995). Glocalization: Time-space and homogeneity and heterogeneity. In M. Featherstone, S. Lash, & R. Robertson (Eds.), *Global Modernities* (25–44). Thousand Oaks, CA: Sage.

Sassen, S. (2000). Spatialities and temporalities of the global: Elements for a theorization. *Public Culture* 12(1), 215–32.

⎯⎯⎯⎯⎯⎯⎯. (2007). *A sociology of globalization*. New York: W.W. Norton & Co.

Tomlinson, J. (1997). Cultural globalization and cultural imperialism. In A. Mohammadi (Ed.), *International Communication and Globalization: A Critical Introduction* (170–90). Thousand Oaks, CA: Sage.

Tsing, A. (2000). The global situation. *Cultural Anthropology* 15(3), 327–60.

UN Population Fund. (2007). State of world population. New York: UN Population Fund.

UN Habitat. (2008). State of the world's cities 2008/2009: Harmonious cities. Sterling, VA: Earthscan.

Wallerstein, I. (1974). *The modern world system.* New York: Academic Press.

Whiteman, D. (2006). Anthropological reflections on contextualizing theology in a globalizing world. In C. Ott & H. Netland (Eds.), *Globalizing Theology* (52–69). Grand Rapids, MI: Baker Academic.

Section 2: Historical and Theological Perspectives on the City

Basil of Caesarea: An Early Christian Model of Urban Mission

Edward L. Smither
esmither@ciu.edu

"The hungry are dying. ... The naked are stiff with cold. The man in debt is held by the throat" (Basil, Sermon 6.6 in Holman 2001, 103). This is how Basil (AD 329–379) described his city, Caesarea of Cappadocia, in the late fourth century, especially amid a lingering famine that plagued his region. As the twenty-first-century church ministering in the world's cities continues to deal with problems such as hunger, usury, corruption, unemployment, displaced peoples, and even slavery, it seems useful to consider some models of urban mission from the church's past. In this article, I will explore the approach to urban ministry by the well-known church father and bishop Basil who is remembered mostly for his contributions to fourth-century Trinitarian theology. Following a brief survey of his life and call to ministry and the context in which he ministered, I will discuss his practical strategies and theology of mission regarding ministry in the city. In conclusion, I will begin a reflective conversation between Basil and modern practitioners on ministering in urban contexts.

Basil's Life and Ministry

Basil was born into a wealthy Christian family and his grandparents were influenced by the ministry of Bishop Gregory Thaumaturgus (ca. 213–ca. 270), the most prominent evangelist in Asia Minor in the third century (Rousseau 1998, 1, 12). More than an average nominal Christian family in the post-Constantine era, Basil's family followed the example of his famous grandmother Macrina and practiced asceticism as a household (Gregory of Nazianzus, Oration 43.12; Rousseau 1998, 4–5; Sterk 2004, 35). Basil was educated in the classical tradition and studied rhetoric (communication) and philosophy in Cappadocia, Constantinople, and later Athens. After a brief stint in teaching, he traveled east in 356 pursuing the mentorship of the ascetic Bishop Eustathius of Sebaste (Rousseau 1998, 27; Sterk 2004, 39–40; Ayres 2009, 121). However, Basil later broke fellowship with his spiritual leader for theological reasons as Eustathius subscribed to a moderate Arian position (Basil, Letter 223). Basil was baptized in 357 and then retreated with his close friend Gregory of Nazianzus to his family's estate in Pontus in pursuit of a communal (coenobitic) monastic experience. Apparently, Basil was convinced by his sister (also named Macrina) that a monastic way of life was superior to the more academic path that he had begun to take following his return from Athens (Rousseau 1998, 9–11; Sterk 2004, 36).

Though Basil was a monk, he did not reject the opportunity to be ordained as a minister in the church at Caesarea. He was set apart as a reader in 360, a presbyter in 364, and then finally as bishop of Caesarea in 370. While his preference would have been to remain in ascetic retirement in Pontus, Basil was compelled to accept ordination in large part because of the Arian heresy that was threatening the churches of Asia Minor (Basil, Letters 207.2, 223.5; Rousseau 1998, 2, 68–69, 84–85, 93; Sterk 2004, 43, 74–76). By combining his monastic and ecclesiastical callings, Basil played a part in one of the most intriguing developments of the fourth and fifth centuries—the phenomenon of the monk-bishop—that included other leaders such as Eusebius of Vercellae (283–371), Martin of Tours (316–397), Gregory of Nazianzus (329–ca. 390), John Chrysostom (347–407), and Augustine of Hippo (354–430). Unlike many monks in his day, Basil regarded the city as both his context for monastic living and Christian mission. Though he rejected Eustathius's theology, Basil did emulate his mentor's concern for urban ministry (Sterk 2004, 25–27). In addition to leading the church in his city of Caesarea, which included the tasks of preaching, administering the sacraments, and ministering to the poor, Basil served as a metropolitan bishop, meaning that he oversaw the work of some fifty other bishops in Cappadocia. One of his responsibilities included convening an annual council of bishops in which theological issues and practical church matters were addressed (Basil Letters 92, 98, 204–205; Sterk 2004, 44–46, 73–74; Smither 2008, 62–64).

Basil's Context: Cappadocian Caesarea

Let us now consider Basil's ministry context—Caesarea, the capital of the Roman province of Cappadocia in Asia Minor. Originally called Mazaca, the city was renamed Caesarea by the Emperor Claudius and it became the provincial capital in AD 17. It remained the largest and most important city in Cappadocia through the fourth century. Though precise population statistics are not available, the presence of fifty bishops leading congregations in the region of Caesarea—a reflection of the Roman administrative system—suggests that the population was significant (McHugh 1999, 213; Ramsay 1972, 281).

From an economic perspective, Caesarea was not terribly prosperous. Though olives, grapes, grain, and livestock were successfully harvested at times, the Cappadocians largely struggled with agriculture (Holman 2001, 70; Rousseau 1998, 133). In addition, the pre-Roman feudal system created such a strong sense of dependency that when the Romans did gain control of the region, the Cappadocians asked them for a king. These conditions were only worsened by multiple earthquakes in the third century that destroyed parts of Pontus and Cappadocia (McHugh 1999, 213–14).

Despite these difficulties, Caesarea was an important city because of some key Roman roads—trade routes that stretched from Constantinople to Syria—that ran through the city. On one hand, this was beneficial to Caesarea because traveling merchants would stop in the city, lodge there, and spend money in its establishments. On the other hand, the roads also brought the Roman army, including some troops that commandeered local food sources and other supplies, creating stress for the local inhabitants. Understanding Caesarea's strategic geographic location, the Roman government established the city as one of its key administrative centers. Finally, the city's location also made it an important intercultural crossroads as diverse peoples from Asia Minor, Armenia, Syria, Persia, and the Northern Gothic regions regularly spent time and interacted in Caesarea (Rousseau 1998, 133–34; Holman 2001, 69–70).

Spiritually speaking, Caesarea was initially evangelized in the first century. However, the most significant church growth and expansion occurred in the third, fourth, and fifth centuries. Mentioned previously, the most effective third-century evangelist was Gregory Thaumaturgus, who enjoyed a fruitful ministry in Cappadocia (Basil, On the Holy Spirit 74; Harakas 1999, 201–202; McHugh 1999, 213). Not unlike much of the church in the Roman Empire in the pre-Constantine period, Cappadocian Christians were persecuted for their faith by the Governor Serenianus in the mid-third century (Frend 1984, 309–310; McHugh 1999, 214).

What were the specific challenges that Basil faced in Caesarea in the fourth century? First, though Christianity had been tolerated and even preferred in Rome in the fourth century, Basil still experienced conflicts with political leaders. The most obvious was with Emperor Julian (361–363)—the so-called "apostate" who attempted to revive paganism. Annoyed by the growing number of Christians in Cappadocia, Julian's revival also involved persecuting the church, which included confiscating church property and even drafting church leaders into the army (Sozomen, History of the Church 5.4; Holman 2001, 70; Ramsay 1972, 304). While the conflict with Julian made sense, Basil also had conflict with the Arian Emperor Valens. During Basil's tenure as bishop, Valens divided Cappodocia in half, effectively limiting Basil's influence over the churches and citizens of the region. As we will see shortly, Basil had no problem confronting the political establishment over such decisions. In fact, if Basil had not been so popular with the people, he probably would have been spent time in exile as other fourth-century bishops like Athanasius and Ambrose did when they clashed with the authorities (Basil, Letters 74–76; Gregory of Nazianzus, Oration 43.56; Ramsay 1972, 283; McHugh 1999, 214; Sterk 2004, 72).

A second challenge that Basil faced had to do with theology. Though the Council of Nicaea of 325 had condemned Arius' heresy, Arianism was quite prevalent and taught by many of the bishops in Asia Minor. As Basil and the other Cappadocian fathers (Gregory of Nazianzus and Gregory of Nyssa) battled Arianism through preaching, writing, and church councils, it was this theological conflict that led to Basil's political conflicts with Valens (Basil, Letters 80, 82, 90.1, 91, 92.2–3, 203.1, 242.1, 243.4, 244.8, 256; Basil, On the Holy Spirit 30.76–77; Sterk 2004, 45). Gregory of Nazianzus described the emperor as "a cloud full of hail, with destructive roar, overwhelming every church upon which it burst and seized ... Valens, most fond of gold and most hostile to Christ." Describing the struggle, he continues:

> Furious indeed were his first acts of wantonness, more furious still his final efforts against us. What shall I speak of first? Exiles, banishments, confiscations, open and secret plots, persuasion, where

time allowed, violence, where persuasion was impossible. Those who clung to the orthodox faith, as we did, were expelled from their churches; others were imposed upon, who agreed with the imperial soul-destroying doctrines, and begged for testimonies of impiety. (Gregory of Nazianzus, Oration 43.30, 36)

A third major issue that Basil dealt with was poverty. In an insightful study on the nature of poverty in the early Christian centuries, Susan Holman writes:

In the Greek texts of the first four centuries C.E., there are two common words for the poor person, penes and ptochos. Ptochos traditionally designated the destitute beggar who is outside or at the fringes of society, the "street person," the extreme poor. Penes, on the other hand, is used to indicate the individual whose economic resources were minimal but who functioned within society, the "working poor." The penetes differ from the ptochoi in that their social ties within the community remain intact: they retain their dwellings, families, and responsibilities, including their debts. Penes could also be a derogatory term for anyone forced to engage in manual labor for survival. (Holman 2001, 5)

Generally concurring with this distinction, Basil asserts, "I consider that a ptochos is he who falls from wealth into need; but a penes is he who is in need from the first and is acceptable to the Lord" (Basil, Short Rules 262 in Holman 2001, 6). While both types of poor people lived in Caesarea, Basil's sermons (i.e., Sermon 8) suggest that the ptochoi represented the most common type of poverty. Sadly, this included desperate families who were abandoning children on the doorstep of the church at Caesarea (Holman 2001, 78–80).

The biggest factor that contributed to Caesareans slipping into poverty was the famine that hit Cappadocia in 368. In fact, it is impossible to understand Basil's ministry without describing this period of tragedy. Gregory of Nazianzus wrote:

There was a famine, the most severe one ever recorded. The city was in distress and there was no source of assistance. ... The hardest part of all such distress is the insensibility and insatiability of those who possess supplies. ... Such are the buyers and sellers of corn. (Gregory of Nazianzus, Oration 43.34 in Holman 2001, 65)

Holman adds:

> Basil's famine sermon refers back to an extremely cold, dry winter that had been followed by an unusually hot, dry spring, and this led to catastrophic agricultural crisis as wells and rivers dried up and crops failed. Those able to hoard grain increased their vigilance and the market prices. Laborers began to starve. Schools closed down. The populace came to church to pray for rain. The poor who worked in the fields and wandered along the roads took on the appearance of living cadavers. Possibly the poor resorted to exposing their children, or selling them, while the rich haggled with them over the purchase price. Gregory of Nazianzus implied that the situation was heightened by the difficulty of importing emergency food supplies to a landlocked region. (Holman 2001, 68–69)

Based on evidence from Basil's letters, the famine probably lasted for four years and resulted in additional difficulties (Basil, Letter 31). In 372, there was a riot in Caesarea. As shown, some responded by hoarding grain while others resorted to stealing (Basil, Letter 86; Holman 1999, 339). From Basil's sermons, we are also given a picture of the slow and horrible death that some were dying from starvation—"the hungry are dying."

Basil's Approach to Ministry

Given this historical, political, and cultural background of Cappadocian Caesarea as well as the specific challenges that Basil faced, let us now consider some key elements of Basil's ministry in his urban context. Four areas of ministry are most apparent: preaching and evangelism; a prophetic discourse toward oppressors; advocacy for the poor; and practical care for the poor in response to the famine and in the establishment of the basileas ("new city").

Preaching and Evangelism

A key aspect of Basil's ministry was evangelism and preaching. As noted, Basil praised the ministry of Gregory Thaumaturgus, the bishop who helped transform Cappadocia in the third century through his evangelistic preaching (Basil, On the Holy Spirit 29.34; Sterk 2004, 37). For Basil, an important element of his pastoral ministry was preaching in order to train believers and to reach non-believers with the gospel—aspects of ministry that he emphasizes to his disciples in his work Morals (Basil, Morals 70.9–11, 31–34). Finally, while describing Basil's humanitarian efforts, Gregory of Nazianzus suggests that spiritual teaching and gospel proclamation were Basil's priorities:

> [Basil] provided the nourishment of the Word and that more perfect good work and distribution being from heaven and on high; if the bread of angels is the Word, whereby souls hungry for God are fed and given to drink, and seek after nourishment that neither diminishes nor fails but remains forever; thus [i.e., by his sermons] this supplier of grain and abundant riches [he who was] the poorest and most needy [person] I have known, provided, not for a famine of bread or a thirst for water, but a longing for the truly life-giving and nourishing Word, which effects growth to spiritual maturity in those nourished well on it. (Gregory of Nazianzus Oration 43.36 in Holman 2001, 65)

Prophetic Discourse

As social, economic, and political issues plagued Caesarea, Basil's preaching was also characterized by a prophetic discourse in which he challenged the rich, poor, and political leaders to pursue righteousness. Indeed, it was the famine of 368 that prompted Basil to preach his most famous sermons on hunger and poverty—Sermons 6-9 and two sermons on Psalm 14 (Holman 1999, 338). Brian Daley asserts that Basil—not unlike other preachers trained in rhetoric—put his communication skills to work in an effort to influence his hearers toward holy living (Daley 1999, 438).

Basil's first audience included money lenders—those who were exploiting the poor during the economic crisis and lending "to the financially desperate at highly usurious rates" (Patitsas 2008, 269–70; Holman 2001, 118, 121; Rousseau 1998, 136). While declaring in one sermon that money lenders were worse than dogs, Basil preaches from Psalm 14 that "usury involves the greatest inhumanity. ... seeing a man by necessity bent down before his knees as a suppliant ... [the creditor] does not pity him who is suffering misfortune ... he takes no account of his nature; he does not yield to his supplications" (Basil, Sermon 2.2; Ramsey 1985, 187; Ihssen 2008, 417; Basil, Sermon Ps. 14b.1 in Holman 2001, 120). He builds his entire message around the single phrase, "[the righteous man] does not lend out his money at interest" (Holman 2001, 114). Similarly, in Sermon 8, Basil invited those involved in price gouging and usury to repent publicly of their sin. Holman notes that Basil goes even further and calls "usurers—anyone who lends at interest" to stop oppressing the poor and to offer interest-free loans instead (Holman 2001, 78, 114).

In the same sermons, Basil aims part of his message at the poor themselves. He urges them to repay their debts, to refrain from borrowing more, and to be content in their simplicity (Holman 2001, 114; Ihssen 2008, 420–21). Reiterating his understanding of how Caesareans slipped into poverty (ptochoi), Basil preached, "the debtor is … one who has borrowed and adopted a lavish lifestyle which he could not otherwise afford" (Basil, Sermon Ps. 14 in Ihssen 2008, 417). Finally, in Sermon 8, Basil reminds the poor that they are not so desperate that they cannot be generous themselves (Basil, Sermon 8.6).

A third group that Basil condemned through his sermons were those who hoarded food during the famine. Through storing grain in barns and in caves around Caesarea, Basil preached that the wealthy "would rather burst themselves eating than leave a crumb for the hungry" (Basil, Sermon 6.2 in Holman 2001, 103). Though the rich were materially well off, Basil asserted that they were the truly poor ones:

> You turn away from those you meet lest you be forced to let even a morsel escape your clutches. You have only one phrase: "I have nothing to give; I am a poor man." You are indeed poor; and in need of every good. You are poor in love for your fellow man; poor in humanity; poor in faith in God; poor in the hope of eternity! (Basil, Sermon 6.6 in Holman 2001, 103)

Instead of fearing the poor, Basil urged them to fear God, who will judge those who fail to act justly. Further, he encourages them to imitate God in his goodness and the Patriarch Joseph in his love for his fellow man. He adds: "Make your brothers sharers of your grain; and what may wither tomorrow, give to the needy today. For it is greed of the most horrible kind, to deny to the starving even what you must soon throw away!" (Basil, Sermon 6.6 in Holman 2001, 103; Holman 1999, 349).

Similarly, Basil chastised the wealthy for their failure to be generous with the poor. Preaching about the rich young ruler in Matthew 19, Basil largely directed Sermon 7 toward the wealthy. Asserting that accumulating wealth was an indication of misguided love and ultimately a vain endeavor, Basil reminded them that they are merely stewards of their possessions—not owners (Daley 1999, 444–45). He adds, "Consequently, the one who loves his neighbor as himself possesses nothing in excess of his neighbor's. However, you obviously have many possessions. ... clearly your wealth and superabundance indicates a lack of charity" (Basil, Sermon 7.1 in Holman 2001, 105). While warning that hoarding wealth would lead to further social problems in Caesarea, Basil invites them to participate in the joy of giving—a sure outcome of their salvation in Christ. In this sense, he commends to them the example of the Good Samaritan and charges them to be good neighbors to the poor and oppressed in Caesarea (Basil, Sermon on Ps. 14a.3; Holman 2001, 105, 109, 112). In short, for Basil, authentic faith should transform Caesarea's economic system as generosity overcame greed while the rich and poor worshiped together in Christian community (Basil, Sermons 332.2, 323.5; Rousseau 1998, 178–79).

While much of Basil's prophetic discourse was directed at the issues of poverty and hunger, he also confronted the social sin of slavery. Slavery was not a new issue to Asia Minor as the Goths had attacked the region in the fourth century and taken some Cappadocians captive—including the family of the famous Arian missionary Ulfilas [ca. 310–383] (McHugh 1999, 214). Though, as noted, some parents were abandoning their children to the care of the church during the famine, many others were selling their children into slavery. In Sermon 8, Basil called parents to repentance for these tragic choices (Holman 2001, 81). Elsewhere, arguing that all creatures were subservient to God—not one another—Basil categorically denounced slavery as a human condition (Basil, On the Holy Spirit 20.51; Ramsey 1985, 67; Frend 1984, 570). While he preached against slavery, he wrote many other letters to communicate prophetically about this social sin (Basil, Letters 72, 73, 177–78, 273–75, 307).

Finally, Basil was not opposed to confronting Roman officials in a prophetic manner, especially those with Arian leanings that were putting pressure on the church. Gregory of Nazianzus records an exchange that Basil had with the Roman Prefect Modestus, who openly challenged Basil for not respecting the Emperor Valens. Basil related that he only followed the teachings of a true Sovereign—the Lord. When Modestus asked if Basil feared him, the following exchange occurred:

> "Fear of what?" said Basil, "How could it affect me? ... confiscation, banishment, torture, death. Have you no other threat?" said he, "for none of these can reach me ... Because ... a man who has

nothing, is beyond the reach of confiscation; unless you demand my tattered rags, and the few books, which are my only possessions. Banishment is impossible for me, who am confined by no limit of place, counting my own neither the land where I now dwell, nor all of that into which I may be hurled. ... As for tortures, what hold can they have upon one whose body has ceased to be? ... Death is my benefactor, for it will send me the sooner to God." Amazed at this language, the prefect said, "No one has ever yet spoken thus, and with such boldness, to Modestus." "Why, perhaps," said Basil, "you have not met ... a bishop ... where the interests of God are at stake, we care for nothing else, and make these our sole object." (Gregory of Nazianzus, Oration 43.48–50)

Advocacy for the Poor

Basil went beyond merely preaching about the spiritual and physical needs in Caesarea; he used his position as a bishop to be an advocate for the poor, needy, and suffering in his city. In addition to integrating a monastic and ecclesiastical calling, Basil also combined his pastoral office with that of a Roman patron—one endowed with authority and influence to impact society. While patrons were a normal part of the Roman social fabric, in the post-Constantine era, bishops were accorded a level of authority and often functioned as judges and mediators in the court system. In light of Caesarea's needs, Basil did not reject this opportunity to influence political leaders and even model for the government how to solve important social and economic problems (Sterk 2004, 66–69; Rousseau 1998, 170–71; Holman 2001, 98). Sterk writes:

> In Basil's capacity as a patron he endeavored to act consistently with his understanding of both monastic vocation and episcopal responsibility [and] attempted to apply the principles of the Gospel in confronting the social and political realities of his day, even ... [using] ... the tactics of petition and mediation. (Sterk 2004, 68–69)

Peter Brown adds, "Nowhere was the Christian representation of the church's novel role in society more aggressively maintained than in the claim of Christian bishops to act as 'lovers of the poor'" (cited in Holman 2001, 18). Through his letters and personal meetings, Basil lobbied to secure tax relief for the poor, tax exempt status for priests, and tax exemption for his basileas ministry, which will be discussed shortly (Basil, Letters 88, 104, 110, 303, 308–309, 316–17; 86-87; 142–44; Sterk 2004, 67–68; Rousseau 1998, 142–43, 159). In addition, he appealed to the wealthy to gain an eternal perspective on material possessions and leave part of their estates to the poor (Rousseau 1998, 139; Frend 1984, 569). Though Basil experienced conflict with Valens, the bishop still managed to secure a donation from the emperor for his ministry to the poor (Gregory of Nazianzus, Oration 43.63; Sterk 2004, 70; Rousseau 1998, 140; Holman 2001, 75).

Practical Response: To Famine

Andrew Dinan correctly notes that Basil's ministry was not limited to preaching and advocacy as "Basil's solicitude for the welfare of his people was manifest in concrete ways" (Dinan 2009, 135). In an extended description, Gregory of Nazianzus describes Basil's courageous leadership and generosity in response to the famine of 368:

> By his word and advice [Basil] opened the stores of those who possessed them, and so, according to the Scripture, dealt food to the hungry and satisfied the poor with bread ... and in what way? ... He gathered together the victims of the famine with some who were but slightly recovering from it, men and women, infants, old men ... and obtaining contributions of all sorts of food which can relieve famine, set before them basins of soup and such meat as was found preserved among us, on which the poor live. Then, imitating the ministry of Christ ... he attended to the bodies and souls of those who needed it, combining personal respect with the supply of their necessity, and so giving them a double relief. Such was our young furnisher of corn, and second Joseph ... [But unlike Joseph, Basil's] services were gratuitous and his succor of the famine gained no profit, having only one object, to win kindly feelings by kindly treatment, and to gain by his rations of corn the heavenly blessings. (Gregory of Nazianzus, Oration 43.34–36 in Holman 2001, 65)

Unlike the proconsul of Carthage (North Africa), who personally profited from the famine during this period, Basil upheld his conviction for generosity toward the poor and hungry. Again, according to Gregory, Basil liquidated some of his own inherited assets to help meet the needs of the Caesareans. He writes:

> [Basil] ungrudgingly spent upon the poor his patrimony even before he was a priest, and most of all in the time of the famine, during which he was a ruler of the church, though still a priest in the rank of presbyters; and afterwards did not hoard even what remained to him. (Gregory of Nazianzus, Against Eunomius 1.10 in Holman 2001, 66)

Though Basil's brother Gregory of Nyssa likened him to Elijah, Gregory of Nazianzus presented him as a Joseph for the people of Caesarea. Basil seemed to agree with the latter description. In Sermon 6, he interpreted and applied the Joseph narratives from Genesis toward his ministry in Caesarea: "I shall open my barns. I shall be like Joseph in proclaiming the love of my fellow man" (Basil, Sermon 6.2 in Holman 2001, 128).

Practical Response: The Basileas

A second concrete expression of Basil's ministry to the poor in Caesarea was the establishment of the basileas ("new city")—"a complex of buildings constructed at the edge of Caesarea during the early years of Basil's episcopate" (Sterk 2004, 69). Built on land owned by Basil's family or perhaps donated by the emperor, the complex was first called the basileas by the fifth-century church historian Sozomen, who recorded: "the basileas, the most celebrated hospice for the poor. It was established by Basil, bishop of Caesarea, from whom it received its name in the beginning, and retains it until today" (Sozomen, Ecclesiastical History 6.34.9). While Basil was influenced by others to act on behalf of the poor (his pious family, his sister Macrina, and Eustathius), it seems that the devastation caused by the famine of 368 drove him to launch the basileas project (Basil, Letters 94, 150, 176; Daley 199, 432; Patitsas 2008, 269; Sterk 2004, 40, 69; Dinan 1999, 137–38; Holman 2001, 76).

What were the specific ministries of the basileas? First, the complex included a home for the poor. Some of residents probably included children that had been abandoned by their parents during the famine (Gregory of Nazianzus, Oration 43.35; Holman 2001, 80). Second, the facility had a hospital that cared for the sick. Sterk suggests that some patients were suffering from leprosy (Sterk 2004, 69). Third, the basileas offered the poor an opportunity to work and to develop job skills (Patitsas 2008, 269; Holman 2001, 74). Fourth, as noted, the complex included storehouses with food supplies administered by the "Joseph" of Caesarea (Rousseau

1998, 142). Finally, as Caesarea was located on a crossroads between Asia Minor, Syria, Armenia and the Gothic regions, the basileas included a hospice for travelers (Rousseau 1998, 133). Basil insisted that his disciples be able to show hospitality to minister to other believers but also as a means to witness to non-Christians. In his Long Rules, he writes:

> Has a guest arrived? If he is a brother ... he will recognize the fare we provide as properly his own. What he has left at home, he will find with us. Suppose he is weary after his journey. We then provide as much nourishment as is required to relieve his weariness. Is it a secular person who has arrived? Let him learn through actual experience ... and let him be given a model and pattern of frugal sufficiency in matters of food. ... In every case, care must be taken for a good table, yet without overstepping the limits of the actual need. This should be our aim in hospitality—that the individual requirements of our guests may be cared for. (Basil, Long Rules 20)

For Basil, the basileas ministry was perhaps the clearest expression of what it meant for him to be a monk-bishop ministering in the city. Indeed, his monasticism was characterized by voluntary poverty following the example of John the Baptist (if one has two coats, give the other away), Jesus (sell all you have and give it to the poor), and the early Christians in Acts (selling their goods and sharing everything in common) (Basil, Letter 150; Frend 1984, 631; Daley 1999, 439). In his instruction to Christian leaders in Morals, he stated, "one who is entrusted with the preaching of the Gospel should possess nothing more than is strictly necessary for him" (Basil, Morals 70.27).

As a coenobitic monk, Basil's monastic vision also relied largely on community. McGuire helpfully notes that "Basil is the first monastic writer in the East to be totally convinced that a common life provided the best way of bringing individual men to God" (McGuire 1988, 31). In addition to the monasteries that Basil oversaw in Caesarea, the basileas also provided a communal context of spiritual growth for Basil's disciples (Basil, Letter 150; Smither 2008, 56).

Basil's expectation was that the monastic community would be a community that served others. Distinguishing his communal monastic vision from those who withdrew into isolation, he simply asked: "Whose feet will you wash? For whom will you care? In comparison with whom will you be the least?" (Basil, Long Rules

7 in Ramsey 1985, 180). Dinan helpfully notes that the goal of Basil's manual labor was charity—loving God and loving one's neighbor (Dinan 1999, 147–49).

Finally, Basil was convinced that an important task of a bishop or Christian leader was caring for the poor. Basil instructed spiritual leaders in his Morals that "the preacher of the Word should be compassionate and merciful, especially toward those who are suffering distress of soul" and be "solicitous even with regard to the bodily needs of those in our charge" (Basil, Morals 70.19–20). While it is clear that clergy in Caesarea were quite involved in administrating the work of the basileas, Basil also encouraged church leaders in Cappadocia and Asia Minor to make ministry to the poor a priority in their churches (Basil, Letters 142–43; Sterk 2004, 74; Patitsas 2008, 269, 282; Daley 1999, 440; Rousseau 1998, 143). Though at times this admonition was met with some resistance by some church leaders, there is evidence that a number of smaller projects for the poor developed in Cappadocia under the leadership of bishops that Basil supervised (Basil, Letters 141.2, 223.3; 142–44; Rousseau 1998, 149; Sterk 2004, 69–70).

Sterk summarizes: "for Basil, then, involvement in such a foundation was what committed ascetics as well as bishops ought to be doing. Such activity on the part of monks, bishops, and laity alike made the Gospel a living reality in the city" (Sterk 2004, 71). Basil's efforts appeared to be sustainable as the basileas facility remained intact and ministry to the poor continued for over a century after his death (Holman 2001, 75).

Conclusion

Basil died at the age of forty-nine, yet he lived a very full life. He was a theologian par excellence who also presented a winsome model for Christian leadership. Having discussed the political, theological, and social issues that he faced in fourth-century Caesarea, I have argued that Basil was a Christian leader who was quite engaged with his context and ministered in a relevant manner. While apparently prioritizing the ministries of preaching and evangelism, he ministered courageously to the needs of the poor in Caesarea. He read the Joseph narratives in quite a functional manner and found meaningful application for them in his context. Finally, his ministry to the poor was a concrete expression of his monastic and pastoral theology. He chose a lifestyle of voluntary poverty in community with others and, in turn, this community lived out the gospel in word and deed in Caesarea.

As evangelical Christians participate in urban mission today, what can be learned from Basil? In closing, I would like to stimulate some dialogue for modern practitioners by discussing Basil's four approaches to urban mission.

1. Preaching and Evangelism. Central to being an evangelical is proclaiming the gospel. In his work as a theologian and conflicts with the Arian political authorities, Basil showed great resolve to maintain the purity of the gospel. Even as he ministered during the famine, he seemed to make proclamation his priority. As evangelicals move forward in urban mission today, how will we safeguard this priority? As many good and legitimate ministries in an urban context demand our energy and focus (i.e., nutrition, community health, sports, literacy, job skills training), how will we keep our urban mission Christian? (Little 2008; McQuilkin et al. 2008; Stott 1982).
2. Prophetic Discourse. Basil was a preacher by trade. Not only did he disciple his congregation through preaching, but he also aimed his biblical exegesis at the social evils of his day and confronted usurious money lenders, the discontent poor, the indifferent wealthy, and heretical political leaders. What does our prophetic discourse look like today? Should we blast government decisions and leaders that fall short of a biblical standard? Are we engaged enough with our urban contexts to preach relevantly toward the city? How do we preach against social sins and remain focused and grounded on a biblical exegetical foundation?
3. Advocacy. Basil used his position as a bishop in the Roman Empire to be an advocate for the poor. Yet, what does advocacy look like in the twenty-first-century, post-Christendom era? To be sure, many pastors and missionaries in the present global urban context do not have the clout to appeal to the authorities about the poor or other injustices. As we assess the role of North American Christians in global missions in the twenty-first century, advocacy seems to be a real strength of North Americans and a place in which they may reasonably contribute. Groups such as International Christian Concern are doing a formidable job of telling the story of the persecuted church around the world and lobbying on their behalf to political leaders. Even as I write this paper, some American Christian leaders waged a campaign on

Twitter and successfully lobbied for the release of an Afghani Christian sentenced to death for his faith.

4. Practical response in the *basileas*. Basil was engaged with his urban context through the *basileas*—a community that cared for the poor and hungry, the sick, and travelers passing through. Most evangelicals today involved in urban mission are not monks, yet what monastic principles observed in Basil's ministry are meaningful for evangelicals today? Evangelicals who have started or served in hospitals, orphanages, schools, food pantries, and clothes closets can relate to the major components of the *basileas*. However, can we identify with the ministry of hospitality that Basil championed? How does hospitality relate to mission?

References

Ayres, L. (2009). The Cappadocians. In A. D. Fitzgerald (Ed.), *Augustine through the ages: An encyclopedia* (121–24). Grand Rapids, MI: Eerdmans.

Basil of Caesarea. (1962). Long rules, short rules, morals. In M. M. Wagner (Trans.), *Saint Basil's Ascetical Works, Fathers of the Church 5*. Washington, DC: Catholic University Press.

_____. (1951). Letters, Volume 1 (1–185). In A. C. Way (Trans.), *Fathers of the Church 13*. Washington, DC: Catholic University Press.

_____. (1955). Letters, Volume 2 (186–368). In A. C. Way (Trans.), *Fathers of the Church 28*. Washington, DC: Catholic University Press.

_____. (1980). *On the Holy Spirit*. (D. Anderson, Trans.). Crestwood, NY: St. Vladimir's Seminary Press.

Daley, B. E. (1999). Building a new city: The Cappadocian fathers and the rhetoric of philanthrophy." *Journal of Early Christian Studies* 7(3), 431–61.

Dinan, A. (2009). Manual labor in the life and thought of St. Basil the Great. *Logos: A Journal of Catholic Thought and Culture* 12(4), 133–57.

Frend, W.H.C. (1984). *The rise of Christianity*. Philadelphia: Fortress Press.

Gregory of Nazianus. (n.d.). Oration 43. In Nicene and Post-Nicene Fathers 2.7, *Christian Classics Ethereal Library*. Retrieved from http://www.ccel.org/ccel/schaff/npnf207.iii.xxvi.html.

Harakas, S. S. (1999). Caesarea in Cappadocia. In E. Ferguson (Ed.), *Encyclopedia of Early Christianity* (201–02). London: Routledge.

Holman, S. R. (2001). *The hungry are dying: Beggars and bishops in Roman Cappadocia*. New York: Oxford University Press.

_____. (1999). The hungry body: Famine, poverty, and identity in Basil's Hom. 8. *Journal of Early Christian Studies* 7(3), 337–63.

Ihssen, B. L. (2008). Basil and Gregory's sermons on usury: Credit where credit is due. *Journal of Early Christian Studies* 16(3), 403–30.

International Christian Concern. (2011). http://www.persecution.org.

Little, C. (2008). What makes mission Christian? Christian mission today: Are we on a slippery slope?" *International Journal of Frontier Missiology* 25(2), 65–73.

McGuire, B. P. (1988). *Friendship and community: The monastic experience 350–1250*. Kalamazoo, MI: Cistercian Studies 95.

McHugh, M. P. (1999). Cappadocia. In E. Ferguson (Ed.), *Encyclopedia of Early Christianity* (213–15). London: Routledge.

McQuilkin, R. et al. (2008). Responses to Christopher Little's "What makes mission Christian? *International Journal of Frontier Missiology* 25(2), 75–85.

Patitsas, T. (2008). St. Basil's philanthropic program and modern microlending strategies for economic self-actualization. In S. R. Holman (Ed.), *Wealth and Poverty in Early Church and Society* (267–86). Grand Rapids, MI: Baker Academic.

Ramsay, W. R. (1972). *The historical geography of Asia Minor*. New York: Cooper Square Publishers.

Ramsey, B. (1985). *Beginning to read the fathers*. Mahwah, NJ: Paulist Press.

Rousseau, P. (1998). *Basil of Caesarea*. Berkley, CA: University of California Press.

Smither, E. L. (2008). *Augustine as mentor: A model for preparing spiritual leaders*. Nashville, TN: B&H Academic.

Sozomen. (2011). Ecclesiastical history. In Nicene and Post-Nicene Fathers 2.2, *Christian Classics Ethereal Library*. Retrieved from http://www.ccel.org/ccel/schaff/npnf202.iii.xi.xxxiv.html.

Sterk, A. (2004). *Renouncing the world yet leading the church: The monk-bishop in late antiquity*. Cambridge, MA: Harvard University Press.

Stott, J. R. W. (1982). Evangelism and social responsibility: An evangelical commitment. Lausanne Occasional Paper 21. Retrieved from http://www.lausanne.org/all-documents/lop-21.html

Jacques Ellul's Contribution to an Evangelical Theology of the City

Stephen Strauss
sstrauss@dts.edu

Ministry must always begin with theology. Any ministry that is not rooted deeply in the soil of Scripture will soon wither away for lack of power or stumble into short-term expediency that yields short-lived results. This is especially true in the difficult task of reaching the world's cities for Christ. Ministry in the cities must be grounded in a solid theology of the city if it is to be long-lasting and effective. C. Henk Koetsier argues that one of the main reasons churches in Europe "have not been able to cope with the situation in the cities" is because of "theological withdrawal." "Churches have not been able or willing to reflect critically and creatively on the challenges posed to them by the cities. There is little theological analysis and reflection on what is actually happening. It seems as if theology has lost interest in the world of the modern city" (1986, 46). It is vital that the massive task of evangelizing and discipling the world's cities is grounded in a solid theology of the city.

A helpful vantage point from which to reflect on a theology of the city is the work of sociologist and theologian Jacques Ellul. Ellul's writings on the city are comprehensive and profound. At first glance one might think Ellul's writings must be out of date since they were written twenty to forty years ago. But a careful reading of Ellul reveals that he is still highly significant for the second decade of the twenty-first century. This chapter will seek to summarize Jacques Ellul's thought about modernity and the city and reflect on his continued contribution to a theology of the city in the church's third millennium.

The Technical Society: Ellul's Understanding of Modernity and Urbanization

Ellul's sociology of modernity and urbanization is centered around the concept of *technique*. By technique Ellul means more than technology. He borrows H. D. Lasswell's definition of technique "as 'the ensemble of practices by which one uses available resources in order to achieve certain valued ends'" (Ellul 1964, 18). "The technical phenomenon" occurs when "tentative, unconscious, and spontaneous" acts become "clear, voluntary, and reasoned concepts" to obtain better results (ibid., 20). Technique is "the one best means in every field," and "in every field men seek to find the most efficient method" (ibid., 21). Technique is the assumption that technical progress is always good, leading to a never-ending, self-perpetuating search for the "best" way to achieve results.

Prior to the nineteenth century, people used technology, but it "was applied only in certain narrow, limited areas" (ibid., 64). Technologies were local, evolved slowly, and had a limited purpose. "The search for greater efficiency ... was one factor among several" (ibid., 73). But today most Western value systems are controlled by the idea that seeking better technology to achieve better results is inherently good. Their worldview is controlled by "technique."

Ellul makes his case for technique as a central feature of the modern worldview by describing a number of characteristics of modern technique. Most people today automatically seek the best way of doing things, and "the worst reproach modern society can level is the charge that some person or system is impeding this technical" progress (ibid., 80). "Modern men are so enthusiastic about technique, so assured of its superiority, so immersed in the technical milieu, that without exception they are oriented toward technical progress" (ibid., 85). Furthermore, though the technicians claim to have the betterment of humanity as their goal, better technique has become an end in itself.

> *Technical civilization* means that our civilization is constructed by technique (makes a part of civilization only what belongs to technique), for technique (in that everything in this civilization must serve a technical end), and is exclusively technique (in that it excludes whatever is not technique or reduces it to technical form). ... *Technique has taken over the whole of civilization.* (ibid., 128)

Ellul demonstrates the pervasiveness of technique in economics, government, and human relations. In the field of economics, the emphasis on the elimination of waste, economic "laws," growth, and production have turned people into no more than pieces in an economic machine, both as producers and consumers. Government has become geared to constant improvement and better organization, all of which works to give someone power over someone else. Legal systems are so enamored with technique that social order has become more important than justice. And in human relations, the goal has become "through psychological means to draw from man his last measure of effort and at the same time compel him to bear up under the disadvantages with which the new society hinders him." Technique, then, has become the integrating center of the modern, Western worldview. "Every human initiative must use technical means to express itself" (ibid., 420).

Reflections on "Technique"

Ellul's observations on technique provide tremendous insight into Western worldview. Indeed, "technique" is so much a part of the way people now look at the world that is it difficult for those who are a part of modern, urbanized societies to conceive of any other way of thinking. Ellul helps Westerners realize that they *presume* technique. He opens their eyes to see that there are other ways of looking at the world rather than constantly planning for the best way to achieve tangible results.

It could be argued that Ellul's observations on technique are out of date. The emptiness of the technical society is one cause for the birth of a post-modern worldview, a worldview that acknowledges the transcendent and makes interpersonal relationships and personal fulfillment a substitute for the constant organizing and improving that is the hallmark of technique. However "modern consciousness is rather hard to get rid of. Its definitions of reality and its psychological consequences are dragged along even into the rebellions against it, providing the ironic spectacle of an assault on modernity by people whose consciousness presupposes the same modernity" (Berger 1973, 215). The modern worldview is so thoroughly self-integrated and self-perpetuating that it cannot be easily deconstructed. Even as Westerners begin to absorb postmodernism, pursuit of progress and whatever is "best" remains part of their core, worldview assumptions. It might even be argued that post-modernism is itself a form of technique, the striving for a "better" environment, a more holistic, "better" self.

Ellul himself reflected on technique in his later life, as postmodernism gained an increasing hold on Western worldview, and stated that he had "no need to correct or modify anything" he had written earlier (1990, xii). Rather, he saw technique extended even deeper into Western society. "It is still the same technical system. It is richer and more complex" (ibid., 6). Though he died before e-mail and the Internet became ubiquitous, one can almost hear him pointing to these as the most recent examples of how technique becomes an end in itself, perhaps asking, "Has the speed of e-mail and the volume of information on the Internet *really* made your lives more fulfilling, or are they simply part of the impulse to always do more and do it faster?"

Postmodernism may be an example of "late modernity" (Rommen 2011) that retains the assumed "good" of progress or it may be a truly different worldview. In either case, technique does seem to still be a significant part of the Western worldview; Ellul performs a useful service in identifying it. But the emptiness created by the technical worldview has drawn mankind to question it and to search for something more. Evangelicals can identify this postmodern search as an example of Augustine's "God shaped vacuum" in human beings; technique leaves people feeling that there must be more to life than better results and greater efficiency.

The Meaning of the City: Ellul's Theology of the City

Ellul's ideas about the pervasiveness of technique could elicit a great deal more comment, but for the purposes of this chapter, they primarily form the background to his second book, *The Meaning of the City*, which Ellul himself described as "the theological counterpoint" to *The Technological Society* (Ellul 1970, vii).

The City in the Old Testament: Rebellious Independence from God

Ellul begins his theology of the city by surveying the Old Testament attitude about the city. Throughout the Old Testament he sees the building of cities as an act of rebellious independence from God. This begins with Cain. When Cain is expelled from Eden, he is condemned to a life of wandering. "Cain does two things to make his curse bearable. … He will satisfy his desire for eternity by producing children, and he will satisfy his desire for security by creating a place belonging to him, a city. … He is far from the Lord's face, and so he will shift for himself" (ibid., 5). Cain names his city Enoch, which means "inauguration," "initiation" or "dedication." In opposition to God's creation, Eden, Cain inaugurates his own city. "Now a start is made, and it is no longer God beginning, but man" (ibid., 6).

Nimrod and the people of Babel continue this rebellious independence from God when they build their cities. Nimrod names one of his cities Resen (Gen 10:12), which means "bridle." The horse represented "human power glorified," and by naming his city "bridle," Nimrod is symbolizing his control of nature. Ellul says that Resen "is the city of technique, of invention, of domination over nature" (ibid., 14). In the same way, the people of Babel built their city to make a name for themselves, a way of earning their independence from God. "It is only in an urban civilization that man has the metaphysical possibility of saying 'I killed God'" by excluding him and replacing his creation with their own (ibid., 16). Ellul believes that the point of the Babel story is not the beginning of different languages, but the introduction of a lack of understanding among people. In the city, people try to unite themselves to exalt themselves, but in the end are even more at odds with one another. "By the confusion of tongues, by noncommunication, God keeps man from forming a truth valid for all men. Henceforth, man's truth will only be partial and contested." "In and because of the city men can no longer understand each other and get along" (ibid., 19).

Ellul then turns to the nation Israel and traces her relationship to cities. Again, he finds that the building of cities typifies rebellion and independence from God. In Genesis, Israel did not build cities, only altars. It was in captivity that they learned to build cities, cities of slavery. When Israel built cities in Canaan, it was "the imitation of what she had learned in Egypt, before the deliverance" and so was "the sign of a curse, and the proclamation of slavery renewed" (ibid., 25). Ellul sees this return to rebellion in the conquests of Abimelech, the building programs of Solomon and Rehoboam, and the rebuilding of Jericho. The sermons of the prophets were directed against this return to the slavery of Egypt symbolized by the cities. In fact, according to Ellul, the book of Chronicles is edited specifically to emphasize that "the construction of cities is in itself an expression of separation from God" (ibid., 39).

The City as Epitomized by Babylon: Cursed by God

Ellul believes that throughout the Old Testament the city is an autonomous entity to which God speaks. Though God offers mercy to the individuals in the city, when speaking to the city as a corporate being, God only has words of condemnation. This is true of every city, but especially for Babylon, which becomes the figure of all other cities. "She is the second creation and wants autonomy. In all her activities she affirms that her strength is all-sufficient. ... She excludes God because she is for herself her own sufficient spirituality. ... The city has chosen her special role by specifically and voluntarily shutting herself off from any divine intervention. Stubbornly, obstinately, of her own will, she applies all her attention to herself" (ibid., 52, 54).

Based on Isaiah 47:9–14, Jeremiah 51:8–9, and Revelation 18:14, Ellul believes that the city as an institution, epitomized by Babylon, cannot be redeemed. "The city cannot be reformed. Neither can she become other than what men have made of her" (ibid., 57). So what should be the response of the people of God who live in the city? Not to escape, for they cannot. Not to destroy the city, for that is God's job. Ellul finds the believer's response in Jeremiah 29:4–7, 10. Believers are to work for the city's good and to pray for the city. And, as Jonah did for Nineveh and Jesus commanded his disciples to do in Matthew 10 and Luke 10, they are to call the city to repentance. The presence of God's people in the city is one example of God's grace toward the city. But the city is still condemned.

Jerusalem:
The Witness City

Ellul sees Jerusalem as a special city. She is a holy city, holy because of the temple, and because God chose her and dwells in her even though people do not want him there. She bears his name and "is therefore his power" (ibid., 102). Nevertheless, she is still a city. "She never escapes from all the characteristics of the city, as is indicated by the accusations constantly aimed at her," her bloodshed, and her idolatry (ibid., 97; Ezek 16; Jer 21). And so, Jerusalem is a witness to both God's condemnation of and grace toward the city. "Her presence announces that all that she is must disappear and that man's goal in creating the city will be found in the city, but in another city, that city which must replace Jerusalem" (ibid., 108).

Jesus does not alter the curse on Jerusalem. He holds out the promise of grace and salvation, and he has compassion on the individual people of the city, but "he never proclaims grace for man's work. All he recognizes is its devilish quality, and his only reaction is to struggle against the power of the city trying to hinder his work" (ibid., 113; Matt 11:20ff). And when Jesus was crucified in Jerusalem, she ceased to be the holy city. Jesus himself has taken her sacred role (ibid., 138–139). So what is now the responsibility of the followers of Jesus in regard to the city? He has not abandoned the city and neither must they. Instead, in Luke 21:20ff, he calls his disciples to abandon the *values* of the city, the independent security apart from God that can breed so easily in the city.

The city, then, "is man's greatest work" (ibid., 154). People are magically attracted to cities because they are the places where ideas flourish and where it is possible "for man to do what he wants when he wants" (ibid., 152). But this shows that the true character of the city is still what it was when Cain built the first city. It remains a combination of man's prideful work and evil spiritual powers.

The Heavenly Jerusalem: God's Work to Manifest Himself

Because of the evil nature of the city, mankind will never be able to transform it. "Poor little man. You failed to notice that you are not dealing with flesh and blood, but with Thrones, and Powers and Dominations which are attacking you … and that the Devil's last trick is to make you think that you can put order back into this chaos, that you are going to get spiritually big enough to control the world" (ibid.,166–167). Instead, it is God himself who will bring about the renewal of the human race in the renewal of the city. Even as God used human means of communication to give the Bible, he will "take over for himself man's invention of the city. … His Jerusalem will be the fulfillment of all that man expected. It is in Jesus Christ that God adopts man's work" (ibid., 176).

The New Jerusalem is first and foremost a work of God. It is God "taking possession of the world from which man wanted him excluded" (ibid., 190). It is God, no longer hidden in the city, but revealing himself through the city and glorifying himself through the city. What man had inaugurated as a means and monument of rebellion, God will recreate to reveal and glorify himself.

Until God recreates this New Jerusalem, believers must remember that they "have [their] job to do in the city" (ibid., 181). Even though they can never bring the New Jerusalem to earth, for that is the work of God alone, and even though they can expect "rejection by the city," they must remain "faithful witnesses to God's work" in the city (ibid., 182).

Reflections on Ellul's Theology of the City

What does Ellul contribute to a biblically balanced theology of the city? What important elements are missing from his theology? The remainder of this paper will reflect on Ellul's contribution to a theology of the city.

The Importance of a Careful Hermeneutic

Any biblical theology must begin with a careful hermeneutic. Whenever one approaches Scripture with a predetermined set of concerns (such as the city), it is easy to miss the meaning of the text intended by the author and read into the text a message that is not there. This is especially true of a subject like the city, for there are few passages in Scripture exclusively devoted to a theology of the city. And so,

> the temptation is strong to make restricted biblical passages on the city say more than they do. Hermeneutical carelessness can miss larger biblical themes into which urban concerns are gathered. An urban typology can emerge that is artificially imposed on passages chosen for emphasis. Modern readers' interests can divorce the text from the intentions of its divinely inspired author. (Conn 1992, 14)

At times Ellul seems to fall into this trap. He finds a reference in the Bible to a city, but instead of beginning with careful exegesis to determine the meaning of the text in its original context, he makes a methodological leap and applies a detail of the text directly to today. For example, he interprets Jesus' warning to flee from Jerusalem to the mountains in Luke 21:20ff as a call for believers today to abandon the values of the city. As Conn suggests, the heart of a biblical theology of the city must not be proof texts, but "larger biblical themes into which urban concerns are gathered."

The City as a Center of Human Sin and a Focus of God's Grace

Introduction: Humanity in Concentration and Complexity

Perhaps the place to begin a biblical theology of the city rooted in the exegetically-based themes of Scripture is by seeing the city as a concentration of humanity and a complexity of human social systems. The Bible has a lot to say about humanity.

First, Genesis teaches that men and women were created in the image of God (Gen 1:26–28; 5:1–2) and, despite the Fall, people continue to bear that image (Jas 3:9). Second, Romans 5:12–21 and Ephesians 2:1–3 remind us that all human beings have been touched with the sin of their first parents; Romans 1:18–3:20 adds that all people are themselves sinners. Finally, Scripture teaches that, in his mercy, God has made a measure of his grace common to all mankind (Acts 14:17: 17:26–27; 2 Thess 2:6–7; 2 Pet 3:9). Human beings are sinners by birth and personal responsibility, but still bear God's image and receive his unmerited favor.

Cities are concentrations of human beings relating to one another in complex human social systems. Because human beings are concentrated in the city, their sin and depravity is concentrated in the city. Filled with rebellious sinners seeking to be independent from God, cities can exhibit their greatest acts of pride and rebellion. Moreover their sin and depravity infect the complex social systems of the city, resulting in systemic evil that goes beyond individual personal sin. Ellul argues that the city is an autonomous "entity in itself," cursed by God (1970, 44). But, as Kaiser responds, "to depict the city as evil would be to miss the problem of sin and the fact that Scripture locates sin's roots in the hearts of men and women" (1989, 6). If cities are evil, they are only evil because they are home for depraved human beings and their social systems.

But the individuals who congregate in the cities are not only sinners. They are also concentrations of human beings who bear the image of God. The context of Genesis 1 explains humankind as created in God's image in two ways: to rule over creation (1:26) and with the capacity for complementary relationships (1:27). Because God gave people the capacity and mandate to rule the earth, they themselves are willing and able to be creative. Because God gave people the capacity for relationships, they are willing and able to form intimate bonds with one another. Cities are centers of the creative and relational energy God gave to people created in his image and which he ordained them to use. Ellul's insight into cities as "man's greatest work" (1970, 154) to which "people are magically attracted" (152) because they are places where ideas flourish is suggestive of the energy cities possess as concentrations of people created in the image of God. As such, they are a special focus of his love and grace. God loves people, and so he loves the city because it is the center of humanity.

The Sin of the City: Personal and Systemic

There are two distinct kinds of sin in the city. First, there is the personal sin of vast numbers of people.

> Much of a city's evil is personal. When such sin accumulates among its people (as it did in Sodom), the city itself becomes overwhelmed by and possessed by such sin. Thus, in a profound sense the sin takes on corporate dimensions because it is being very slavishly indulged in by a vast number of that city's citizens. (Linthicum 1991, 41)

Cities sometimes seem to be such evil places for this reason. Vast numbers of sinful human beings living close together will multiply the effects of their sin. Furthermore, the very size of the city makes personal sin easier. Unlike rural areas and villages where everyone knows everyone else, it is easy for a person to get lost in the anonymity of the city. Anonymity can make people feel free from group inhibitions and that can increase sin. As Ellul says, the city offers "liberty, that is, the possibility for man to do what he wants when he wants" (1970, 152).

But there is a second kind of sin in the city. This is the evil that can take hold of the city's social systems. "A city's evil is far greater than the sum of the sin of the individuals. The very systems of a city ... become corrupt, grasping, oppressive, and exploitive" (Linthicum 1991, 46). "Social, political, economic and legal structures—indeed, the whole of life—are permeated with sin. Economic exploitation of the poor and political oppression of human beings by their fellow men are urban realities that cannot be denied" (Conn 1987, 140). Sociologically, cities are a complex web of human social systems and relationships. As individual sin infects those systems on a massive scale, the systems themselves become oppressive and unjust.

This is the context in which to understand Ellul's perspective on Babylon. Ellul correctly sees Babylon as the epitome of human sinfulness, as a "symbol of all that stood opposed to God and his reign" (Kaiser 1989, 14). But is Babylon sinful because she is the ultimate city? Linthicum's understanding seems better. He sees Babylon as the city of Satan because 1) "she had committed herself to the worship of another god" and 2) "she had given herself to the unconditional exploitation of the world in order to foster her own economic security and luxury" (1991, 279, 281). Babylon is not the epitome of sinfulness because she is a city, but because, as an evil, corporate community of individuals, she is opposed to God's law, his covenant people, and his covenant purposes.

Cain, Nimrod, and Babel

Ellul sees the cities in the early chapters of Genesis as "human power glorified" as people seek to dominate nature. He looks "at the city as a symbol of the technology he fears" (Conn 1992, 13). But the Scripture never condemns people, or cities, for planning and using their resources to obtain the best, most efficient result (Ellul's "technique"). Indeed, making the best use of resources would seem to be included in humankind's mandate to be stewards of the earth for the betterment of humanity and the creation. Ellul seems to be overstretching his sociological analysis of modernity when he sees "technique" in the early chapters of Genesis, and he seems to be overstretching his theology in his assumption that technique is equal to rebellion against God. However, the early chapters of Genesis do seem to connect cities with mankind's desire to rebel and build a world apart from God. Nimrod's city "had become more than a place of protection and safety; it was now a center from which an autocratic abuse of power and force could exert itself over an empire." Also, in seeking a name for themselves, the builders of Babel were setting "themselves in opposition to the rule of God" (Kaiser 1989, 10–11). Later on the prophets condemned Israel's trust in the security offered them by high-walled cities instead of entrusting themselves to the protection offered by God. However, "the problem did not reside in the cities, their walls, towers or their fortifications; the problem instead was in the trust that the urbanites placed in these things rather than in the Lord" (Ps 127:1; Kaiser 1989, 13).

Ellul has rightly perceived a negative portrayal of cities in the early chapters of Genesis. But it comes because of the rebellious independence and pride of people, not because they had become people of technique.

God's Grace to and through the City

Ellul lists several examples of God's grace to the city, including the sending of Jonah to Nineveh, the city as an instrument of God's judgment, the city as a place of refuge, and the presence of God's people living in the city, praying for the city, and calling the city to repentance (1970, 63–94). Ellul seems to appreciate God's work of grace for the city more than what some of his critics give him credit for. Nevertheless, he does not emphasize an important aspect of God's grace toward the city. God loves people, and people are concentrated in cities, so God loves and has compassion on the city. No passage of Scripture better illustrates this than the book of Jonah. Ellul mentions Jonah, but his main concern is to show that God withheld punishment only because there was "the conversion of an entire population and its government," not because some individuals repented or the city experienced social reform (1970, 69). Ellul says nothing about God's heart of concern for the city and the individuals who lived in it, echoed in the closing verses of Jonah. "Nineveh's repentance ... remains a sign of what can happen in cities and neighborhoods when God's message is proclaimed and his Spirit moves" (Greenway and Monsma 2000, 34). Ellul seems to miss completely God's compassion toward the people who live in the city, and his grace that goes to great lengths to reach out to draw them to himself.

Except for his brief mention of the cities of refuge, Ellul also seems to ignore another evidence of God's grace regarding the city: God has given cities to mankind as a blessing from him. It may be overstating the case to say that God intended for "human culture ... to take city form," as Conn asserts (1992, 15). Perhaps it is more balanced to simply say that Adam's creation in the image of God and God's mandate to him would have eventually required the building of cities. How? To be all that they could be as created in the image of God, people would eventually need to congregate in cities. As a concentration of people made in God's image, cities vibrate with unique creative and relational energy. Besides the economic and relational opportunities they offer, cities act like a magnet, attracting people from the surrounding countryside. "The development of human culture and civilization depends on" cities (Greenway and Monsma 2000, 31) and "both the Old and the New Testaments have treated the city as a gift from God" to carry out the cultural mandate (Kaiser, 16). "Despite sin's radical distortion of God's urban purposes, the city remains a mark of grace as well as rebellion, a mark of preserving, conserving grace shared with all under the shadow of the common curse. Urban life, though fallen, is still more than merely livable" (Conn and Ortiz 2001, 87). Ellul misses the scriptural teaching that cities are not only the recipients of God's grace, but they are themselves expressions of God's grace as concentrations of individuals made in God's image.

Jerusalem as a Witness City

Ellul feels that Jerusalem is a witness city which shows both God's grace and his judgment of the city. This seems to be an accurate understanding of the role of Jerusalem in Scripture. Kaiser notes that "Jerusalem is the city of God par excellence, but it is still a city. ... What made her great and what made her the city of God was the presence of God himself. ... [But] Jerusalem would only remain as a place of safety, protection, and worship of the living God for as long as she served the Lord" (1990, 14). Ezekiel 16 is an excellent summary of God's relationship with Jerusalem. He loved her, but she became unfaithful, and so he judged her. However, God will remain faithful to his covenant with Jerusalem, and will one day restore her. In Ezekiel 16, Linthicum sees Jerusalem as a model of God's relationship with the city in four ways: 1) God loves the city and is patient toward her, 2) he longs to see the city become the city of God, 3) humanity often refuses the city of God, and 4) the city that rejects Chris's saving work will inevitably be judged (1991, 115–17). This is very close to Ellul's understanding of the role Jerusalem plays in Scripture.

Spiritual Warfare in the Cities

Since cities are both "the result of common grace" and also "are by nature apostate corporations," cities will be the center of spiritual warfare (Greenway and Monsma 2000, 30). Ellul has a keen sensitivity to the intensity of this spiritual warfare in the cities, affirming that "the spiritual power of the city must therefore clash with the spirit of grace" (1970, 41; cf. also 166–67). Linthicum agrees that reaching the city requires intense spiritual warfare, and so warns that

> the greatest enemy of the urban Christian is not the city and its concentration of noise, power, and evil. Nor is it the church struggling to remain alive and vital, and in that struggle demanding all of its people's and pastor's energies. I am convinced that the greatest enemy of the urban Christian is the Christian himself or herself! ... We urban Christians are the most vulnerable in sustaining ourselves in ministry. (Linthicum 1991, 235)

He goes on to suggest that only through the intense practice of the disciplines of personal spiritual formation, life in community, and participating in God's vision for the city will the believer be able to enjoy victory in the spiritual battle that rages in the city.

Living as Kingdom People in the City

One of the primary biblical themes that contributes to a theology of the city is the kingdom of God. Linthicum goes so far as to say that "the kingdom of God is the primary paradigm for understanding God's call to the church in the city" (1991, 105). Ellul gives very little emphasis to the importance of the believer living kingdom values in the city. He does mention the importance of working for the welfare of the city (citing Jer 29:4–7, 10) and of calling the city to repentance. But he is pessimistic about the believer's ability to effect any real change in the city. Though Ellul calls for believers to remain in the city until it has clearly rejected Christ, it would be easy for the believer to respond to his hopelessness by abandoning the city.

To some extent Ellul's pessimism is biblical. The city will never ultimately be redeemed by human effort. But he badly undervalues the significance of making a difference in the lives of individuals. For example, speaking of Nineveh he emphasizes that individual conversions will never lead to a transformation of the city's social structures (1979, 69). But ministry to individuals and their needs is precisely what the New Testament calls for. "We are not called by God to be committed to dealing with all the needs of the city, but to address only one pain of the world" (Linthicum 1991, 238). Ellul's pessimism about not effecting ultimate transformation of the city is not balanced with the importance of making a difference in the lives of individuals.

Ellul's weak hermeneutic also betrays him at this point, for he fails to balance his pessimism with the broad scriptural emphasis on how the individual believer and the church are to live in the world. "The church must live in the city and implement … the great commission and the great commandment" (Bakke 1989, 11). Ellul does not begin to cover the large number of passages describing the Great Commission and Great Commandment responsibilities of the believer. With Ellul we must emphasize that only God will bring about the ultimate transformation of the city and that only God will establish his kingdom on earth. But believers have the responsibility to incorporate those same kingdom values, to live as kingdom people, here and now (Strauss 2005). For example, Old Testament prophecies of the coming kingdom will be completely fulfilled only when Christ returns and God himself accomplishes his kingdom purposes on earth. But by demonstrating God's ultimate agenda for the city, passages such as Isaiah 65 show kingdom people what their agenda should be for the city today (see Linthicum 1991, 163–192).

Finally, Ellul fails to emphasize the degree to which "the presence of godly people in a city will save it from destruction. ... Just by the consistent, quiet, committed living-out of their faith, the godly people provide for their city both an example and a moderating presence" (Linthicum 1991, 157). His brief mention of Jeremiah 29:7 does not do justice to the full significance of that verse. Babylon was the epitome of rebellious humankind in Scripture, and yet God commands his people to pray for it and work for its welfare, "for in its welfare you will find your welfare" (ESV). The implication seems clear that God's people can make a significant difference in the city! Many believers fail to see that they themselves are God's means of pouring out his common grace on the city. Ellul tells them to stay and minister in the city, but gives them little reason. A fuller biblical theology of the city will remind them that God would have saved Sodom for the sake of only ten righteous people, and that only one righteous preacher, Jonah, led a whole city to repentance. "Jesus continues this principle when he calls Christians the salt of the earth—penetrating its garbage and corruption with conscience and compassion—and the light of the world—demonstrating social and evangelistic witness and influence" (Bakke 1987, 64). Kingdom people living kingdom values in the city can make a difference.

A Biblical Theology of Poverty and Justice

Another broad scriptural theme with special application to the cities, but which is completely ignored by Ellul, is a theology of justice and poverty. The poorest of the poor live in and on the fringes of the city, and the Bible's theology of the poor has special relevance to the city. "If Christians are to reach the world for Christ, we must begin to come to grips with reality. The reality is that people, especially the poor people in the cities, are suffering. They need to be ministered to holistically, body, mind and soul, for they lack everything" (Yuen 1987, 16). The systemic evil, which is concentrated in the city, compounds the problem of oppression and injustice there.

The Scripture's teaching about justice and poverty is not some minor, fringe issue. Over four hundred verses express God's concern for the poor, and over eighty specifically express his concern for justice, most with a particular emphasis on justice for the oppressed (Claerbaut 2005, 8, 10–15). As centers of systemic and individual sin, urban believers must intentionally embrace a priority on mission to the poor and those who suffer from injustice.

Attacking systemic causes of injustice and poverty means that individual believers and churches must carefully engage in political and economic issues.

> There must be regularized vigilance here, such that the church knows how to encourage those political forces that affirm justice and rightness, and how to oppose those that seek only manipulation. This does not mean being a naive pawn of a political party or candidate. Rather, it means studying the issues and problems and affirming positions and programs that bring justice and reconciliation. ... It is important that the church educate itself on key issues, advocating social justice and human rights. (Claerbaut 2005, 24)

This will be new and uncharted territory for some congregations. Careful teaching from Scripture will be an important foundation for encouraging their greater involvement in issues of oppression and poverty. In particular, they need to see that the submission to government commanded in passages such as Romans 13 does not forbid their active involvement in society; instead it affirms it. They need to see that the great commandment needs to be practiced systemically as well as individually. A biblical theology of the city is incomplete without a theology and praxis of justice, especially for the poor.

The City as the Center of Outreach

Ellul gives little or no reflection on the role of the city in the book of Acts and the epistles. This is unfortunate, because in the New Testament "the city now becomes the sphere in which the work of God can be promoted and encouraged. Both Christ and the disciples used the city as the locus of their activity" (Kaiser 1989, 14–15). Paul, who was himself "a city person through and through," consistently began his ministry in a new area by targeting that area's most important cities for intensive evangelism and discipleship (Greenway and Monsma 2000, 38). In contrast to the Essenes, who "described Hellenistic cities as an 'infectious germ,' an unclean world they sought to avoid," Paul saw cities as "strategic centers, not cloisters, from which the gospel would spread" (Conn and Ortiz 2001, 138). When there was a positive response to his evangelism and when he was not forced to leave because of religious or political opposition, he stayed for long periods of time building the church and using it as a center of evangelistic outreach in surrounding areas. His ministry in

Corinth and Ephesus are examples of this. When he was forced to move on because of opposition, he would go to the next significant city in that area and begin preaching there. His ministry in southern Galatia and Macedonia are examples of this. In both cases, he concentrated his work in cities. Greenway and Monsma also point out that Paul's city-centered ministry was built on thoroughgoing conversion through radical discipleship, was family-centered, led to significant social change, encouraged involvement of the new believers in evangelism, and resulted in a communal unity brought only by the Holy Spirit (2000, 38–52). These are important guidelines for today's strategists of urban outreach.

Studies of the churches in Antioch and Ephesus offer special promise for showing how the city church can be a stimulus to wider evangelism. In Acts, Luke presents Antioch as the city that launched the mission to the Gentiles and Ephesus as the city that evangelized western Asia Minor. A study of the church in these two cities shows that in both cases there was serious commitment to Christ in the lives of the believers (Strauss 2011; Greenway and Monsma 2000, 59–60), a strong emphasis on solid teaching, and an inter-ethnic spirit that demonstrated the oneness of the body of Christ and an eagerness to reach out to people of all races (cf. Strauss 2011). To be complete, a biblical theology of the city must show how cities can be the center of evangelistic outreach.

Ellul completely misses the city-centered hope that radiates from the book of Acts. Cities may be centers of human sin, but the book of Acts shows that they can also be catalysts for worldwide outreach.

The New Jerusalem

Ellul is both strong and weak when he begins to talk about the New Jerusalem. His emphasis on the eternal city being wholly the work of God is badly needed today. In the war between Babylon and Jerusalem, ultimately Jerusalem will prevail only because she is a city prepared in heaven by God and given as his gift to mankind. This is not being too "otherworldly"; it is biblical, and it gives hope to embattled spiritual warriors in the city who can be assured of final victory because almighty God guarantees that he will bring about that final victory.

On the other hand, Ellul's weak hermeneutic again manifests itself in his picture of the New Jerusalem. There is nothing in the book of Revelation to support his idea that, in building eternity around a city, God is really taking over man's idea.

And while some of his insights about the symbols in Revelation are helpful, others seem to be groundless speculation. When it comes to understanding these symbols, one is better advised to consult a good commentary on Revelation than to trust Ellul's interpretive impulses.

Conclusion

Jacques Ellul is a realist who has made a significant contribution to the church of Jesus Christ. His sociological insights help contemporary Westerners understand the forces of urbanization and modernity that shape their worldview. His theology alerts believers to the degree of mankind's rebellion and pride when people congregate in cities and to the intensity of the consequent spiritual warfare. His reminder that only the sovereign intervention of God will ultimately bring an end to the destructive effects of sin is sobering and timely.

However, Ellul's theology only shows one side of the story. The Bible's message about the city is a story of grace as well as sin, of changed hearts as well as rebellious pride, of hope as well as toil. The theologian of the city must begin with Ellul's helpful contribution. But he must go beyond him to consider a fuller understanding of what the Bible says about the city.

References

Bakke, R. J. (1987). *The urban Christian.* Downers Grove, IL: InterVarsity Press.

_____. (1989). A theology as big as the city. *Urban Mission* 6(5): 8–19.

Berger, P., Berger, B., & Kellner, H. (1973). *The homeless mind.* New York: Vintage Books.

Claerbaut, D. (2005). *Urban ministry in a new millennium.* Waynesboro, GA: Authentic Media.

Conn, H. M. (1987). *A clarified vision for urban mission.* Grand Rapids, MI: Zondervan.

_____. (1992). Genesis as urban prologue. In R. Greenway (Ed.), *Discipling the city*, 2nd ed. (13–34). Grand Rapids, MI: Baker.

Conn, H. M., & Ortiz, M. (2001). *Urban ministry: The kingdom, the city & the people of God.* Downers Grove, IL: InterVarsity Press.

Ellul, J. (1964). *The technical society.* (J. Wilkinson, Trans.). New York: Vintage Books.

_____. (1970). *The meaning of the city.* (D. Pardee, Trans.). Grand Rapids, MI: Eerdmans.

_____. (1990). *The technological bluff.* (G. W. Bromiley, Trans.). Grand Rapids, MI: Eerdmans.

Greenway, R. S., & Monsma, T. M. (2000). *Cities: Missions new frontier, 2nd ed.* Grand Rapids, MI: Baker.

Kaiser, W. C. (1989). A biblical theology of the city. *Urban Mission* 7(1): 6–17.

Koetsier, C. H. (1986). The church situation in European cities. *Urban Mission* 3(3): 45–47.

Linthicum, R. C. (1991). *City of God, city of Satan: A biblical theology of the urban church.* Grand Rapids, MI: Zondervan.

Rommen, E. (2010). *Get real: On evangelism in the late modern world.* Pasadena, CA: William Carey Library.

Strauss, S. (2005). Kingdom living: The gospel on our lips and in our lives. *Evangelical Missions Quarterly* 41(1): 58–63.

Strauss, S. J. (2011). The significance of Acts 10:26 for the church of Antioch and today. *Biblosacra Sacra* 168(671): 283–300.

Yuen, B. K. (1988). Urban poor-ology: A theology of ministry to the world's urban poor. *Urban Mission* 5(1): 13–19.

Section 3:
Theological Education and Training for Ministry in Today's Cities

Riots in the City: Replacing Nineteenth-century Urban Training Models with Relevant "Urbanized" Training Models for the Twenty-first Century

Larry W. Caldwell and Enoch Wan
lwcald@yahoo.com
ewan@westernseminary.edu

Introduction

Doing urban ministry today is a complex task because urbanization has created new multifaceted and complex urban realities. Those who train urban workers—whether formally in Bible school or seminary, or informally in local church or para-church organizations—must ensure that their training programs are relevant for the task.

In most cases this will mean a radical reworking of existing training programs (most based on nineteenth-century curriculum models) and replacing them with "urbanized" twenty-firstcentury models. In this paper, the term "urbanized" is used in a technical sense referring to "the process of contextualizing to reflect the new multifaceted and complex urban realities of demographic density, ethnic and cultural diversity, religious plurality, and abject poverty in the inner city." These characteristics are true in urban centers worldwide; but in the West there are additional elements of globalization, postmodernity, post-Christianity, transnational migration of diaspora peoples, and so on. Also, the term "urbanized training model" is a reference to a "training program designed to prepare and equip Christian workers to serve in the urban context" in contrast to a "traditional training program" which is based upon "old curriculum models from the nineteenth century with emphasis primarily on classic disciplines of Bible, theology, and church history."

An **urbanized twenty-first-century training model** is contextually appropriate to the new multifaceted and complex contemporary urban realities. In the recent past, most urban ministry training typically meant having a heavy emphasis on Bible and theology, with a smattering of urban studies mixed in. In today's multifaceted urban landscape this approach is fundamentally flawed. In contrast, urban workers today need complex skill sets in order to truly face the challenges of the new reality in urban centers in the twenty-first century. They need to acquire "urbanized" training that will thoroughly equip them for urban ministry.

Historically, urban uprisings have often given rise to radical change in governments and society: riots in Paris during the French Revolution led to the overthrow of the French monarchy; riots of the 1960s in major cities of the United States led to vast changes in American society and politics; and, most recently, the urban people power uprisings in Egypt overthrew the Mubarak regime. The same sense of urgency that these riots engendered in the past is needed in our training institutions for urban workers today in terms of curricular design, faculty qualification, and program emphasis. Hence, this explains the title of this study.

In this paper we will seek to give some preliminary answers to the kind of urban ministry training that is necessary for the twenty-first century: the kind of relevant "urbanized" training required in both the majority world (non-Western) and in North American urban settings. We will do this by first giving a brief historical review outlining how we got to where we are today regarding the "traditional training program" and how it continues to affect the contemporary scene. With this background in mind we will then move on to examine both the faculty and curricula that need to be "urbanized," as well as looking for radically different training models that can enhance existing curricula, including an emphasis upon the new discipline of diaspora missiology. Suggested actions will conclude the paper.

What we say here will be directed primarily toward seminaries. However, Bible schools, local churches, and para-church urban training programs will also benefit from the analysis.

Historical Review

The nineteenth century was the pivotal century for the development of seminary curricula in North America. While schools like Harvard and Yale were the foremost ministerial training institutions of the eighteenth century—and for the first half of the nineteenth century—they eventually became dominated by more generalized undergraduate programs coupled with an increasingly liberal theological bent, both of which eventually eclipsed their original mandate to train ministers. Consequently, in the 1860s and onwards, there was a period of great expansion of new seminaries, both from existing denominations as well as from new denominations that were forming because of the great influx of European immigrants.

Along with these new seminaries came new changes to their curricula. Greatly influenced by the more "modern" European educational systems, North American seminaries in the second half of the nineteenth century saw change in three major areas: 1) a philosophical and arts-based teaching philosophy was replaced by scientific and scholarly study; 2) professors who were skilled at teaching across disciplines were replaced by professors who were narrow specialists within a specific discipline; and 3) the disciplines of Bible, theology, and church history became the "classical fields" of study with everything else left to the less glamorous practical theology department (Miller 2007, 43–62; Banks 1999, 7).

In the eighteenth and nineteenth centuries, and well into the twentieth century, the minister was the most educated individual in the community, trained for a leadership role in society that was firmly grounded in both biblical and theological knowledge. As George M. Marsden (1994, 37) notes, "the clergyman would be the best educated citizen and education would be a key to his authority." This educational superiority was reinforced by the end of the nineteenth century with the three-year Bachelor of Divinity degree (later Master of Divinity) which had by then become the standard professional degree and all seminary graduates were considered professional ministers. Those seminary students who were training for more specialized missionary or Christian education work were still expected to master the classical disciplines (Bible, theology, and church history) as did everyone else. It was thought that leaders, both on the mission field as well as those involved in the educational ministry of the church, had to be well-grounded in these classical disciplines in order that they, too, might influence the communities in which they served.

Likewise, though, the Bible college movement—begun in the early part of the twentieth century—was in part a reaction both to the professionalism of seminary training as well as to the lack of practical training for those training for ministries other than the pastorate (e.g., missionaries, evangelists, Christian education workers, and so on). However, despite this reaction the Bible college movement likewise put heavy emphasis upon the classical disciplines, particularly Bible and theology.

The Contemporary Scenario

Today in the twenty-first century, this "traditional training program" continues to dominate ministry training worldwide, including urban ministry. While missions studies in seminaries over the past fifty years have increasingly aimed at more relevancy—with specialized Schools of World Mission or Intercultural Studies—nevertheless the dominance of the nineteenth-century classical curriculum continues to surface, disregarding the new urban realities of the twenty-first century. Though attempts have been made to point out the deficiencies of this dominance (Ferris 1990; Banks 1999; and from a majority world perspective Harkness 2010), even among missiologists (Conn and Rowen 1984; Elliston 1999; Villafañe 2002; and Theron 2005), there is still a long way to go.

Most seminaries today, even if they have a separate missions department or even school, build their urban ministry training on the foundation of the "traditional training program." For example, most urban ministries MA degrees are built on at least one year of required course work in Bible and theology. One cannot help but ask the key question: "How relevant is the traditional training program at this stage and age and what radical changes are required in curricular design and program implementation in the twenty-first century?"

This question is not to take away from the fact that all those involved in Christian ministry, urban workers included, need to know the contents of the Bible as well as to have a basic understanding of theology. Some foundational courses in Bible and theology must be required of all urban workers. However, we must always critique whether or not our seminaries are really dealing with the realities of the vast urban landscape both in North America and abroad. The "traditional training program" was helpful in its day, but not so in the twenty-first century.

What we need to do today is to radically "urbanize" the curricular design, faculty qualifications, and student preparation to reflect the realities of the contemporary urban context.¹ Indeed, it is time to move from "the age of the horse and buggy" to "the age of the hybrid automobile." It is imperative that we create relevant training models for urban ministry in the twenty-first century.²

In light of the realities of the global phenomenon of urbanization that will only increase in the twenty-first century, everything in seminary training must be re-evaluated with this urban reality in mind. In other words, everything in the seminary curriculum must be redesigned to contextualize to the new urban realities of the twenty-first century. In a real sense, it is a radical throwback to the nineteenth century when the minister was, in Marsden's words, "the best educated citizen" in the community.

In today's incredibly complex and multifaceted urban context the urban ministry worker must be trained to be "the best educated citizen" of the city in order to have effective ministry within the urban context. And this will not be done with either nineteenth-century training models heavily dominated by the classical disciplines or with twentieth-century hybrids that try to blend the classical disciplines with specialized urban ministry components. To the contrary, we have to "go back to the drawing board" once again to try to figure out what is the best "urbanized" training model to produce effective workers for the twenty-first century.

Why is it necessary to address the issue of the relevancy of our urban ministry training? It has much to do with the demographic reality of urban populations. In the year 2008, the United Nations projected that fully one-half (50 percent) of the world's population would be urban, with further projections that this would increase to 60 percent of the world's population by 2030 (United Nations). While North America (and the rest of the Western world) will continue to be highly urbanized, most of this projected increase will occur in the majority world. Furthermore, a significant number of those urban populations will be made up of diaspora peoples: those who moved away from their homelands and/or rural areas. Thus it is imperative that the relevancy of urban ministry training be examined in light of these twenty-first-century worldwide urban realities.

---

1   While we are specially addressing seminaries in this paper, what we are saying applies also to Bible colleges, local churches, and para-church organizations that are also involved in training workers for urban ministry.
2   Roger Greenway (1996) was the first to give the clarion call for this in his brief but seminal article.

In the two sections below, we propose "urbanized twenty-first-century models" that will make urban ministry training more relevant in the contexts of both the majority world as well as in North America.

Relevant Urban Ministry Training Required in the (Non-Western) Majority World: The Need for "Lower-based" Training Programs and "Border" Pedagogies

When confronted with the task of making urban ministry training relevant in the majority world, we must look at the task from the perspectives of both the faculty as well as the courses and curricula of training institutions. We must ask the following two questions:

- Are the faculty in majority world training institutions adequately trained for the urban realities of their majority world urban context?
- Are the courses and curricula in majority world training institutions truly "urbanized" for the majority world urban context?

We will look at each question in turn.

Are Faculty Adequately Trained for the Urban Realities of the Majority World Context?

The answer to this first question may be both yes and no. Yes, if we mean that most of the faculty live and minister in a majority world urban context and that this proximity somehow positively influences their seminary teaching. No, if we mean that living and ministering in a majority world urban context guarantees that these faculty teach in light of the realities of that urban context. The fact is that many faculty who live in the majority world urban context—whether or not they themselves are originally from that context—have not been adequately "urbanized" enough to make sense of their context and adapt their teaching to reflect urban realities.

Furthermore, many (if not the majority) of the faculty of majority world training institutions are to some extent Western-trained, either by Westerners or by having studied in the West themselves. As a result, they have been heavily influenced by the nineteenth-century emphasis upon the classical biblical and theological disciplines.

Furthermore, the influence of the West, especially if they have lived in the West during their years of study, has sometimes made these majority world faculty less sensitive to their own local urban context, especially if those contexts are ones of extreme poverty. In light of the above, it is appropriate to ask whether or not those majority world faculty who have received advanced theological training in the West—or in the non-West through a Western-based curriculum—are really the ones who are best prepared to equip pastors and workers for the urban context.

For in reality many of these faculty members have not had frontline urban church ministry experience either as pastors of urban churches or as workers in an urban context. Though they may be highly talented and competent in their individual areas of study and teaching, it may be unreasonable for us to assume that they will be experts in urban ministry as well. Note that this is an observation rather than a judgment. Most majority world training institutions are filled with such faculty ill-equipped for urban ministry at least partly because of the continuing emphasis in these training institutions upon the nineteenth-century classical disciplines.

Thus we must answer the question posed at the beginning of this section with a resounding "No!" Of course, some majority world training institutions do have superb faculty well-grounded in the urban realities of their contexts and who are adapting their course work to their local urban settings. That being said, however, most of the faculty of majority world training institutions—who are experts in Greek or Hebrew, Old Testament or New Testament, church history or theology—are not necessarily experts at ministry in their urban context, nor in how to make their courses applicable to their local urban settings.

Alongside this lack of urban ministry experience is oftentimes a lack of knowledge and ministry experience with the urban poor, including the diaspora community. Since most majority world faculty tend to be from at least the middle class, this economic disparity may make it especially difficult for majority world faculty to adequately train pastors and workers for ministry among the significant numbers of the majority world urban population who are desperately poor and oftentimes displaced.

Are Courses and Curricula in Majority World Training Institutions Truly "Urbanized" for the Urban Context?

Relevant faculty is one challenge. Directly related to this is the challenge of relevant courses and curricula for the majority world context. I (Larry) was shocked into the reality of this challenge when talking with a majority world seminary faculty colleague years ago. During our conversation my colleague said something that I will never forget: "I don't think any Christian can accurately interpret the Old Testament without at least four years of Hebrew study." I wasn't sure that I had heard correctly, so I followed up by asking: "Certainly this will be necessary for those who are going to teach Hebrew, but do you really believe that four years should be required of all our students?" The answer was an unequivocal "Yes!" Since I had studied Hebrew for only three years, I quickly let the conversation lapse.

Hebrew is indeed a good thing to study, typical of most seminary courses. But is it the best, or most relevant, training? In light of the desperate need for trained pastors and ministry workers for urban contexts throughout the majority world, two questions need to be asked of our extensive seminary courses and curricula: 1) How many? and 2) How much? Most faculty members in majority world seminaries have completed many courses on the Old and New Testaments, Greek and Hebrew, exegesis, systematic and biblical theology, and so on. And I dare suggest that not many of us have seriously questioned the need for all of this extensive training for students in the majority world. We have bought into this nineteenth-century classical system that has been carried over from the West. We have rather blithely assumed that the extensive Western-oriented nineteenth-century training that we received is what our majority world students should also receive in the twenty-first century. But should this really be so? Elsewhere I (Larry) have written:

> It is imperative that we do indeed question the appropriateness of such extensive training, not only for our own lives but for the lives of our students. ... The bottom line question comes down to this: how many and how much? *How many* of our students need to be able to exegete a text in Greek and/or Hebrew? *How much* Greek and Hebrew needs to be required for ministry purposes? *How many* need to be able to write library-based papers comparing and contrasting the views of several commentators on a particular text? *How much* emphasis should be placed on the mastery of the viewpoints of professional scholars? Yes, a small percentage of our students will need to learn a lot of this information. But not everyone; in fact, not many at all. What *everyone* really needs ... are the tools, resources and training that will equip them to relevantly interpret the Bible [and do theology] in the complicated context that is Asia. If we do

not properly equip them, how will Asia truly be reached with the gospel? (Caldwell 1999, 41)

To offer urbanized courses and curricula for the urban ministry context in the majority world will mean a radical rethink of what the majority world urban situation really is and what it is that our pastors and ministry workers really need to learn.[3] This is especially true as we attempt to meet the training needs of those who are, or will be, working with the urban poor (cf. Gunderson 2008).

In thinking about urbanized courses and curricula, we can benefit from recent development theory, especially what is known as "participatory rural appraisal" (PRA). Though PRA was begun with the rural poor in mind, its principles apply as well to majority world urban ministry situations, especially among the urban poor. PRA is the new field practice of putting the first last—in other words, recognizing the natural abilities and giftings of poor people (see Chambers 1997). This practice confronts the dominance of those called "uppers" as opposed to the vast majority of the people who are the "lowers." The uppers see grassroots programs flourish through empowering the lowers to do them. Such a practice is a major challenge for "upper" seminaries and faculty whose courses and curricula are based on "top-down" systems (cf. Friesen 2008).

According to Robert Chambers (1997, 210), top-down systems have "brought bad practice: dominant and superior behavior, rushing, upper-to-upper bias, taking without giving, and arousing expectations which are not met." New lower-based training programs are necessary. Yet such new paradigms imply and demand changes which are institutional, professional, and personal. Institutional change needs a long-term perspective, with patient and painstaking learning and reorientation. Professional change needs new concepts, values, methods, and behaviors, and new curricula and approaches to learning. Personal change and commitment have primacy, and can be sought experientially. Learning to change and learning to enjoy change are both fundamental (Chambers 1997, 210).

---

3   Though coming from the standpoint of working toward the contextualization of good theology in Asia, the following articles are helpful starting points for relevant urban ministry training: LaBute (2006); and specifically for the Philippines context Gener (2004) and Caldwell (2005).

A Case Study from the Majority World: Asian Theological Seminary, Manila, Philippines

This is precisely where I (Larry) have been most challenged in recent years. When I was the Academic Dean at Asian Theological Seminary (ATS) in Manila, Philippines, one of my priority projects was to help develop a new program in urban ministries. But how could we do this in an "upper seminary" with a "top-down" system? The answer eventually turned into the ATS Center for Transformational Urban Leadership (CTUL) that offers courses leading to a Diploma, Graduate Diploma, or MA in Transformational Urban Leadership (TUL). The courses are designed for Christian practitioners among the urban poor. The courses bring together a team of national and international academic and "hands-on" experts currently working with the urban poor. All the TUL courses are combined with extensive field internships among the urban poor.[4]

Built on a foundation of Bible, evangelical theology, and applied social sciences, the TUL curriculum includes a majority of courses that are specifically made for effectively ministering in an urban poor context and among diaspora communities. Diaspora knowledge is increasingly significant because urban ministry in Manila is made even more complex due to the millions of migrants from "the province" (a Filipino expression referring to those from the rural area). These migrants form many distinct diaspora communities in Manila, based on their place of origin, ethnicity, and language. Teaching students to minister effectively among those with a diaspora background requires cultural sensitivity and skills in intercultural communication because of cultural differences and linguistic and ethnic diversity.

For example, the MA in TUL, a forty-five-semester-unit program of study, includes the following courses:

Core Courses:
Doing Hermeneutics with the Urban Poor
Theology 1
Bible Introduction
Urban Spirituality
Theology and Practice of Community Economics
Urban Poor Church Planting

---

[4] For more information see the Asian Theological Seminary Transformational Urban Leadership website at www.ats.ph/ctul_brochure_2008.pdf.

Leadership in Urban Movements
Theology and Practice of Community Transformation

Specialized Courses:
Services to the Marginalized
Urban Reality and Theology
Educational Center Development
Entrepreneurial and Organizational Leadership
Primary Health Care
Advocacy and the Urban Environment
Language and Culture Acquisition (for foreign students)
Diaspora Missiology

Field and Research Courses:
Research in Church and Ministry
Urban Reality and Theology
Thesis/Project
Field Supervision 1 and 2

Notice that these courses in the MA TUL program are not found in the catalogs of typical majority world training institutions (nor of most seminaries in the West).[5] In fact, from a typical seminary's point of view they are indeed quite radical. Where are the classical disciplines? While we did keep three classical courses in the TUL curriculum (Bible Introduction, Theology 1, and a modified Hermeneutics course), we felt that it was imperative that ATS offer courses that were really needed for effective urban poor ministry and that they be taught by those who were actually "doing the ministry." This caused some headaches for our upper resident faculty, but eventually the TUL program was approved as a separate Center of ATS. The main concerns related to government recognition and accreditation issues. However, eventually the government regulating body for education was highly impressed that an evangelical seminary was offering such a practical program; the program is now on track for full accreditation.

---

5   Exceptions to this include those institutions connected with the Encarnacio Alliance of urban poor movement leaders, under the direction of founder Viv Grigg. Three currently affiliated institutions are: Asian Theological Seminary in Manila, Philippines; Hindustan Bible Institute in Chennai, India; and Azusa Pacific University in Los Angeles, USA. For more information on how a North American university is creatively meeting the need for relevant urban ministry workers see Azusa's website at www.apu.edu/clas/globalstudies/urbanleadership/courses.

I was even more challenged by the TUL program when I was asked to teach one of the core courses, Interpreting the Bible With the Urban Poor. I had taught basic hermeneutics courses for twenty-five years, but I had little personal experience with, or exposure to, the urban poor other than living in their midst for over twenty years. I was challenged by the prospect of putting my theories concerning ethno-hermeneutics (multigenerational, multicultural, and cross-cultural hermeneutics) to the test through empowering the lowers and, as a result, seeing grassroots Bible interpretation flourish as the urban poor did it themselves.

This required me to "think outside the box" to develop a "border pedagogy" (the term of fellow cross-cultural hermeneutics expert D. N. Premnath) that goes beyond the traditional classical nineteenth-century approach I had been so fond of:

> The term "border" sharply captures the dominant tendency to establish borders or boundaries based on the either-or binaries within Western thought. ... The dominant group defines, structures and thereby dominates all constituted as Other. Border pedagogy provides a pedagogical alternative for learners to identify and be critical of these borders that are used to set apart entities and peoples. ... [It] seeks to create spaces for ... experiences to be expressed, valued, and thought through by students and teachers alike. (2007, 6)

Border pedagogy allowed me to teach my students reading strategies for exegeting the text of the Bible while at the same time challenging me to help my students develop relating strategies for exegeting the culture of their urban poor audiences. Thus they would better develop their own strategies for exegeting the text of the Bible with the urban poor.[6] This aspect of border pedagogy involves

> the ability to expose the dominant definitions of reality. It enables the learner to recognize cultural codes and social practices that marginalize or even repress alternative ways of perceiving. ... The models of the dominant culture need no longer be the sole basis for defining what constitutes proper knowledge. ... As learners cross borders, alternative forms of knowledge emerge and the dominant definitions of reality come under closer scrutiny. (Premnath 2007, 7)

---

6   For a general overview of how to do this see Caldwell (2008); see also de Wit, et al, (2004) and Caldwell (2005).

As I taught my students, and my students (who, in turn, had been taught by their urban poor communities) taught me, we arrived together at hermeneutical strategies that worked with the urban poor. In almost every class period my students would come back from leading Bible studies with their urban poor groups and report comments that some individuals had made: for example, "I never knew that the Bible was for me," or "I never knew that I could interpret the Bible for myself." It is precisely this kind of interaction between professor, student, and the urban poor and diaspora that is so necessary if evangelical Christianity is to make an impact among the poor of the majority world.

Relevant Urban Ministry Training Required in the North American Context: The Need for Diaspora Missiology

What has already been said about relevant urban ministry training in the majority world in terms of faculty, courses, and curricula is applicable to the North American context as well. In addition, there are elements of globalization, postmodernity, post-Christianity, transnational migration of diaspora peoples, and so on, pertinent to urban centers in North America that are to be understood and addressed. Therefore, "urbanized twenty-first-century training models" in various urban centers in the North American context may vary in their emphasis and focus, specializing in any of the areas listed above. I (Enoch) will focus our attention particularly on the emerging discipline of "diaspora missiology" since the growing numbers of displaced peoples coming to North American urban areas is among the most challenging.[7]

Why Diaspora Missiology?

The realities of today's urban world compel us to address the issue of diaspora peoples. While diaspora peoples have been a part of urban landscapes for centuries, the size and significance of diaspora have increased in the twenty-first century. According to David Lundy (2005, xiv), approximately "3 percent of the global population live

---

7   I (Enoch) have been involved in various North American urban ministry contexts. In the 1970s I conducted research for my dissertation on New York's Chinatown and engaged in pastoral ministry in New York City. I also taught classes there in the last few decades. Furthermore, I draw from my ministerial experience in Toronto in the 1990s: church planting in metro-Toronto and serving as director of the Centre of Intercultural Ministry of Canadian Theological Seminary, coordinating the first national conference of Canada in intercultural ministry. See Enoch Wan (1993).

in countries in which they were not born." Urbanization, international migration, and people displaced by war and famine are all contributing factors. There is the global trend that migrant populations are moving from south to north, and from east to west toward seven of the world's wealthiest countries. These seven countries have less than 16 percent of the total world population yet contain 33 percent of the world's migrant population (cf. Joly 2004).

North America, particularly the United States, has been the recipient of many of these diaspora peoples. Since the implementation of the Immigration and Nationality Acts of 1965 and 1990 the influx of immigrants has been impressive. For example, during the period between 1990 and 2000 over 1,200,000 immigrants landed in New York City. What is true for New York City is true as well for many of the large and medium-sized urban areas throughout North America today. For example, the mid-American small city of Sioux Falls, South Dakota—population 150,000—has seen immigrants from 97 nations and 120 different language groups arrive in the last 10 years or so, and according to the 2010 census figures more than 11,000 people who live in the Sioux Falls metro area were born outside the United States. As a result, it is necessary to develop a missiology tailored to the realities of these diaspora peoples.

What is Diaspora Missiology?

Let us begin to answer this question with definitions of several key terms. "Diaspora" is a reference to "people living outside their place of origin" and "diaspora missiology" is "a missiological framework for understanding and participating in God's redemptive mission[8] among diasporic groups."[9] "Diaspora missions" is "the Christian's participation in God's redemptive mission to evangelize their kinsmen on the move and through them to natives in their homeland and beyond" (cf. Wan 2010b and Pantoja, Joy and Wan 2004; see also Lausanne Committee 2004).

The two ways of working with diaspora are "ministering to" and "ministering through" them. As a result, there are three types of "diaspora missions" (cf. Wan 2007 and Pantoja, Joy and Wan 2004):

- "Missions to the diaspora": reaching the diaspora groups in terms

---

8   "Mission" as used here is defined as "the *Missio Dei* of the Triune God."
9   For more information on diaspora, see Enoch Wan (2012a). See also Wan (2007), (2010a), and (2012b). Cf. Lausanne Committee (2009) and Pantoja, Joy, and Wan (2004).

of pre-evangelistic social service or evangelism and then discipling them to become a worshipping community/congregation;
- "Missions through the diaspora": reaching individuals through the diaspora group's natural network of friendship, kinship abroad, and in their homeland;
- "Missions by/beyond the diaspora": organizing new diaspora converts into worship communities/congregations to engage in cross-cultural missions to the natives in their homeland or host country when they have acquired language facility, cultural sensitivity, and relational competency.

Against this background of diaspora realities and definitions the question to be asked is this: "Has 'traditional missiology'—as taught and practiced in North America—kept pace with this new demographic reality of the phenomenon of diaspora?" By "traditional missiology" we mean the missiology represented by organizations such as the American Society of Missiology and the Evangelical Missiological Society.[10] We must answer this question with a "No." Most North American missiologists are just beginning to realize that "traditional missiology" must be supplemented by the new paradigm of "diaspora missiology." As shown in the two figures below, the two paradigms are very different in focus, conceptualization, perspective, orientation, paradigm, ministry patterns, and ministry styles.

---

10   For more information on these organizations, see their websites: www.asmweb.org and www.emsweb.org.

#	ASPECTS	TRADITIONAL MISSIOLOGY ←→ DISPORA MISSIOLOGY	
1	FOCUS	• polarized/dichotomized • "Great Commission" ←→ "Great Commandment" • saving soul ←→ social gospel • church planting ←→ Christian charity • paternalism ←→ indigenization	• holistic Christianity with strong integration of evangelism with Christian charity • contextualization
2	CONCEPTUALIZATION	• territorial: here ←→ there • "local" ←→ "global" • lineal: "sending" ←→ "receiving" • "assimilation" ←→ "amalgamation" • "specialization"	• "de-territorialization" • "glocal" • "mutuality" and "reciprocity" • "hybridity" • "interdisciplinary"
3	PERSPECTIVE	• geographically divided: • foreign mission ←→ local, urban ←→ rural • geo-political boundary: • state/nation ←→ state/nation • disciplinary compartmentalization: e.g., theology of missions/strategy of missions	• non-spatial, • "borderless," no boundary to worry about: transnational and global • new approach: integrated and interdisciplinary
4	PARADIGM	• OT: missions = Gentile, proselyte: coming • NT: missions = the Great Commission: going • Modern missions: – E-1, E-2, E-3 or M-1, M-2, M-3, etc.	• New reality in the twenty-first century = viewing and following God's way of providentially moving people spatially and spiritually • moving targets and move with the targets

Figure 6.1 The Continuum: From "Traditional Missiology" to "Diaspora Missiology" in four aspects[11]

---

11 Modified from Figure 5 in Wan (2007).

#	ASPECTS	TRADITIONAL MISSIONS ←→ DISPORA MISSIONS	
1	MINISTRY PATTERN	• OT: calling of Gentiles to Jehovah (coming) • NT: sending out disciples by Jesus in the 4 Gospels and by the H.S. and in Acts (going) • Modern missionaries: — sending missionaries and money — self-sufficiency of mission entity	• new way of doing Christian missions: "mission at our doorstep" • "ministry without borders" • "networking and partnership" for the kingdom • "borderless church" (Lundy 2005) • "liquid church" (Ward 2002) • "church on the oceans" (Otto 2007)
2	MINISTRY STYLE	• cultural-linguistic barrier: E-1, E-2, etc. • Thus various types: M-1, M-2, etc. • "people group" identity • evangelistic scale: reached ←→ unreached • "competitive spirit," "self-sufficient"	• no barrier to worry about • mobile and fluid • hyphenated identity and ethnicity • no unreached people • "partnership," "networking," and "synergy"

Figure 6.2 The Continuum: From "Traditional Missions" to "Diaspora Missions" in two aspects[12]

The above figures show that a "diaspora missiology" will require an addition of several new specialized courses to the traditional urban missions curriculum. Such courses will include:

- Introduction to Diaspora Missiology/Missions
- Biblical and Theological Foundation of Diaspora Missiology/Missions
- Demographic Study of Diaspora Communities
- Ethnographic Profile of Diaspora Communities
- Missions to the Diaspora
- Missions through the Diaspora
- Missions by and beyond the Diaspora

---

12 Modified from Figure 6 in Wan (2007).

North American seminaries will do well to consider curricula changes that reflect the diaspora reality.

Actions to Be Taken

This paper has argued that the nineteenth-century model of seminary training which has dominated both North America as well as theological institutions worldwide—primarily based on the classical disciplines of the Bible, theology, and church history—is a relic of the past. In its place we need radically different urban ministry training models based upon the true needs of urban practitioners as well as those in preparation for such a task. We have shown that there are indeed relevant alternatives for both the majority world as well as for North America.

With this in mind, there are practical actions that seminaries, in both the majority world and North America, can take to help make their urban training programs more relevant for their particular urban context. These actions include the following.

Evaluate Local Urban Contexts

Evaluate local urban ministry contexts and develop urbanized courses, curricula, and programs that truly meet the ministry training needs of the urban workers in those contexts, even if this means radical change. As Jesus said, "no one pours new wine into old wineskins" (Luke 5:37). Urban ministry training institutions—whether majority world or North American—must resist the urge to conform uncritically to nineteenth-century faculty, courses, and curricula, as well as to standards that are simply not appropriate for twenty-first-century urban ministry. Seminaries must especially resist the temptation to do everything in light of accrediting bodies and government regulations. If necessary, develop a separate Center that is linked to the existing training institution but still has its own relevant urban ministry training program.

Develop Faculty

Develop new faculty, and engage experienced faculty who are intimately acquainted with the local urban context and who ideally have extensively ministered in that context. Make sure that tenured faculty stay actively connected with the local urban scene.

Practice Partnership

Partner with local urban churches and ministries (especially strategic ones), so that the urban workers that are being trained are appropriate for these churches and ministries and their needs. Creatively work with these urban churches and institutions to ensure that their training needs are enfolded into new or existing seminary training programs: a "win-win" situation for both the seminaries and the local urban churches and ministries.

Offer Practical Training

Offer non-academic tracks and programs to help meet the overwhelming urban ministry needs of the churches of the majority world. Only a very small percentage of majority world urban practitioners have the time, money, and/or qualifications to invest in outdated nineteenth-century MA and MDiv programs. Seminaries must be at the forefront in helping to equip the vast number of these "non-degree urban pastors" through courses and programs facilitated by existing faculty and graduates.

Supplement "Traditional Missiology" with "Diaspora Missiology"

In the training of urban workers supplement "traditional missiology/missions" with "diaspora missiology/missions" due to the new demographic reality of the diaspora peoples found in urban centers around the world, especially in North America. Interestingly, seminaries that do this will find many thriving diaspora congregations in North America, congregations that have much to offer those seminaries that are willing to work with and learn from them.

Conclusion

Developing relevant urban ministry training models for the twenty-first century is an immense topic. We know full well that this paper has just scratched the surface. At the same time we are hopeful that as more seminaries seek to develop truly relevant urban ministry programs—by "urbanizing" their course offerings and curricula—both the majority world and North American urban mission field will be more effectively reached.

The tremendous needs of the cities cry out for urban ministers who have received the training necessary to competently function in the midst of multifaceted and complex urban realities. To fail to heed that cry by using nineteenth-century seminary training models may literally mean more riots in the streets. Instead, metaphorically speaking, we need riots among our seminary faculty and in our seminary classrooms in order to truly meet the realities of urban contexts in the twenty-first century.

References

Banks, R. (1999). *Reenvisioning theological education: Exploring a missional alternative to current models*. Grand Rapids: Eerdmans.

Caldwell, L. W. (1999). Towards the new discipline of ethnohermeneutics: Questioning the relevancy of western hermeneutical methods in the Asian context. *Journal of Asian Mission* (March), 41.

_____. (2005). Towards an ethnohermeneutical model for a lowland Filipino context. *Journal of Asian Mission* (September), 169–93.

_____. (2008). Interpreting the Bible with the poor. In L. Wanak (Ed.), *The church and poverty in Asia* (171–80). Manila: OMF Literature.

Chambers, R. (1997). *Whose reality counts? Putting the first last*. London: ITDG Publishing.

Conn, H. M., & Rowen, S. F. (Eds.). (1984). *Missions and theological education in world perspective*. Farmington: Associates of Urbanus.

de Wit, H., et al. (Eds.). (2004). *Through the eyes of another: Intercultural reading of the Bible*. Elkhart: Institute of Mennonite Studies.

Elliston, E. J. (Ed.). (1999). *Teaching them obedience in all things: Equipping for the 21st century*. Pasadena, CA: William Carey Library.

Ferris, R. W. (1990). *Renewal in theological education: Strategies for change*. Wheaton: Billy Graham Center.

Friesen, S. J. (2008). The blessings of hegemony: Poverty, Paul's assemblies, and the class interests of the professoriate. In C. Briggs Kittredge, E. B. Aitken, & J. A. Draper (Eds.), *The Bible in the public square: Reading the signs of the times* (117–28). Minneapolis: Fortress.

Gener, T. D. (2004). Re-visioning local theology. An integral dialogue with practical theology: A Filipino evangelical perspective. *Journal of Asian Mission* (September), 133–66.

Greenway, R. (1996). World urbanization and missiological education. In J. Dudley Woodberry, C. Van Engen, & E. J. Elliston (Eds.), *Missiological education for the 21st century: The book, the circle, and the sandals* (144–50). Maryknoll: Orbis.

Gunderson, J. (2008). Rethinking holistic ministry: Reflections on the struggle against poverty in Asia. *Journal of Asian Mission* (March–September), 3–15.

Harkness, A. (Ed.). (2010). *Tending the seedbeds: Educational perspectives on theological education in Asia.* Quezon City: Asia Theological Association.

Joly, D. (Ed.) (2004). *International migration in the new millennium: Global movement and settlement.* London: Ashgate.

LaBute, T. S. (2006). Beyond contextualism: A plea for Asian first level theology. *Asia Journal of Theology* (April), 36–56.

Lausanne Committee. (2004). The new people next door. Retrieved from www.lausanne.org/docs/2004forum/LOP55_IG26.pdf.

_____. (2009). The Seoul declaration on diaspora missiology. Retrieved from http://www.lausanne.org/fr/documents/all/175-consultation-statements/1112-the-seoul-declaration-on-diaspora-missiology.html.

Lundy, D. (2005). *Borderless church: Shaping the church for the 21st century.* Waynesboro: Authentic.

Marsden, G. M. (1994). *The soul of the American university.* New York: Oxford University Press.

Miller, G. T. (2007). *Piety and profession: American Protestant theological education, 1870–1970.* Grand Rapids: Eerdmans.

Otto, M. (2007). *Church on the oceans: A missionary vision for the 21st century.* Carlisle: Piquant.

Pantoja, L. Jr., Joy, S., & Wan, E. (Eds.). (2004). *Scattered to gather: Embracing the global trend of diaspora.* Manila: LifeChange Publishing.

Premnath, D. N. (2007). *BorderCrossings: Cross-cultural hermeneutics.* Maryknoll: Orbis.

Theron, Pieter F. (Ed.). (2005). Effective theological education for world evangelization. In D. Claydon (Ed.), *A new vision, a new heart, a renewed call* (3:155–211). Pasadena, CA: William Carey Library.

United Nations, Department of Economic and Social Affairs, Population Division. (2006). World urbanization prospects: The 2005 revision. Working Paper No. ESA/P/WP/200. Retrieved from http://www.un.org/esa/population/ publications/WUP2005/2005WUP_FS1.pdf.

Villafañe, E., et al. (Eds.). (2002). *Transforming the city: Reframing education for urban ministry*. Grand Rapids: Eerdmans.

Wan, E. (Ed.). (1993). *Missions within reach: Intercultural ministries in Canada*. Hong Kong: China Alliance Press.

_____. (2007). Diaspora missiology. Occasional Bulletin of the Evangelical Missiological Society (Spring).

_____. (2010a). Ministering to scattered peoples: Moving to reach the people on the move. Retrieved from http://conversation.lausanne.org/en/conversations/detail/11438.

_____. (2010b). Global people and diaspora missiology. Retrieved from http://www.ustream.tv/recorded/6897559.

_____. (2011). Research methodology for diaspora missiology and diaspora missions. Paper presented at the North Central Regional meeting of the Evangelical Missiological Society, February 26.

_____. (Ed.). (2012a). *Diaspora missiology: Theory, methodology, and practice*. Portland: Western Seminary Institute for Diaspora Studies.

_____. (2012b). Global status of diaspora ministry. Retrieved from https://netforum.avectra.com/eweb/shopping/shopping.aspx?site=exchange&shopsearch=diaspora&prd_key=1781ee1f-0ecd-446c-9898-b5eb7e7e6a12.

Ward, P. (2002). *Liquid church*. Carlisle: Paternoster.

"Let Those in the City Get Out": Making a Way of Escape

Larry Poston
Larry.poston@Nyack.edu

The Problem

> Confuse the wicked, O Lord, confound their speech, for I see violence and strife in the city. Day and night they prowl about on its walls; malice and abuse are within it. Destructive forces are at work in the city; threats and lies never leave its streets. (Ps 55:9–11)

Our planet is undergoing a season of unprecedented urban growth. Numbers tell the story clearly: while in 1800 only 3 percent of the world's population lived in cities, the year 2008 saw the "tipping point" when for the first time in history more than half of the world's people were domiciled in cities with populations of 100,000 or more (Dugger 2007). On every continent, North America included, migration from rural to urban settings appears to be well-nigh unstoppable.

The lure of the city is mainly that of economic survival. It is assumed by a majority of those who join the influx that they will find more opportunities for employment and have greater access to amenities in urban environments than they will in the rural areas from which they come, places where jobs are scarce and living conditions more "primitive."

A truer picture of urban conditions, however, is found in the shantytowns, ghettos, and barrios that form a mock "suburbia" at the edges of many of the major cities of the world. As of 2007, more than a billion people—almost a sixth of the planet's population—lived in such environments. Conditions in these areas, both physical and psychological, are squalid in the extreme. Cardboard homes, open latrines, tainted water supplies, joblessness, and lack of opportunities for meaningful activities form a breeding ground for disease, drugs, crime, prostitution, and "rape gangs" (McClelland 2011).

In response to these phenomena, evangelical Christianity has sought over the last several decades to develop an emphasis on "urban ministry." The works of Roger Greenway, Ray Bakke, Harvie Conn, and others have been standardized as textbooks in religiously-oriented educational institutions and have been required reading in many a college classroom. It is troubling to this writer, however, that nearly all of these works assume that we as Christians must simply acknowledge the phenomenon of urbanization and "meet urban peoples where they are," implying that we simply leave them there. We are told that we are to seek to develop evangelistic techniques, discipling ministries, and church involvement among urban residents in the midst of the conditions that surround them. One even hears urban ministry spoken of in terms of "sacrifice" and sees it endowed with a quasi-romantic aura that makes voluntary city residency a sort of "living martyrdom."

I am consistently surprised at how little is said regarding the evil aspects of urban life by persons who are interested in relief and development work, the goal of which, it would seem, is to improve the standard of living and raise the quality of life of all persons in general and Christians in particular. True, there are some few who seek through litigation and similar means to introduce changes in the overall environment at the macro level, but such attempts have been relatively few and have enjoyed little success. More normatively, what I find is that upon experiencing the new birth and the initial joy and transformation that accompanies a genuine conversion to Christ, nearly all newborn brothers and sisters are left alone in the midst of an excruciatingly difficult environment and almost inevitably come to fulfill the biblical description of recidivism: "'A dog returns to its vomit,' and, 'A sow that is washed returns to her wallowing in the mud'" (2 Pet 2:22). Leaving new Christians in the midst of the urban environments in which they are found, including environments that feature illegal addictive substances, sexual promiscuity, theft, abuse, unemployment, gang warfare, and the like, makes it nearly impossible for them to grow successfully in their newfound faith. Can people who live in such environments be expected to gain the momentum necessary for significant progress in Christian discipleship?

Christian Approaches to the Phenomenon of Urbanization

In centuries past, Christians have almost exclusively been negatively disposed toward cities and city living. Biblically speaking, humanly constructed cities are never presented as "positive" in any respect. Cain, who murdered his brother and who was cursed by God to be a "restless wanderer on the earth," refused the exilic punishment God had commanded for him and instead built a city to surround himself with others of his kind—men and women who would support and encourage each other in a life of rebellion and sin (Gen 4:10–24). The city of Babel with its "tower reaching to the heavens" became symbolic of mankind's stubborn drive toward complete autonomy and independence from God (Gen 11:1–9). The "cities of the plain" were the site of Abraham's wars for the sake of his kinsman Lot, Abraham having left the mighty Ur of the Chaldeans for the more rural Canaan (Gen 14:8–24). Sodom and Gomorrah serve as a byword for and the epitome of human degradation and sin so far advanced and deeply rooted that not even a half dozen "righteous" persons could be found within them (Gen 19:1–29). For Jesus, the city of Jerusalem—named for "shalom" (peace)—was associated with blood and the murder of prophets (Matt 23:37). And John's revelational depiction of "the adulterous Babylon" has become the symbol of ruthless, relentless, and ultimately senseless evil (Rev 18:1–24). It is fair to say that until the last two chapters of the final book of the New Testament canon, cities fare very badly in the eyes of God.

The above portrayals have not gone unnoticed. Perhaps the best exposition of the Bible's attitude toward urban environments is found in French theologian Jacques Ellul's modern classic The Meaning of the City. Excerpts from this work reflect Ellul's observations concerning the hopelessness of the city in general and "urban renewal" in particular. He begins from the premise that Cain's construction of a city was in rebellion against God's plan for humankind, and extrapolates from this interpretation a belief that when Israel built their own cities, it was always for them the sign of a curse, and the proclamation of slavery renewed. And the prophecies of those long-haired prophets who were a constant reminder of the innocence of the nomadic life as opposed to urban life were based on that first apprenticeship: Israel bound herself to slavery, and, even more, to the land of sorrow and sin; by the cities she built, cities that were always the imitation of what she had learned in Egypt, before the deliverance. (Ellul 1970, 25)

Ellul notes that "every city must suffer the effects of the curse; it is always considered a good and holy work for Israel to utterly destroy a city (Num 21:2), for this is an act of God" (Ellul 1970, 46). Rural living is to be preferred to urban residence, as evidenced not only in the Bible but even in contemporary sociological studies:

Sociologists know that every city has its own personality, and that a man's mental make-up changes when he goes from the country to the city and again from one city to another ... of course the farmer is dependent on other factors, has his own sins, takes other risks. But his destiny does not appear from Scripture to be so inescapably bound in with an environment which is only the work of man. (Ellul 1970, 22)

The urban "personality" mentioned in the previous citation has a seductive quality to it, and this is what makes cities so supremely dangerous to those who seek to live a godly life: "Standing before a city, man finds himself faced with such a perfect seduction that he literally no longer knows himself, he accepts himself as emasculated, stripped of both flesh and spirit" (Ellul 1970, 30). And despite some persons' hopes that cities might yet be redeemable, Ellul dismisses such thoughts as sheer fantasy, for

the city cannot be reformed. Neither can she become other than what men have made of her. Nor can she escape God's condemnation. Thus in spite of all the efforts of men of good will, in spite of all those who have tried to make the cities more human, they are still formed of iron, steel, glass, and cement. The garden city. The show city. The brilliant city ... They are all cities of death, made of dead things, condemned to death, and nothing can alter this fact. The mark of her builders and the judgments of God weigh her ruthlessly down. (Ellul 1970, 57)

Lest some object that all of the above are Old Testament sentiments, Ellul points out that even with the inauguration of the New Covenant, there is continuity between the views of Old Covenant prophets and those of Jesus himself:

> Jesus Christ has no conciliatory or pardoning words for the cities. ... When he speaks to the cities, he never has anything but words of rejection and condemnation. He never proclaims grace for man's work. All he recognizes is its devilish quality, and his only reaction is to struggle against the power of the city trying to hinder his work. (Ellul 1970, 113).

And for these reasons, Jesus' ministry was mainly "outside the camp":

> The crowd came to Jesus, but the astonishing point, clearly indicated in the Gospels, is that Jesus did not meet it on its own ground. He did not meet it in the city. Rather we find that when the multitude had left the cities, they followed Jesus into the desert (e.g., Matt 14:13). (Ellul 1970, 131)

Therefore, Ellul is convinced that the people of God must not remain in urban environments.

> [S]omeday we must leave, when the wait is ended, and then there can be no hesitation. The Scriptures give us remarkable details concerning this departure. It is not an escape, we will not be leaving as conquered forces driven from the triumphant city that man created for this very triumph, for this separation, for this expulsion of everything which might remind him of God. Rather, it is only an escape in which the city is being punished before the last day, as a sign. (Ellul 1970, 80)

Secular Confirmation of Biblical Teaching Regarding the City

It should come as no surprise that the New Testament's warnings regarding cities are corroborated by "secular" documentation. Sociologists have shown time and time again that urban environments wield a power that is almost impossible to escape. A large proportion of those who try to renounce a dysfunctional or criminal lifestyle while remaining ensconced in urban environments are inexorably drawn back to those lifestyles. For instance, in a study conducted concerning murder in the city of Chicago in 2004, it was ascertained that "there seem to be murders emanating from a recidivist population that cannot escape a criminal past and a socialization and street culture orientation and values" (Horton 2007, 25). The most common factors contributing to this recidivism were "street gang altercations, armed robbery, and gang-related narcotics activity" (Horton 2007, 16). Two out of three of these factors involve gang associations, a sociological phenomenon that is found almost exclusively within urban environments. While rural towns and villages may be said to have their own set of sociological disadvantages, these pale in comparison with those to be found in urban settings. Indeed, Arthur Horton notes that several items contributing to recidivism are specifically urban, including laws (police corruption) and community norms favorable to the (recidivist) behavior; extreme economic depression, neighborhood disorganization, family (as opposed to individual) alcohol and drug use, and association with drug-using peers (Horton 2007, 26–27).

Another study conducted in the major cities of the United States demonstrated that even after extensive drug rehabilitation, an average of 27.5 percent of all urban offenders return to their drug habit in the first two years after their original apprehension (Roman 2003, 10). Since drug use is so prevalent among those who commit crimes of all kinds, the fact that recidivism rates are high shows the difficulty of escaping one's past when one remains in an environment in which drug use may be said to be normative. Indeed, a national survey has shown that upwards of 20 percent of crimes are committed in order to procure drugs or to support a drug habit, and two-thirds of criminals are on drugs at the time of their arrest and incarceration (Mumola 1999, 2).

Leaving the North American continent we find that the statistics grow increasingly dismal. Looking at Europe, for instance, we find in a study conducted in Portugal that a much wider range of crimes occurs in urban environments. This clearly results from the fact that there are far more goods available in cities to be stolen and sold. However, it also reflects the fact that increasing numbers of people have moved to the cities in recent decades, only to find themselves living in rundown areas in situations of social exclusion. In fact, today, crime is associated with societies that have great disparities of wealth and quality of life. For people on lower incomes, such factors may make it easier to turn to crime as a form of subsistence and way of acquiring goods that would otherwise be out of reach, thereby increasing one's social status. Finally, urban environments also offer less social control and more anonymity, which can benefit criminals. (Esteves 2009)

We find in studies conducted in South Africa, certainly one of the more "advanced" countries of sub-Saharan Africa, that 80% of all offenders who were caught, imprisoned, rehabilitated, and returned to society relapse into a life of crime (Swart 1994). Recidivism rates are also astronomically high in the cities of Asia. In Malaysia, 49%. In New Zealand, 57%. And in Japan, 42% of those incarcerated for criminal activity return to prison for new offenses (APPCCA 1995, 57–58). It should be clear from the studies cited above, and from a multitude of others, that allowing men and women to remain in an environment that is an almost perfect breeding ground for sin enormously reduces the possibility that they will be able to throw off former associations and addictions.

A Christian Response to Urban Converts

It is deeply troubling that most Christians appear to believe that a dramatic conversion experience will be enough to overcome any and all of the obstacles described above. The truth of the matter is that persons claiming to have undergone the new birth described by Jesus experience just as many difficulties breaking addictions as non-Christians do. There is often a "honeymoon period," of course—a time during which it appears that a new convert has been able to throw off his or her former lifestyle and associations and has adopted a new way of living. But Jesus' parable of the soils gives two examples of persons who fail either to attain full salvation or to be sanctified: first, the seed that fell on rocky places, which "sprang up quickly, because the soil was shallow. But when the sun came up, the plants were scorched, and they withered because they had no root." Secondly, there was the seed that fell among thorns, "which grew up and choked the plants" (Matt 13:5–7). These examples can easily be applied to new Christians in urban settings.

The difficulties of establishing a successful long-term urban ministry may be illustrated by the experiences of A. B. Simpson (1843–1919), the founder of the Christian and Missionary Alliance. Simpson established his Missionary Training Institute (now Nyack College) in midtown Manhattan in 1882, hoping to draw from the multitudes of people in the Western hemisphere's then-largest city.

But as Ellul and others have noted, urban environments exercise their own powers over inhabitants, and the students of Simpson's institute were no exception to this rule. Apart from the expense of trying to arrange facilities for classrooms and living quarters, there were two other negative factors. First, many of the students were drawn off and distracted by the various circumstances connected with city living. Those who had come from sordid backgrounds prior to their salvation experience were forced to deal with the constant temptations connected with their former lifestyles. For many there was no choice other than to live with or remain in the company of non-Christian relatives, companions, and neighbors. Continuing in their "old contexts" often resulted in a reversion to former sinful habits and patterns.

For those who were able to resist such temptations, another problem presented itself: that of being constantly surrounded by acute needs. The compassionate nature of newborn Christian converts often led to absenteeism from classes due to a propensity for prioritizing ministry functions and the meeting of socioeconomic needs over studies. In several instances, students were unable to fulfill the requirements for graduation due to their failure to complete class requirements.

Consequently, fifteen years after its founding the Missionary Training Institute was relocated to suburban Nyack, New York, where facilities were erected as financial conditions allowed. At the time of the move it was noted in *The Christian and Missionary Alliance Weekly* that "the country affords much greater quiet and opportunity for study and saves students from a certain class of distractions which have been found to seriously interfere with solid work" (Institute 1897, 362).

Simpson and his wife had also established the Berachah Home for Healing on Manhattan's 34th Street as a shelter and "halfway house" for homeless persons and others who needed temporary or even long-term housing. Their goal was to minister to "street people," including prostitutes and those who lived outside the bounds of what most would call a more "normal" social environment. But Berachah was relocated to the Nyack hillside as well, allowing persons to be removed from their former environments and giving them an opportunity to overcome addictions, to develop new and healthier relationships, and to learn usable work skills. The Simpsons rightly recognized that for some, a break from the old habitat was essential to accomplish Christian sanctification.

A Proposal for the Present: Two Fronts with a "Pipeline" Extending Outward

It is the thesis of this essay that Christians must leave off their passive acceptance of "city-living" and modify the kind of "urban ministry" that has been advocated for the last several decades. This is not to say that ALL of the suggested ways of doing ministry in cities have been incorrect. Many of the strategies put forth by Bakke, Greenway, Cox, and others have laudable aspects, and these ways of working have proved to be highly functional and productive.

But there is another side to urban ministry that is often ignored. A terrible disservice is done to many of those that are brought to Christ in the midst of urban environments if they are simply left in those environments. I believe that **it is essential that we develop a "pipeline" of sorts that allows certain classes or categories of newborn Christians to exit the city**. Persons with addictions—be they substance addictions, sexual addictions, or other kinds of ingrained habits that are essentially sinful—will have an infinitely better chance of recovery if they are separated from the familiar environments where they have ready access to the items to which they are addicted. If such persons can be brought out of their former neighborhoods to unfamiliar or isolated locations, temptations to indulge in old habits may be much less. Persons with specific associations—be these gang members, drug rings, or even influential family members and friends—will be able to progress much more successfully if they are separated from such associations.

Consequently, I would suggest that **we must arrange an urban ministry that functions on two fronts**. The first "front" will be within the confines of target cities themselves. Many missiologists and urban strategists have developed practical and workable programs for this front, and such programs are not the subject of this essay. It is the second "front" that I wish to highlight. The goal of this second front will be to relocate certain categories of new Christians to a place that is sufficiently distant to allow them to grow and develop as the "new creations" they have become. Of what would such a program consist?

"Let Those in the City Get Out"

This plan would call for missions organizations to pour at least half their urban resources into developing what may be called "retreat centers" far enough away from urban environments that there is no possibility of persons returning to their former domiciles on their own. Ideally, such retreats would be rural or at least suburban "compounds" that are semi-isolated and that construct an environment that is essentially the diametric opposite of the urban environment from which the relocated persons have come.

The first step to such a plan would be to develop a detailed philosophy of "recovery and discipleship" that includes specific goals and objectives for the envisioned retreat center. For what purposes are people brought out of the city? Let me suggest that the primary purpose should be to **reacquaint and reengage former city residents with the "Cultural Mandate" of Genesis 1 and 2 as it was given to humankind in our pre-Fall circumstances.** Of what did/does this mandate consist?

1. *We were to "fill the earth"—to pair off in family units and to reproduce our kind* (Gen 1:28). As human beings created in the image of God we were to establish and develop proper family relationships and exercise the biblical, holy purposes of our God-given sexuality. In the cities, more than anywhere else, the family has become sundered and ruined. Sex has become a game, a form of entertainment, a recreational pursuit, an activity to fill the time, something to mitigate the boredom and meaninglessness of city life. In many respects, cities reduce human beings to levels of existence that are below the level of animals.
2. *We were to "subdue" the earth*—to tame and domesticate the wildness that exists around us naturally (Gen 1:28). We were to take that which grows in wild and chaotic fashion and bring order to it, following the lead of our God who is a "not a God of disorder but of peace" (1 Cor 14:33). But there is very little "nature" to bring order to within city environments.
3. *We were to "rule over the fish of the sea and the birds of the air and over every living creature that moves on the ground"* (Gen 1:28). We were to function as stewards over the beasts, offering

protection and shelter to them. Such connection with animals is all but impossible in cities.
4. *We were placed in a garden and commanded to "work it and take care of it"* (Gen 2:15). This aspect of the mandate is an amplification of the second characteristic noted above. Our original parents were created to be "gardeners"—working and preparing soil, planting seed, tending a variety of growing crops, harvesting and preserving those crops.

We understand, of course, that in our fallen state a complete reacquisition and fulfillment of this mandate is not possible. The curse to Eve affected the first aspect of the Cultural Mandate, introducing painfulness to reproductivity and changing the relationship between husband and wife, thereby altering God's original intent for family life. The curse to Adam affected the second aspect of the mandate, dooming men to live "by the sweat of their brow" and producing "thorns and thistles" in their attempts to "subdue the earth" (see Gen 3:16–19). The killing of animals that was required to make "garments of skin" (Gen 3:21) for the now-sinful humans affected the ability of men and women to exercise authority over the animal kingdom, and the expulsion from the Garden seen in Genesis 3:23–24 made literal fulfillment of the fourth aspect of the mandate impossible.

And yet as human beings who still in some sense bear the Imago Dei—a ruined, shattered, distorted, and wrecked image to be sure, but some semblance of the image nonetheless—these aspects of "humanness" are still part of all men and women. Our desires to procreate, i.e., to "fill the earth," remain. Our longings to make order out of chaos remain. Our love of animals and our desire to relate to them remain. And our pleasure at "tending and keeping" gardens endures. This, of course, is the tragedy of fallen humanity: our Adamic natures are still with us, but these natures cannot fulfill the Cultural Mandate as originally intended.

Not even in a "secondary" or "second-best" sense can most of these tasks or activities, with the possible exception of the first, be fulfilled within urban environments. There is no "earth" to subdue; there are instead only the man-made creations of brick, steel, concrete, and glass, or of plastic, cardboard, and fabric. There are no animals over which one can "exercise authority"; beyond pigeons and an occasional squirrel there are few animals to be seen. There are no gardens that one can "work and take care of" other than perhaps some potted plants on a windowsill or a balcony. And so those who have lived as prostitutes, drug addicts, thieves, alcoholics, domestic abusers, and the like and who have now bowed the knee to Christ must be brought out of the evil and unnaturalness of their urban environments and introduced to an altogether new approach to "life." They must be removed from their former associations—be those pimps, drug suppliers, "fences" (i.e., receivers of stolen goods), fellow "drinkers," and in certain cases family members with whom they have dysfunctional relationships. They must instead be settled into areas of greens (i.e., grass and trees) and blues (i.e., sky and water). For "studies have assessed the influence of the physical environment upon violence, highlighting the contribution made by green spaces (i.e., the existence of trees and grass) in reducing the incidence of aggressive and violent behavior in residents who live in the vicinity, particularly in inner-city social housing estates" (Santana, 2009).

Again, we will not be so naive and theologically unsophisticated as to believe that "sin" and "evil" will disappear when one exchanges an urban for a rural environment. Sin, of course, is innate in individual human beings; when one leaves the city one carries one's sinfulness with him/her. But there are advantages to "letting those in the city get out," advantages that all—both "sacred" and "secular"—readily recognize.

"Strengthening the Feeble Hands"

The prophet Isaiah bids us to "strengthen the feeble hands, steady the knees that give way; say to those with fearful hearts, 'Be strong, do not fear; your God will come'" (Isa 35:3–4). Let us envision, then, a piece of real estate, purchased and managed by a Christian missions organization and set within a rural environment, distant from all that is meant by the word "city," both in a physical sense and in a "spiritual" sense as well. This center will be separate even from "sub-urban" settlements that still contain a "city" mentality. Ideally, such real estate will include the following:

- residential facilities, preferably a series of detached homes with multiple bedrooms that can be used to create a "family-like" atmosphere of biblically-oriented domesticity;
- "work" facilities, including workshops for various activities having to do with the second, third, and fourth aspects of the Cultural Mandate; sheds for the housing of tools and agricultural machinery and for the storage of produce; as well as any other buildings deemed necessary for the transformation of urban personalities;
- "animal" facilities, including barns, stalls, coops, pigsties, and the like—for housing domesticated animals in accordance with the

third aspect of the Mandate;
- fertile and cultivable land;
- wooded areas that may be used for activities ranging from sugar-mapling to the gathering of firewood to sustenance hunting during appropriate seasons;
- a sizeable stream or pond.

The primary goal for these facilities would be the creation of a community that is as nearly as possible self-sustaining, providing within that self-sustenance the means for **training spiritually-reborn urbanites in the arts and crafts of subsistence living in accordance with each facet of the Cultural Mandate.** The artificiality and unnaturalness of the sinful lifestyle that comprised the inhabitants' former existence would be replaced with a life consisting of biblically-mandated tasks that will confer meaning, dignity, and a sense of connectedness with God that very few urban dwellers ever truly attain. In order to fulfill these goals, the following must be provided:

1. housing that is simple, clean, and inexpensive. A level of simplicity would be provided that for the formerly homeless would include basic necessities and assure proper diet, proper hygiene, sufficient warmth or coolness (depending on the season), and overall, an environment consisting of non-chaotic days and nights.
2. for those who were urban homeowners or renters and who were accustomed to the rank materialism often associated with the life of a gang member or "drug lord," a simpler, subsistence-level lifestyle would be introduced that would become a means of "weaning" such persons from the material gluttony that characterized their former lives.
3. a measure of peacefulness and quietness that will afford opportunity for meditation and time with God for those who were formerly surrounded by the nearly-constant din of traffic, sirens, stereos, and other media. As the Apostle Paul commanded: "Make it your ambition to lead a quiet life, to mind your own business" (1 Thess 4:11).
4. access to physicians and/or nurses who will be able to deal with physical addictions to various substances as well as counselors to deal with psychological maladjustments. Also available as live-in residents must be disciplers and "pastors" to help in

the process of spiritual growth and to guide each individual's progress in adopting a more biblical lifestyle.

5. implementation of a schedule for a typical day, one that is a mixture of physical, mental, and spiritual "exercises." Pursuing a modified form of the Cultural Mandate would allow a "blending" of these three aspects of an individual's humanity. Physical exercise would be obtained through the "chores" that are involved in the development and maintenance of homestead living: feeding and milking cows, feeding and tending chickens; plowing, tilling, harrowing, irrigating, and ultimately harvesting the products of the soil; construction and maintenance of buildings; felling of trees, cutting and splitting firewood, cultivation of new tree plantings, preparation of meals; and the like. As Paul continues in the passage quoted above: "and to work with your hands, just as we told you" (1 Thess 4:11). Assuming that residents are literate, mental exercise would be provided by required readings on subjects related to the various aspects of homestead living, supplemented by works of literature. For those who are illiterate, the basics of an elementary education would be substituted until sufficient proficiency is acquired to allow for individual assignments. Spiritual exercises would consist of individual and communal Bible study, prayer, and readings in such areas as biblical commentary, theology, the history of Christianity and the like.

6. one-on-one counseling sessions that seek to address the often severe mental and psychological disturbances rooted in lifestyles associated with city living. Such disturbances may be due to a broken or otherwise dysfunctional family situation. They may be due to elementary and secondary educational environments that not only failed to provide the basic elements of literary skills and resources for the development of a worldview and personal identity, but which may have actually created a culture of fear and intimidation that is carried on into adulthood. Such counseling sessions would provide tailor-made programs aimed at producing growth and an individual independence in accordance with New Testament principles. Continuing Paul's theme, " … so that your daily life may win the respect of outsiders and so that you will not be dependent on anybody" (1 Thess 4:12).

7. addressing of educational deficiencies through classroom instruction that will help each convert acquire the minimum

of a GED high school diploma and in certain cases provide a foundation for post-secondary education.

There are, of course, several aspects of inner city living that few give thought to, items that one is not taught to address in a typical ministerial education. My own experiences with urbanites who have experienced the new birth and exited the city have made me aware of the following:

1. The necessity of resetting a person's body clock due to an urban life schedule that transformed day into night and vice versa. A person who escapes from such an environment and seeks to enter the nine-to-five workforce is faced with the difficulty of falling asleep when he/she should be awake and being awake at the time when the majority of human beings sleep.
2. The necessity of educating a person regarding the management of finances. A drug dealer who has undergone conversion suddenly finds himself in a drastically different financial situation. The thousands of dollars that he was accustomed to having at his disposal are suddenly absent, and he seeks to maintain his accustomed lifestyle by means of credit cards. These, of course, in very short order become maxed out, are hence unusable, and leave the cardholder under a staggering load of debt. Helping such people cope with their new financial realities can be an extremely difficult, but also very rewarding, task.
3. The necessity of helping a person adjust to a thoroughgoing abstention from alcohol, tobacco products, recreational drugs, pornographic materials, and the like. While this may sound like a return to a legalistic fundamentalism reminiscent of the early twentieth century, it is still true that all of these substances are highly addictive and bring about less-than-healthy conditions of life. Issues of physiological and psychological dependency must be addressed, despite the insistence of some Christians regarding the protection of our "liberties in Christ."
4. The necessity of achieving a transformation of views regarding women (and sometimes regarding men) along with a transformation of views concerning sexuality in general. In urban environments women are often regarded as nothing more than play-toys or "eye candy," and sexual intercourse is an act casually engaged in for purposes of self-gratification and recreational pleasure without commitments of any kind.

The personnel who are the resident directors of our envisioned "retreat center" must be highly creative and patient men and women. They must be willing to rejoice at each sign of incremental success and be able to deal with the frustration of excruciatingly slow progress and even failure at various points.

Implementation of a plan that involves work on two separate fronts will, of course, involve greater financial outlays than work on a single front. And at a time when finances are more scarce than they have been in decades—at a time when mission agencies and their personnel are already strained to the breaking point—such a recommendation may seem completely impractical. But failure to adopt such a plan on a worldwide basis will doom all efforts in the field of urban ministry even while the headlong rush to the cities gathers momentum.

Sending Them Back?

Is the self-imposed exile from the city to be permanent, or should "fully recovered" and spiritually grounded persons be automatically returned to their former environments? This question can only be answered on a case-by-case basis.

First, the desires of each individual must be considered: does he/she want to return to the city from which he/she came (or to some other urban environment)? Whether the answer is affirmative or negative, the sponsoring organization must assume responsibility for ascertaining the motivations that lie behind each individual's answer. The organization must decide in advance which motivations are justifiable reasons for either returning to a city or remaining outside. Fear of returning, for instance, could be interpreted in more than one way. A fear of returning to city life that arises from an honest evaluation of oneself as being too weak to withstand the temptations of one's former environment could be regarded as courageous.

If, on the other hand, a person desires to return to the urban environment from which he or she came, it is equally important to ascertain the reasons for this desire. If one's heart burns with a longing to see family members and former neighbors come to Christ, such motivation could well be sufficient to prevent a return to one's former lifestyle once the opportunity to do so is at hand. If one is merely "curious" to see how things are, or to "test" oneself to see if one can actually withstand the temptations of the urban environment, such motivations would be cause for caution and should elicit a warning and/or advice to remain in the rural environment that has made growth and progress possible.

Some who have recovered from their previous lifestyles and who are now grounded in Christ may be recruited to remain at the "retreat center" to be of help to newly converted urbanites that will be brought to the facilities. Such personnel can provide newcomers with both a model and motivation for undergoing the physical, mental, and spiritual disciplines that will bring about their healing.

Conclusions

Luke 21:21, in which Jesus commands "Let those in the city get out," is an eschatologically-oriented passage that premillennialists will read as being intended primarily for those within the Great Tribulation period. But even for premillennialists there may be a secondary application to be derived from this warning: in circumstances of extreme danger, one should "flee to the mountains," as it were, leaving an urban environment for the relative safety of a rural region. As argued in this essay, this secondary application should be used to the greatest extent possible if it is desired that spiritually reborn urban dwellers successfully experience Christian sanctification. While this may not be true for all, for a large majority it will be necessary to experience the kind of environment connected with the type of retreat center described here, for the purpose of re-centering and reestablishing an urban Christian in soil that will allow the seed of salvation to germinate and flourish.

Failure to implement the principle taught by Luke 21:21 may result in the experience described in Hebrews 6:4–6: "It is impossible for those who have once been enlightened, who have tasted the heavenly gift, who have shared in the Holy Spirit, who have tasted the goodness of the word of God and the powers of the coming age, if they fall away, to be brought back to repentance, because to their loss they are crucifying the Son of God all over again and subjecting him to public disgrace." Urban dwellers who undergo the new birth and who remain in the midst of drugs, alcohol, prostitution, gang activity, and other generally enslaving aspects of city living will in many cases—perhaps even in most cases—find it difficult or impossible to escape the temptations of their former lifestyles. The ubiquity and ready availability of sinful activities and godlessness will grind down newborns until they "fall away" and return to their previous ways of living.

Not all suffer this fate, of course, for "land that drinks in the rain often falling on it and that produces a crop useful to those for whom it is farmed receives the blessing of God" (Heb 4:7). But perhaps more often than not, city dwellers will within a relatively short period of time become "land that produces thorns and thistles" and suffer the ignominy of being considered "worthless" and "in danger of being cursed" (Heb 4:8). As men and women entrusted with the care of younger brothers and sisters in Christ, we must make every effort to see that this sad fate does not befall anyone in our purview.

References

Asian and Pacific Conference of Correctional Adminsitrators. (1995). APPCCA statistics: Correctional statistics for Asia and the Pacific, 1995. Proceedings of the 15th Asian and Pacific conference of correctional administrators, (57–58). Available at http://www.apcca.org/stats/1995/appca_statictics_1995.htm.

Dugger, C. W. (2007, June 27). Half the world soon to be in cities. *New York Times.* Retrieved from http://www.nytimes.com/2007/06/27/world/27cnd-population.html.

Ellul, J. (1970). *The meaning of the city.* Grand Rapids, MI: Eerdmans Publishing Company.

Esteves, A. (1999). *A Criminalidade na cidade de Lisboa: Uma Geografia da Inseguranca.* Lisbon: Edicoes Colibri. Cited in Santana, P., Santos, R., Costa, C., Roque, N., & Loureiro, A. *Crime and Urban Environment: Impacts on Human Health.* Coimbra, Portugal: Institute for Geographical Studies, University of Coimbra. Available from http://www.cityfutures2009.com/PDF/26_Santana_Paula.pdf.

Horton, A. (2007). Murder in the city: Embedded, intractable and treatment resistant? *Journal of Human Behavior in the Social Environment* 16 (August 1), 25.

McClelland, M. (2011). Aftershocks: Welcome to Haiti's reconstruction hell. *Mother Jones* (January/February), 30–41.

Mumola, C. J. (1999). Substance abuse and treatment of state and federal prisoners,1997. Washington, DC: Bureau of Justice Statistics. Retrieved from http://www.iapsonline.com/sites/default/files/Substance%20Abuse%20and%20Treatment%20of%20State%20and%20Federal%20Prisoners,%201997.pdf.

Roman, J., Townsend, W., & Bhati, A. S. (2003). Recidivism rates for drug court graduates: Nationally based estimates, final report. United States Department of Justice Document 201229 (July). Retrieved from https://www.ncjrs.gov/pdffiles1/201229.pdf.

Santana, P., Santos, R., Costa, C., Roque, N., & Loureiro, A. (2009). *Crime and urban environment: Impacts on human health.* Coimbra, Portugal: Institute for Geographical

Studies, University of Coimbra. Retrieved from http://www.cityfutures2009.com/PDF/26_Santana_Paula.pdf.

Swart, D. & Naude, C. (1994). A proposed structure for the reintegration of released offenders in the Republic of South Africa. *Acta Criminologica* 7: 9–18.

The Missionary Institute. (1897). *The Christian and Missionary Alliance Weekly* (April 6): 362.

Section 4: Contemporary Case Studies on Today's Cities

Examining Evangelical Concentrations and International Migrations in the US and Canada: A Call for More and Better Urban Research

J. D. Payne
jpayne@brookhills.org

Evangelicals in the United States, historically, have not placed much confidence in research. It was not until the middle to latter half of the twentieth century that biblically guided missiological research came to be seen as a blessing and not a bane by a large number of people. Over the past few decades, evangelical researchers have produced some amazing reports reflecting outstanding missiological research to guide missionary strategy.

Research helps the church cut through the fog of uncertainty. While abuses and too much dependency on research exist, research has significantly shaped the face of missions in the latter twentieth and early twenty-first centuries. It was the emphasis placed upon research that helped launch and define the Church Growth Movement. It was the value of research that led the editor of *Mission Frontiers* to place on the cover of the January–February 2008 issue the title, "God Cannot Lead You on the Basis of Information that You Do Not Have." It was the value of research that led to the formation of the World Christian Database, the Joshua Project, and the Global Research Department of the International Mission Board.

While evangelicals have come a long way from Carey's emphasis on the value of research noted in his *An Enquiry*, we have a great distance yet to travel. One of the places where this journey is still long is found in North America. While evangelicals have a fairly good understanding of who are the peoples residing in the non-North American countries of the world, their evangelical statuses, and what groups are ministering among them, here in the United States and Canada, evangelicals face a different situation. We have little to no knowledge of the peoples in our neighborhoods.

The United States and Canada are two of the world's most diverse countries and two of the world's most researched countries. Multitudes of scholars have studied North America from a variety of sociological and anthropological angles. While we have statistics galore on both the magnificent and the mundane and the macro and the micro, evangelicals in the United States and Canada lack the missiological research to guide wise missionary strategy. We have excellent information on a small unreached people group "over there," but have little to no understanding of the peoples living in our backyards.

While the Lord leads his church, even when she is ignorant to reality, how much better is it when the church understands her context? How much better stewardship is involved when she understands the Somalis living across town, the Quebecois across the river, or the Anglos moving into the new apartment complex down the street?

It is difficult to hit a target if one does not know that target. The church may have a great zeal to reach others with the gospel and plant churches; but zeal with ignorance is not healthy for the kingdom. The writer of Proverbs reminds us, "Desire without knowledge is not good, and whoever makes haste with his feet misses his way" (Prov 19:2 ESV).

Purpose

My purpose in writing this paper is to extend a call to evangelicals to begin conducting more and better urban research in the United States and Canada. I plan to show support for this need by drawing attention to two research projects that I have conducted over the past couple of years. The first project was a study of evangelical concentrations found across the United States and Canada, with particular examination of the metropolitan areas. The second project draws from my people group research in my forthcoming book *The Strangers Next Door: Global Migrations and the Great Commission Opportunity for You and Your Church*. By revealing the limitations in my research, I hope to provide a much better perspective on the dearth of urban research needed for strategic planning that impacts missional endeavors both in North America and throughout the world.

Case Study #1: Evangelical Concentrations in the US and Canadian Metropolitan Areas

To begin, it is necessary to provide a general statistic for evangelicals in the United States and Canada. According to the U. S. Religious Landscape Survey of 2008 released by the Pew Forum on Religion and Public Life, among all US adults, evangelicals consisted of 26.3% of the population (Pew Forum on Religion and Public Life 2008, 5). Jason Mandryk in Operation World noted that evangelicals comprised 7.7% of the Canadian population (Mandryk 2010, 194). In an e-mail message to the author on December 7, 2009, Rick Hiemstra with the Center for Research on Canadian Evangelicalism estimated the average percentage across the provinces being 12%, with Quebec consisting of 2–3%.

What We Know

The statistics on US evangelicals have been made available for free and on-line to the public since 2006 through The Association of Religion and Data Archives (ARDA). Prior to that time, the data was available for purchase in 2002, appearing in the book *Religious Congregations and Membership in the United States: 2000* published by the Glenmary Research Center. While such information has been readily available for anyone wanting to search through and compile the findings on evangelicals, I am not aware of any organization that collected these findings and disseminated them widely to the larger evangelical body so they could develop evangelism and church multiplication strategies accordingly. Therefore, I decided to collect, organize, and disseminate the findings in a way that would better guide missionary strategy in the United States.

While this data is presently a decade in age, it is the most extensive and best research available on congregations and memberships in the United States. The 2010

Religious Congregations and Membership Study will provide the next comprehensive religious portrait of people in the United States.

Outreach Canada has been a champion for evangelical research in Canada. In 2005, Murray Moerman edited the book *Discipling Our Nation: Equipping the Canadian Church for Its Mission* with an extensive amount of tables revealing a wealth of data presenting the church planting needs across the country. This information was based on 2001 statistics. Lorne Hunter with Outreach Canada shared with me their 2006 data for my research project so that I could include the Canadian data as well.

Using this data, I was able to produce the following information as related to the urban contexts:

- A list of US metropolitan areas with less than a 10 percent evangelical population
- A specific list of US metropolitan areas with less than a 3 percent evangelical population
- The number of evangelical churches and the evangelical church to population ratios in selected Canadian metropolitan areas (2006)

The Evangelical Benchmark

When conducting missiological research in order to better understand what percentage of the people in an area are followers of Jesus and are the most likely to continue to share the gospel with others, missiologists often attempt to discern the number of evangelicals present. Now, clearly not all evangelicals are regenerate and are faithful in sharing the good news with others. Also, there are people who do not consider themselves evangelicals, but are faithful followers of Jesus and faithfully share the gospel with others. However, by most definitions, an evangelical is someone who professes to have had a conversion (regenerate) experience by grace through faith in Christ and believes in the importance of telling others about the good news of this salvation. Therefore, missiologists need a benchmark to attempt to gain a better understanding of how many people have had a conversion experience and are calling others to Jesus as well. This is the reason the generic category of "evangelical" is the focus of this research project.

Other Concerns to Consider

In addition to using evangelicals as a benchmark, there are a few other matters for consideration. The findings of this study for the US were limited to the data found on the ARDA's website. The findings of this study for Canada were limited to the data collected and shared by Outreach Canada. It should also be noted that while the Canadian data is from 2006, the best public US data is from 2000. Though the US data is more than a decade old, this information is a good beginning point for such research today.

The definition of evangelical is worth mentioning here as a limitation. From a sociological perspective, the definition of evangelical used when collecting the data published in *Religious Congregations and Membership in the United States: 2000*, would be fairly accurate. While there are a few limitations noted by those disseminating the data, most researchers would be mostly in agreement with what groups were considered evangelical. From a conservative, evangelical missiologist's perspective, and more importantly, from a kingdom citizen's perspective, I am not comfortable with the original definition of "evangelical" found in *Religious Congregations and Membership in the United States: 2000*. While the original researchers did separate mainline churches, world religions, and cults from evangelicals, the definition on which the research was based is too broad for an accurate understanding of the number of kingdom citizens present and involved in engaging their communities with the gospel.[1] Also, the definition of evangelical "adherents" in the data set is also more problematic when attempting to determine the estimated number of evangelicals in a particular area of the US. According to the Association of Religion Data Archives' website: "Congregational 'adherents' include all full members, their children, and others who regularly attend services. The historically African American denominations are not included in the 2000 congregation and membership totals" (ARDA).

With these facts in mind, it is assumed that the number of regenerate people in all of these locations in the US is much lower than presented in this research; therefore, the need for the gospel in all of these areas is much greater than what is represented here. Since I do not know the evangelical groups counted by Outreach Canada, I cannot comment on possible realities in Canada. The US counties that were studied were selected from the ARDA's website because of their lower evangelical populations.

---

[1] For a list of the evangelical Protestant congregations included in the Religious Congregations and Membership Study 2000 see http://www.thearda.com/mapsReports/reports/evangelical.asp; accessed 12/10/2009.

It should be noted that the counties presented do not necessarily represent all of the US counties with less than 10 percent evangelical populations. These are only presented to give an idea of the realities in the United States.

From 35,000 Feet to 15,000 Feet

This report on evangelicals in the United States and Canada is an attempt to assist the church in moving its missiological perspective of these two countries from what I refer to as a high altitude perspective to a lower altitude perspective. World maps showing the global status of evangelical Christianity are usually color coded to provide the reader with a quick understanding of the percentages of evangelicals in countries across the world.[2] Red areas are the least reached areas while the dark green areas are the most reached areas. While such maps and color codes are good and needed for both a proper understanding of evangelicals and global strategy development, there is an inherent problem. The major limitation is that the perspective provided does not offer the realities in the communities within those countries. Rather, an average approximation is provided.

Again, such mapping is helpful and necessary. However, the church must not stop at the 35,000-foot perspective. Rather, it is important to move to a lower altitude and eventually land the plane in order to know truly what is going on in the communities.

This presentation of the research is an attempt to change perspectives on the United States and Canada from being seen as simply green countries, and thus "reached" with the gospel. By moving into the state/provincial, metro, and county levels, church planters will get a better perspective of the reality of lostness in these two countries. It should be noted that in no way does this presentation attempt to diminish the fact that by far the world's greatest areas of need are found outside of these countries. Rather, my hope is that this information would sound the alarm to the realities and opportunities facing the church in the United States and Canada.

---

2   For example see the pdf document at http://www.imb.org/globalresearch/downloads/GSECMap.pdf.

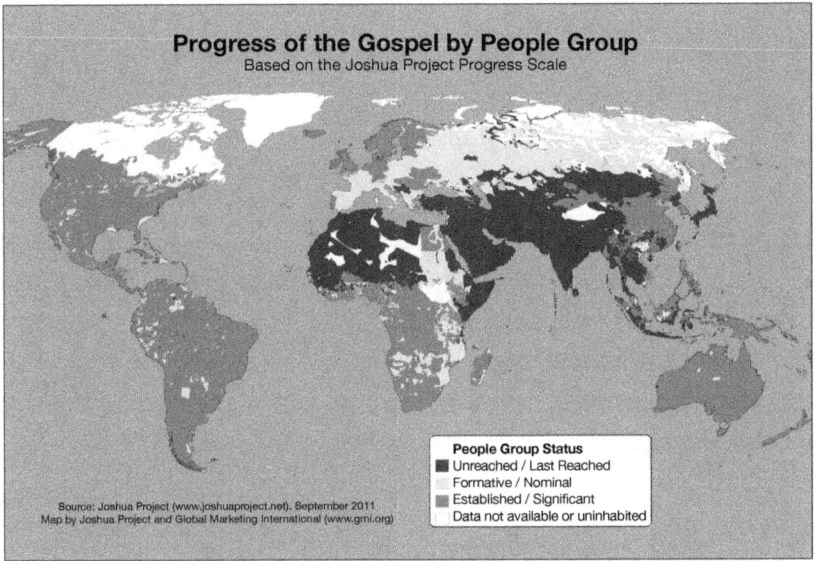

Figure 8.1 Progress of the gospel by people group

What Is Not Here and Why Better Research Is Needed

First, this project does not reveal the ground-level realities, but only the perspective from 15,000 feet. Pockets of significant lostness are not represented in this study. For example, the slides of Kentucky reveal that this state is 34 percent evangelical with a ratio of one evangelical church for every 788 people—a high evangelical percentage and a fairly low church to population ratio. If we only looked at this information, we could easily assume that there is not much of a need for evangelical churches in this state. However, such a perspective does not reveal the apartment complex down the street with only 3 percent of the resident population being followers of Christ. It does not provide us with numbers related to subdivisions, mobile home and condo communities, etc.

Second, at the 15,000-foot perspective we do not see the reality of least reached minority people groups. For example—to return to Kentucky—in Louisville, Kentucky, there are many Nepali and Somali peoples (two of the world's least reached people groups) with few known believers in Louisville at the time of this writing (none among the Somali), and no churches among either group. Also, many Bosnians have chosen to reside in Bowling Green, Kentucky. Again, here is one of the world's least reached people groups and no Bosnian believers (to my knowledge at the time of this writing) in Kentucky, and no church. From the 15,000-foot perspective we miss the number of least reached minority people groups, subcultures, and population segments.

The Findings

The findings in this study are visually displayed in a corresponding PowerPoint presentation. This presentation can be downloaded for free from the "Articles" section of www.NorthAmericanMissions.org.

The following two tables provide a quick glimpse of certain metropolitan areas in the United States and Canada, along with important statistics on the number of evangelicals present.

US Metropolitan Areas	Total Evangelical %	Evangelical Churches to Population Ratio
Provo-Orem, Utah	0.6%	1:18,427
Pittsfield, Massachusetts	1.5%	1:9640
Barnstable-Yarmouth, Massachusetts	1.5%	1:8889
Providence-Warwick-Pawtucket, Rhode Island	1.7%	1:8230
Springfield, Massachusetts	1.9%	1:9814
New York-Northern New Jersey-Long Island, NY-NJCT-PA	2.3%	1:8517
Salt Lake City-Ogden, Utah	2.3%	1:9808
Boston-Worcester-Lawrence-Lowell-Brockton, Massachusetts	2.5%	1:7786
New London-Norwich, Connecticut	2.5%	1:6477
Hartford, Connecticut	2.7%	1:7557
Albany-Schenectady-Troy, New York	2.7%	1:5837
Allentown-Bethlehem-Easton, Pennsylvania	2.8%	1:6577
Burlington, Vermont	2.9%	1:6630
Dubuque, Iowa	3.1%	1:6857
Glens Falls, New York	3.1%	1:4288

Scranton-Wilkes-Barre-Hazelton, Pennsylvania	3.1%	1:4733
Utica-Rome, New York	3.4%	1:4837
Philadelphia-Wilmington-Atlantic City, PA-NJ-DE	3.6%	1:5704
Syracuse, New York	3.7%	1:5049
Bangor, Maine	3.8%	1:3535
Portland, Maine	3.8%	1:4580
Laredo, Texas	3.9%	1:4598
Reading, Pennsylvania	4%	1:4018
Rochester, New York	4.1%	1:5084
Binghamton, New York	4.4%	1:3504
Reno, Nevada	4.6%	1:4715
Salinas, California	4.7%	1:3686
Lewiston-Auburn, Maine	5%	1:4152
Pittsburgh, Pennsylvania	5%	1:3978

Figure 8.2 US metropolitan areas of 5 percent or less evangelical

There are at least twenty-nine US metropolitan areas with an evangelical population less than or equal to 5%. The Provo-Orem, Utah, area is by far the least evangelical metro area in the country. Evangelicals comprise 0.6% of the 368,536 people living there. There are twenty evangelical churches in the area, making the church to population ratio 1:18,427. The runner-up category is a tie between two Massachusetts areas: Pittsfield and Barnstable-Yarmouth, Massachusetts, are only 1.5% evangelical. The church to population ratio in Pittsfield is 1:9640, and for Barnstable-Yarmouth, 1:8889.

Metro Area	Province	Evangelical Church To Population Ratio
Quebec City	Quebec	1:23,331
Saguenay	Quebec	1:21,733
Trois-Rivieres	Quebec	1:9508
Montreal	Quebec	1:8688
Sherbrooke	Quebec	1:8668
St. John's	Newfoundland	1:6718
Ottawa-Gatineau	Ontario	1:6129
Oshawa	Ontario	1:5381
Toronto	Ontario	1:5229
Great Sudbury	Ontario	1:4764
Calgary	Alberta	1:3818
Windsor	Ontario	1:3773
Victoria	British Columbia	1:3674
Hamilton	Ontario	1:3654
Kingston	Ontario	1:3604
Halifax	Nova Scotia	1:3539
Edmonton	Alberta	1:3420
London	Ontario	1:3351
Vancouver	British Columbia	1:3269
Thunder Bay	Ontario	1:3214
Winnipeg	Manitoba	1:3169
Regina	Saskatchewan	1:3148
St. Catherine's-Niagara	Ontario	1:2390
Saskatoon	Saskatchewan	1:2331
St. John	New Brunswick	1:2099

Figure 8.3 Selected Canadian metro areas where the evangelical church to population ratio is greater than 1:2000

The overall percentage of evangelicals in Canada is much smaller than that found in the US. Figure 8.3 reveals the church to population ratios in metropolitan areas across the country. The five greatest ratios are found in Quebec, with Quebec City at 1:23,331, and Saguenay at 1:21,733 dwarfing the other cities. It should be noted that at the time of this research, data was not provided for any of the Canadian Territories, or the overall evangelical percentages in each province or metro area.

Case Study #2:
The Strangers Next Door

In my forthcoming book, *Strangers Next Door: Immigration, Migration, and Mission*, I note the nationalities and the numbers of the world's unreached peoples living in Western countries. The second piece of evidence that I wish to submit for consideration is that while many of the world's unreached peoples are moving to the urban areas of the United States and Canada, little helpful information is known about them.

What We Know

The United States and Canada rank among the countries with the highest numbers of international migrants. The United States is by far the world's largest migrant receiving nation, absorbing 20 percent of the 214 million people who are on the move outside of their homeland. While Canada receives a much smaller portion, it is a much more ethnically diverse country, with a much larger percentage of its residents being born in another country.

Country	Estimated number of international migrants at mid-year, 2010	As Percentage of Global Total
United States	42,813,281	20
Canada	7,202,340	3.4

Figure 8.4 Numbers of international migrants in the United States and Canada, 2010

Consider the following statistics as related to the numbers of international migrants to the United States and Canada:

1. Between 2000–2010, the United States gained 8 million international migrants and Canada 1.6 million (United Nations 2008, 1).

2. In 2005, countries with at least 20 million inhabitants where international migrants constituted high proportions of the population included Australia (20%), Canada (19%), France (11%), Germany (12%), Saudi Arabia (26%), Spain (11%), Ukraine (15%), and the United States (13%) (United Nations 2009).
3. Between 2000–2007, the number of international students more than doubled to over 2 million. The main destination countries were the United States, the United Kingdom, Germany, France, and Australia (NBB Museum 2010).
4. In 2010, migrants comprised 22% of the total population in Australia, 21.3% of Canada, 13.5% of the United States, 10.4% of the United Kingdom (United Nations 2008).
5. By 2017, one Canadian in five could be a visible minority person (Berlanger and Malenfant 2005, 19).

Students

Every year, large numbers of international students travel to Western countries to study, with the United States and Canada receiving large portions of such students. The following table contains data from the Institute of International Education. It should be noted that students from China and India comprised over one-third of the international students studying in the United States during the 2009–2010 academic year.

Rank	Country	2009/10	Percent of Total
	World Total	690,923	100
1	China	127,628	18.5
2	India	104,897	15.2
3	South Korea	72,153	10.4
4	Canada	28,145	4.1
5	Taiwan	26,685	3.9
6	Japan	24,842	3.6
7	Saudi Arabia	15,810	2.3
8	Mexico	13,450	1.9
9	Vietnam	13,112	1.9
10	Turkey	12,397	1.8

11	Nepal	11,233	1.6
12	Germany	9,548	1.4
13	United Kingdom	8,861	1.3
14	Brazil	8,786	1.3
15	Thailand	8,531	1.2
16	Hong Kong	8,034	1.2
17	France	7,716	1.1
18	Indonesia	6,943	1.0
19	Columbia	6,920	1.0
20	Nigeria	6,568	1.0
21	Malaysia	6,190	0.9
22	Kenya	5,384	0.8
23	Pakistan	5,222	0.8
24	Venezuela	4,958	0.7
25	Russia	4,827	0.7

Figure 8.5 Top places of origin for international students in the US, 2009–2010[3]

Refugees and Asylees

Another important source fueling international migration is that of refugees and those seeking refugee status (asylees). The table below shows the numbers representing these two groups for the United States and Canada in the year 2009.

Country	Refugees	Asylum-Seekers (pending cases)
Canada	169,434	61,170
United States	275,461	63,803

Figure 8.6 Refugees and asylum-seekers in the United States and Canada as of 2009 (UNHCR 2009)

In 2009, the largest numbers of refugees and asylum-seekers to the United States came from Iraq, Burma, Bhutan, and Iran. The information in Figure 8.7, taken from

---
3 Taken from http://www.iie.org/en/Research-and-Publications/~/media/Files/Corporate/Open-Doors/Fast-Facts/Fast%20Facts%202010.ashx (accessed 28 February, 2011).

the United States Department of Homeland Security, reveals the largest numbers of refugees, by country of nationality:

Country	Number
Iraq	18,838
Burma	18,202
Bhutan	13,452
Iran	5,381
Cuba	4,800
Somalia	4,189
Eritrea	1,571
Vietnam	1,486
Congo, Democratic Republic	1,135
Burundi	762
Other	4,786

Figure 8.7 Refugee arrivals in the United States by country of nationality, 2009 (Martin 2009, 3)

How Many Unreached People Groups Are in the United States and Canada?

Figure 8.8 displays the numbers of unreached peoples living in the United States and Canada as tallied by Joshua Project and the Global Research Department. Since the latter organization uses a less than 2 percent evangelical definition for an unreached people group, I decided for comparison's sake to provide an additional column showing the Joshua Project numbers, using the same statistical definition. Joshua Project notes that 114 unreached people groups reside in the United States and Canada as compared to 541 unreached people groups according to the Global Research Department. While the difference lessens whenever "Adherents" is removed from the Joshua Project definition revealing 374 unreached peoples, there is still much discrepancy between these databases.[4]

---

4   It should be noted that Joshua Project and the Global Research Department use differing definitions for what constitutes certain people groups (for more information see http://www.joshuaproject.net/how-many-people-groups.php).

While I recognize the strategic reasons the Joshua Project subscribes to defining an unreached people in consideration of their adherence level, theologically and missiologically, I am not comfortable with such a guideline. Since membership within the kingdom demands the regenerative work of the Holy Spirit involving repentance and faith, and not simply a person's subscription to a traditional or cultural understanding of Christianity, I am more comfortable working with the 2 percent or less definition. Also, the inclusion of the adherence level as a defining characteristic for a group being "reached" or "unreached" keeps the church at the 35,000-foot perspective. By comparing the third and fourth columns in Figure 8.8, it is possible to come to a better approximation of the number of unreached peoples in the United States and Canada. While additional limitations will be noted in the next section, it is likely that there are somewhere between 374 and 541 unreached people groups living in the United States and Canada.

Country	UPGs, Joshua Project	UPGs, Joshua Project (with Adherent % removed)	UPGs, Global Research
Canada	41	132	180
United States	73	242	361
Totals	114	374	541

Figure 8.8 Unreached People Groups in Canada and the United States, Joshua Project, Global Research[5]

X Factors Affecting Urban Strategy

There are several limitations in my research on international migration to the United States and Canada. Each of the following matters provides a limitation to the development of robust urban mission strategies. With the development of diaspora missiology and growth of international migrations, it is even more critical that the church have a better understanding of what is presently taking place in these two countries.

---

5   As of March 28, 2012.

Unknown People Groups and Evangelical Percentages

The irony is that while the United States and Canada are two of the most researched countries in the world, the present data on these nations regarding the number of unreached peoples is very limited. For the most part, the Joshua Project has focused on countries other than the United States and Canada, where the numbers of evangelicals present and access to the gospel is more limited. In a recent conversation with Dan Scribner, Director, Joshua Project, I was told that their data for the United States and Canada are representative, but not comprehensive. While their information is a starting point for understanding the present realities, it is based primarily on census data and does not provide the details for an accurate understanding of the people groups. In other words, just because Nigerians show up in a national count, the research has not been accomplished to provide the people groups among them.

I received a similar response from Jim Haney, director of the Global Research Department. At the time of this writing, the Global Research Department of the International Mission Board has the exclusive assignment of researching every country of the world except the United States and Canada. Because their research also has been focused on other countries, they are not confident in their ability to provide accurate people group counts and the evangelical percentages of the various peoples living in the United States and Canada, or information as to whether or not anyone is engaging such peoples with the gospel and planting churches among them. Despite this limitation, the Global Research Department is able to provide the names and estimated populations of several hundred unreached peoples residing in these countries. However, the status of these groups being considered unreached is partially based on the assumption that since they are clearly unreached in other countries of the world, then it is assumed that it is highly likely they are also unreached in the United States and Canada.

According to the Southern Baptist Convention's policy, the North American Mission Board is assigned to missionary activity in the United States, Canada, and their respective territories. Unfortunately, very little research has been conducted by the North American Mission Board on their assigned region of the world.

Therefore, at the time of this writing, accurate information on the unreached people groups living in the United States and Canada does not exist. Not only do we not know who is living in our communities, but we do not know their evangelical statuses or who may be working among them as church planters. The data does not exist because the research has not been conducted. We have better data on an unreached people group living on the backside of the Himalayas than we do on that same people group living across the street from us in New York, Toronto, Chicago, or Montreal. Such is an extremely pathetic reality, and reflective of much of the missiology found throughout North America.

Unknown Receptivity Levels

Hardly any research has been conducted in recent years on the receptivity levels among immigrants (Baptist Press Staff 2010). This is an area that is pioneer territory for the urban missiologist.

Unknown Global Social Networks

International migrants usually remain in close contact with friends and relatives "back home." Oftentimes, those who have migrated frequently send remittances back to loved ones in other lands. These social networks are important when it comes to developing integrated strategies that focus on reaching people "here" so others can be reached "over there." Additional research is needed for a better understanding of the ongoing transnational social relationships.

Unknown Laborers in the Fields

Again, very little research has been attempted in order to determine what churches, networks, and denominations are engaged in evangelistic and church planting activities among the international migrants living throughout North America. Recently, the North American Mission Board and Lifeway Research conducted one such study to determine what groups are presently laboring among first generation migrants (ibid.).

A Proposal to Move Evangelicals in the Direction of More and Better Urban Research

There are at least four important steps that should be taken to help move evangelicals forward in the realm of conducting more and better urban research. The following are offered as starting points.

Evangelicals must develop a missiology that values urban research for North America. Here is the area in which many evangelicals fall short in the United States and Canada. Most of the missiology serving as a foundation for missional activity in North America fails to value research as a tool to assist in strategy development and contextualization.

Evangelicals must recognize that better urban research at home has significant implications for missions abroad. Many of the world's unreached peoples are moving to the urban contexts of the United States and Canada. Unfortunately, most evangelicals continue to embrace a missiology that dichotomizes missions according to geographical boundaries: "International" missions happen "over there," "domestic" missions take place "here," and never shall the two meet.

Transnational migrations, high speed transportation, and instant communication have reduced the appearance of distance between countries. Peoples migrate and continue to be active in the social and political realms in their countries of birth. Mission strategy needs to integrate strategies developed by missionaries "over there" with those developed by missionaries "over here." Many of the peoples residing in North America are gateway peoples to reaching unreached peoples in other lands.

Evangelicals must encourage, develop, and sustain support networks for a cadre of urban researchers at both the professional and volunteer levels. Evangelicals need to come together and form networks for urban research. Since the number of potential researchers is likely to begin as a small number, part of their responsibilities will include recruiting and training additional researchers. Room must be made for collaborative work between both the professionals and the volunteers.

Evangelicals must collaborate with one another to conduct, share, and disseminate findings as quickly as possible. Differing groups and denominations will likely form their own networks of urban researchers. While this matter is not a bad thing, the hoarding of findings, feeding egos, competition, and lack of cooperation are detrimental to the process necessary to provide healthy urban missiological research. The United States and Canada are too large for any one group to study. There must be collaborative efforts related to the study of the peoples of the cities. Without such cooperation among evangelicals, the desperately needed work will likely remain unaccomplished.

References

Baptist Press Staff. (2010). First-generation immigrants: Survey assesses scope of outreach in N. America. Retrieved from http://www.sbcbaptistpress.org/bpnews.asp?id=32595.

Bélanger, A., & Caron, E. (2005). Ethnocultural diversity in Canada: Prospects for 2017. *Canadian Social Trends* no.19 (Winter 2005). Retrieved from http://www.statcan.gc.ca/pub/11-008-x/2005003/article/8968-eng.pdf.

SOPEMI 2010. (2010). International Migration Outlook [PDF document]. Retrieved from http://www.nbbmuseum.be/doc/seminar2010/nl/bibliografie/kansengroepen/sopemi2010.pdf.

Mandryk, J. (2010). *Operation world: The definitive prayer guide to every nation.* Colorado Springs, CO: Biblica.

Martin, D. C. (2009). Refugees and asylees: 2009: Annual flow report, Office of Immigration Statistics.

The Pew Forum on Religion and Public Life. (2008). U. S. religious landscape survey 2008. North American Missions.org. Retrieved from http://northamericanmissions.org/files/2008%20America's%20report-religious-landscape-study-full.pdf.

United Nations High Commissioner for Refugees. (2010). 2009 Global trends: Refugees, asylum-seekers, returnees, internally displaced and stateless persons. *United Nations High Commissioner for Refugees* (UNCHR). Retrieved from http://www.unhcr.org/4c11f0be9.html.

United Nations, Department of Economic and Social Affairs, Population Division. (2009). Trends in international migrant stock: The 2008 revision. Retrieved from United Nations database. Available at http://www.un.org/esa/population/migration/UN_MigStock_2008.pdf.

_____. (2009). International migration report 2006: A global assessment. Retrieved from http://www.un.org/esa/population/publications/2006_MigrationRep/exec_sum.pdf.

Extreme Makeover: Church Addition (Church Mergers as an Opportunity for Urban Missions)

Derek Chinn
dchinn@multnomah.edu

There Goes the Neighborhood—
The Impact of Urbanization on the Church

In the movie *Gran Torino*, Walt Kowalski lives in a changing community. His Anglo neighbors have moved, giving way to Asian immigrants. Kowalski not only has to cope with how he feels about the demographic shift, but how he will interact with his new neighbors and the change they introduce to the neighborhood, whether he likes it or not.

Churches located in an urban setting confront similar challenges. When a neighborhood changes, churches must consider how they will adjust to the transformation of the environment they physically reside in (Bakke 1997, 86–89). Congregations with land and a facility can respond in a few ways—do nothing, leave or sell the property, or adapt. If churches are unable to minister to the changing population, they eventually "die" because they lack "replacement" membership. The church, as a piece of real estate, will be assimilated by the community.[1]

---

1 An Internet search of former churches becoming private residences or businesses demonstrates how the marketplace will "reclaim" land to meet the needs of the community.

The decision to stay and be a part of a changing community is not an easy one. It is a question every church faces when its internal and external communities change. In her landmark work, *The Death and Life of Great American Cities*, Jane Jacobs describes one church's reaction to urbanization:

> The history of the Episcopal chapel a few blocks down the street tells the tale of the slum's formation, almost a century ago in this case. The neighborhood had been a place of farms, village streets and summer homes, which evolved into a semi-suburb that became embedded in the rapidly growing city. Colored people and immigrants from Europe were surrounding it; neither physically nor socially was the neighborhood equipped to handle their presence—no more, apparently, than a semi-suburb is so equipped today. Out of this quiet residential area—a charming place, from the evidence of old pictures—there were at first many random desertions by congregation families; those of the congregation who remained eventually panicked and departed en masse. The church building was abandoned to Trinity parish, which took it over as a mission chapel to minister to the influx of the poor who inherited the semi-suburb. The former congregation re-established the church far uptown, and colonized in its neighborhood a new quiet residential area of unbelievable dullness; it is now a part of Harlem. The records do not tell where the next pre-slum was built by these wanderers. (Jacobs 1993, 359–60)[2]

In this situation, a church emigrated to a "safer" location. Its departure was a response to the urbanization of the city and neighborhood. Jacobs reports that the stagnation and "decline" of the area gave rise to a slum. If a stalwart few from the congregation had stayed to maintain a presence in the community, would things have been different? Only God knows, but it raises important questions about the role, mission, and efficacy of Christ and his people (that is, the local church) in an urban environment.

Michael Emerson and Rodney Woo suggest three motives for change in a church (Emerson and Woo 2006, 55–61)[3]—mission, resource calculation, and external

---

2   Jacobs' work was originally published fifty years ago indicating that the challenge of urbanization on the mission of the church is not a new phenomenon.
3   While their model specifically addresses churches becoming multiracial, the criteria they use fit the urban church as well.

authority structure.⁴ Based on this author's experience, a "merge" option (due to limited resources) (Emerson and Woo 2006, 60),⁵ will be advocated in this paper. Specifically, a church in decline because its community is changing should consider joining with a church that effectively ministers to the local population but lacks resources to further its ministry. As it relates to urbanization and mission in an urban context, this represents a unique opportunity to reach immigrants and/or ethnic minorities through the redistribution of resources from the majority culture.

Fourth Street United Methodist Church in Brooklyn, New York, typifies the collision that can occur with urbanization. A small Latino congregation owns the church building, which was originally established to minister to the Norwegian community—the dominant ethnic group in the neighborhood a century ago (Macaulay Honors College at City University of New York). The Spanish-speaking church hosts a growing, 1,500-plus Chinese congregation to sustain the smaller congregation (Carnes 2010).

> Financially pinched congregations—especially those in mainline denominations like the Methodists—increasingly make ends meet by moving in together. In Jamaica, Queens, a Methodist church split between Latin American and Caribbean congregations has just made room for a small Pakistani one (Dolnick 2010).

> Unfortunately, because of differences in language, culture, theology, and philosophy of ministry, acrimony describes the relationship between the two congregations. Their dilemma is a divisive, kingdom-limiting problem (Dolnick 2010).

While the ill feeling in Brooklyn will probably not be solved by joining the congregations together now, could a different starting point have helped? Was it a relationship doomed to failure? What if the denomination had provided "marriage counseling" for the congregations instead of asking the churches to cohabitate?

The journalist covering the story about Fourth Street UM Church observes,

---

4 Emerson and Woo describe mission as a congregation's goals or "its theological, cultural, and/or symbolic orientation." Resource calculation is when a church adapts to change because its resources/assets have or need to be reallocated. Some congregations are subject to the authority of an external authority structure and their reason for change is outside of their control.
5 Emerson and Woo describe this as "survival merge."

> The standoff mirrors a tug of war that has played out for generations in New York, where immigrant groups—some established, some newly arrived—jostle on crowded sidewalks and in narrow tenements for space, housing and jobs. (Dolnick 2010)

With urbanization, the church has an opportunity and a problem. Ministry opportunities abound to reach people moving to the city for such things as improved access to employment, basic necessities, housing, and safety (National Geographic). Unless the church reconsiders how it will handle the influx of new people, it will squander an opportune moment.

For the context of this paper, the discussion about urbanization is limited to the United States.

Extreme Makeover by Church Addition— Join Churches Together to Advance the Kingdom

Emerson and Woo observe that several factors can influence the formation of multiracial congregations (Emerson and Woo 2006, 53). With urbanization, changing demographics can impact churches' numbers and dramatically affect their resources—financial and human capital. Emerson and Woo describe this impetus for change as one of

> resource calculation, typically due to declining membership as the neighborhood racial composition changed. Oftentimes, when neighborhoods change, congregations sell their church building and move, or they stay and close their doors when members no longer remain. (Emerson and Woo 2006, 59)

Churches wanting to survive can change how they do ministry in order to be "relevant" to their new neighbors, or they can combine with another church (Emerson and Woo 2006, 60). Merging becomes more attractive if survival is questionable because of diminished resources and/or the church fails to attract new congregants after making significant changes. The point of merging is not to simply sustain a ministry, but to combine resources to do more than what the churches were doing alone.

This author is part of a congregation that merged two churches. A significant reason for joining together was that the congregations struggled to expand their respective ministries and lacked critical mass to get beyond "maintenance mode." By combining resources, both churches created a new ministry that exceeded what the stand-alone congregations aspired to do.

How Firm a Foundation— A Theological Basis for this Approach

While the idea of merging churches sounds idyllic, it should not be pursued whenever the opportunity arises. Something more compelling than a pragmatic solution must drive the decision. The work involved needs a biblically grounded vision to rally congregants and sustain them in the difficult times.

This paper offers five reasons for considering a church merger in an urban setting—to bless the city, to reach all people, to model compromise and reconciliation, to strengthen the body of Christ, and to evangelize and transform.

To Bless the City

> But seek the welfare of the city where I have sent you into exile, and pray to the LORD on its behalf, for in its welfare you will find your welfare. (Jer 29:7 ESV)

In Jeremiah 29:7, God calls his people, Israel, to be the shalom, welfare or peace and prosperity, of the city in which they are captives. God wants to bless and sustain his people so they will ultimately pursue him. Israel's pursuit of peace will be a testimony to the enemies of God, and require heart change in his people. This call from the prophet is unexpected and resistance is anticipated as God warns his people against false prophets who would counter this call to be a blessing to Israel's enemies.

Robert Linthicum comments about how a church can transform a city: "Our calling as God's people into whatever situation which God might call us is to seek that city's shalom, its peace, prosperity, well-being, wholeness, fullness, reconciliation" (Linthicum 2005, 88).

In their work, *Redeeming the City*, Pasquariello, Shriver, and Geyer state,

> the mission of the church is to seek the shalom of the city. ... Shalom always is a corporate virtue signifying good relations between persons, families, peoples. It conveys abundance and success in human life such as material prosperity, bodily health, happiness, and the use of resources for positive well-being. (Pasquariello, Shriver, and Geyer 1982, 30–31)

1 Peter 2:13ff and Romans 13:1–7 describe Christian citizenship and conduct. What the apostles prescribe for individuals applies to the corporate body as well. Local churches, as a whole, testify and represent Christ in how they live and interact with their community.[6] With this in mind, how *shalom* is manifested by God's people is relevant. Merging churches offers salient points to deliver peace to the local community—presence, peacemaking, stewardship, community, and evangelism.

To Reach All People

> Though I am free and belong to no man, I make myself a slave to everyone, to win as many as possible. To the Jews I became like a Jew, to win the Jews. To those under the law I became like one under the law (though I myself am not under the law), so as to win those under the law. To those not having the law I became like one not having the law (though I am not free from God's law but am under Christ's law), so as to win those not having the law. To the weak I became weak, to win the weak. I have become all things to all men so that by all possible means I might save some. I do all this for the sake of the gospel, that I may share in its blessings. (1 Cor 9:19–23)

Randy White observes a progression of flight that occurs in cities as people flee to the suburbs—white middle class and black middle class (White 2006, 18). The urban church faces a dilemma when its congregants move away to "better" environs. Should the church in this circumstance follow its constituency? Is there biblical support for a church to vacate a community?

If the Apostle Paul is, for the sake of the gospel, willing to become all things to all men, how does 1 Corinthians 9 impact the decision for a church to stay or leave?

---

6   In 1 Corinthians 6, Paul admonishes the church in Corinth for lawsuits that church members have brought against one another. The apostle challenges their testimony and what these lawsuits represent in the view of unbelievers.

Living the reality of this text, a church should adjust and reflect the demographics (such as gender, race/ethnicity, age, class, education, income) of the neighborhood in which it resides. A church could assimilate demographically by merging with another congregation.

A church moving out of a neighborhood because it has outgrown its space is understandable, especially if it is limited by the facility or geographic location. However, it is a different issue when the congregation is shrinking.[7] Leadership should be sensitive to the concerns of congregants alarmed at their languishing ministry. But what does it take to help the church stay put?

Joining congregations together can expand a church's reach into a specific demographic quickly. For instance, an older Anglo congregation with a building in a changing neighborhood could join with the Hispanic congregation renting their church or using a facility in the area. The resulting combined congregation would have property, people who speak the language of immigrants, and critical mass of volunteers to make outreach and relationships possible.

To Model Compromise and Reconciliation between Churches

> So let's stop condemning each other. Decide instead to live in such a way that you will not cause another believer to stumble and fall. I know and am convinced on the authority of the Lord Jesus that no food, in and of itself, is wrong to eat. But if someone believes it is wrong, then for that person it is wrong. And if another believer is distressed by what you eat, you are not acting in love if you eat it. Don't let your eating ruin someone for whom Christ died. Then you will not be criticized for doing something you believe is good. For the Kingdom of God is not a matter of what we eat or drink, but of living a life of goodness and peace and joy in the Holy Spirit. If you serve Christ with this attitude, you will please God, and others will approve of you, too. So then, let us aim for harmony in the church and try to build each other up. (Rom 14:13–19 NLT)

Bringing churches together to form one body is an extraordinary opportunity to model compromise and reconciliation between congregations. In a time when churches divide over preferences, polity, and/or doctrine and theology, uniting

---

7 The issue of racial and ethnic "flight" because of changing demographics of a community is a topic worth exploring, but beyond the scope of this paper.

congregations is countercultural. It serves as an example of healthy relationships in a society accustomed to divisive conflict in many spheres of life such as politics, social norms, religion, science, and public policy. A researcher of cultural diversity observes, "Churches are among the few institutions in the United States that regularly bring immigrants, social isolates, minorities, and even socially maladjusted people into contact with the 'mainstream'" (Angrosino 2001, 48).

How can modeling happen? Romans 14 and 15 offer a prescription for compromise and reconciliation. Furthermore, in 2 Corinthians 5:14–18, Paul plainly states the reason for seeking to be reconcilers—to point to Christ. Recognizing the difference between core essentials and preferences is important when tackling issues of dispute. Working through conflict is important to relationship building because it helps congregants understand one another, especially as they work toward a healthy resolution (Chinn 2009, 151). Humility is vital to resolving differences on issues of strong preference (Chinn 2009, 159–161).

The power of reconciliation within a congregation blended together for the sake of the gospel can have a significant impact on outsiders. At Wilcrest Baptist Church, visitors with "issues," who were "divorced, single parents, alcoholics and drug addicts … believed that if Wilcrest was open enough to accept racial diversity, it might also be open to accept them" (Emerson and Woo 2006, 109). The implication is that if a church could welcome and reconcile races and ethnicities, then surely they would be welcoming to sinners.

To Offer A Broader Understanding of How the Body of Christ Functions and Lives

> Now you are the body of Christ, and each one of you is a part of it. (1 Cor 12:27)

By bringing two or more congregations together united under one roof and meeting at the same time, there are a number of benefits for all its members. Building up the body for the common good through spiritual gifts is significant. The composition, with a view toward heterogeneity, of the local body has profound impact on spiritual formation.

When congregations come together, both churches can be revitalized and rally around a new sense of purpose (Chinn 2009, 165–66). In addition, there is more opportunity to see the diversity of spiritual gifts exercised for the good of the church. The breadth of these gifts is probably broader than one might expect.

With a greater range of cultures (e.g., race, ethnicity, age, gender, class, and/or education), the spiritual gifts will manifest themselves in unique ways. For instance, consider how the spiritual gifts of teaching or hospitality are expressed by male or female, Chinese or Mexican, teen or elderly, Dalit or Royal, etc. As the gifts draw from a larger pool of believers and serve a bigger audience, diversity expands the ability of the body to strengthen and grow itself.

Merging congregations encourages and expects congregants to embrace believers who are different from themselves. Just expanding a circle of relationships takes people outside of their accustomed comfort zone. When the relationships are with people of different cultures, then the church can catch a hint of the magnitude of the universal church.

In both 1 Corithinians and Ephesians, the Apostle Paul describes the importance of the individual members of the body of Christ—they need one another. Diversity in the church is not simply pursued because it is the nature of the body. Rather, being with people who are different is vital because we need people who have encountered Christ through the lens of their background, shaped by such things as ethnicity, class, education, socioeconomics, country of origin, and gender. Their respective encounters with Christ reveal a different facet of Christ others do not know. These facets can enhance and expand our understanding of God. Discovering an unknown personal aspect of God serves to magnify a finite understanding of an infinite God.

To Be Evangelistic and Transformational

> But if an unbeliever or someone who does not understand comes in while everybody is prophesying, he will be convinced by all that he is a sinner and will be judged by all, and the secrets of his heart will be laid bare. So he will fall down and worship God, exclaiming, "God is really among you!" (1 Cor 14:24–25)

In 1 Corinthians 14, Paul describes the culmination of what chapter 12 (spiritual gifts) and chapter 13 (love) can accomplish for the kingdom of God. In verses 22–26, Paul describes what can happen when an unbeliever comes into the midst of believers worshipping together. Verse 24 describes the impact on an unbeliever who witnesses believers loving and building up one another[8]—the unbeliever is convicted by the Holy Spirit and acknowledges God's presence. The fruit of a merged congregation can be the gospel personified—reconciliation between people that speaks of the greater reconciliation that Christ brings about between God and mankind.

The value of merging congregations is not simply to rescue two or more churches from dying and/or hindered growth. It is more than keeping ministries afloat. Linthicum argues from the book of Nehemiah:

> The task of the church in today's world, in the final analysis, is not simply to win souls to Christ, nor is it to plant or to build up the church, nor is it to organize around issues of the people and to work for justice. ... But the full and authentic mission of the church ... is to work for the building of the shalom community in our congregations, our communities, and our cities. (Linthicum 2005, 243)

Linthicum goes on to suggest that rebuilding the walls of Jerusalem was a step toward spiritual healing (Linthicum 2005, 246). Applying Linthicum's principle, building a "new" congregation by merging churches, should compel congregants to be Christ-focused. The difficulty of joining churches together points to our need for God and the power of his transformative work.

The redemptive aspect of this ministry depends on the relationship. Linthicum explains,

> All truly transforming change—whether in a neighborhood or a city or your congregation—must be built upon the building and maintaining of strong relationships. But relationships that change people and systems are not superficial, uncommitted relationships.... Relationships that change society or even a church must require intentional, deep, and demanding commitments. (Linthicum 2005, 125)

Going back to 1 Corinthians 14, if a church models what Paul describes, the congregations that join together in an urban setting can be redemptive. Jesus' words

---

8   The text notes that the believers are exercising the gift of prophecy. What good is this? Going back to verse 3 of 1 Corinthians 14, Paul tells us that the one who prophesies is doing it to strengthen, encourage, and comfort the brethren. The practice of a spiritual gift coupled with love (described by v. 3) proclaims and advances the kingdom.

in John 17:21 are foundational for the testimony of a united body of Christ—"that all of them may be one, Father, just as you are in me and I am in you. May they also be in us so that the world may believe that you have sent me."

Home Improvement—Churches That Have Taken this Approach

Redemption Church in Phoenix, Arizona launched in January 2011. It is a multisite church that has an urban and two suburban campuses. In a personal interview, Pastor Justin Anderson said the churches came together to expand their respective ministries together and reach the city for Christ. The two churches, Praxis Church and East Valley Bible Church, asked, "Are we better together than we would be apart? Are we better able to accomplish our goals, to expand God's Kingdom, to reach more people—can we do it better together than we could apart?" It was a unanimous decision to come together because they could do more together.

Anderson adds that the two parent churches were different geographically and demographically—young urbanites and older suburbanites. A significant concern for the younger church was that it would be swallowed up by the suburban megachurch due to a disparity in size—numbers and leadership composition. The leaders resolved the issues well by communicating intent, allowing people to air their concerns, and addressing the points raised.

Emmanuel Hope of Glory Wesleyan Church is the product of a Filipino church comprised mainly of young families joining an aging Anglo congregation with a building. The joining together was mutually beneficial because as Pastor Melvin Baliton describes it, in a personal interview, the merge "played to people's strengths" from the respective congregations. The Filipinos, by culture, were caring, loving, and respectful to their elders. The older congregants had spiritual maturity, financial resources, and the building.

Because the Filipino congregation was bigger and had the pastor, they needed to be sensitive to the older congregants' feelings. An important component for success was compromise and empathy. Baliton says they are always blending what they do. They kept the hymns and encouraged the participation of the elderly. While the younger generation prefers upbeat music, Baliton has given the pianist and organist a prominent role with communion and the offertory.

One Church in Lynnwood, Washington, is a young, multiracial immigrant church community that joined an established church "struggling to survive challenging times in a changing community." Both congregations were sharing a pastor, and the younger congregation did not have a church facility. Mutual necessity brought them together.

When Thame Fuller, the pastor of One Church, was helping both congregations discern God's call for their ministry, he gave them a vision for what their church could become. He notes, in personal correspondence, that in their city, "there are various Asian communities (East—Korean, Japanese, etc./South—India, Pakistan, etc.), African communities (Nigerian, Kenyan, Ugandan, etc.), European communities (Western—French, etc./Eastern—Russian, Ukrainian)." Therefore, their ministry as a "Christ-centered intercultural church occurs at the intersection of multiple locally represented cultural communities." In other words, in a city where many ethnic communities reside, the diverse congregation of One Church is uniquely positioned to proclaim Christ. The merge that gave birth to One Church gave it an inroad to reaching a growing immigrant population.

In response to the urbanization of their community, One Church bridges cultures with English as the lingua franca for the church. The appeal of One Church is that they relate to and understand "[t]hose who are connected to an immigrating cultural community, have fluency in the heart language of that community and are comfortable speaking English." Furthermore, as Pastor Fuller commented in a personal interview, they feel that those who are "well-adjusted to America often enjoy worshipping in a diverse intercultural context and have potential to take the gospel much deeper into the cultural communities of their origin than others."

The Table in the Portland metro area is a unique multisite ministry. They have four campuses, with three of their sites resulting from a church merge. Their campuses are located in urban, suburban, and rural settings. Each situation has its own set of challenges.

Pastor Geoff Hartt points out that urbanization doesn't just affect churches in the urban setting. Rural churches are impacted as well. As people move to the city, the rural population shrinks and, consequently, rural churches experience a decline as well. Hartt notes that rural churches are candidates for merging, too. The merge could involve closing a church and creating multisite locations. He also describes a hypothetical scenario where three churches "merge" and share staff (a pastor and administrator) and leadership—it is simply "one church with different locations."

These four churches faced opportunities and challenges arising from a demographic shift in the urban community. God gave the leadership a vision to merge their respective church communities for the sake of expanding the kingdom. A God-inspired vision is fundamental for providing a foundation for the new church to be formed (Chinn 2009, 146–48).

This Old House—Some of the Realities of Renovation

Drawing from the experiences of churches that have merged, there are words of encouragement and caution. The following are some observations from leaders who have taken their churches through the merge process.

Merging Congregations is Redemptive

> Universally, there is a firm conviction that churches merging reflect the heart of God. When the norm for the church seems to be conflict, church mergers is a refreshing notion. It is encouraging to hear of congregants who welcome change and set aside personal preferences to make the "marriage" work. "'Change doesn't always come easy for older folks,' 74-year-old [Rev. Lawrence] Biermann says. 'But they've accepted it well. We're two independent congregations trying to reach the community in the same way, and I think that's encouraging during a time when there is so much division.'" (Paitsel 2010)

Furthermore, participants in the merge see hope for the new church because of new energy and resources. As one pastor describes it, "'Most churches nowadays are spending most of their energies just getting by, paying the salaries and the bills,' he continued. "If we merge with Emmanuel, we'll get beyond that 'survival mode' and into what I call 'mission mode.' That means we'll be able to spend our energy on doing the work that God wants us to do. I mean, Jesus doesn't talk about raising money to repair a roof" (Baker 2011).

As described by Emerson and Woo, merging can rescue a God-given resource (Emerson and Woo 2006, 60). Around 1891,

> [a] modest wooden church was built to house a Methodist Episcopal congregation. By 1959, the Methodists had moved on. Ukrainian

Orthodox Christians had taken their place, installing a three-bar cross on the church steeple. By 1968, the building was home to the Church of the Living God, a historically African American congregation that thrived for a time. But in recent years, membership dwindled. Last fall, unpaid debts meant the church property faced foreclosure and the prospect of being sold at auction in front of the Multnomah County Courthouse. (Haught 2011)

In December 2010, for a little over $200,000, a Buddhist organization purchased this building to establish a permanent home for their spiritual community. After 120 years of ministry for the sake of Christ, this church has undergone change its founders would not have imagined. What could have been done to keep this church building in the service of Christ?

Communication Is Vital

In a merge, parent churches undergo substantial change. The congregants might already be resistant to change so the lack of information can heighten suspicions even if there is nothing to be suspicious about. Making sure stakeholders have the opportunity to understand what is going on is critical (Chinn 2009, 160).

Pastor Baliton was given the "power" by the denomination to take over an older congregation that had a building and property. Rather than taking over and moving people out, he worked to bring two churches together. To facilitate the joining of congregations he promoted the idea as "blending." He conveyed to the congregants that the strengths and attributes they each brought would have a part in building the new church.

Even when things are communicated well, there is a good chance for misunderstanding or, at least, people will hear what they want or expect to hear. Hartt encountered this dilemma when The Table joined up with Stafford Baptist, a rural church. In the first week of being together, fifty percent of the congregation at Stafford left. In spite of what was said, Hartt notes wisely, "People hear something totally different."

Someone Will Be Unhappy

As Anderson puts it, "Everyone loses something." When the churches come together, there must be compromise. As equal partners, someone will give up something for the sake of others, either for someone from their "home" congregation or a person in their "new" family.

Dissatisfaction and conflict will happen. It is important to be prepared to deal with how people respond and have a process for working things out (Chinn 2009, 90–94).

From Hartt's experience with two church mergers he observes, "You will definitely lose fifty percent, give or take, in the merger." He comments realistically, "it [the merger] is not the magical answer" for saving a church.

Success Does Not Come Readily

It is easy and foolish to think that because the merge is God's call that things will go smoothly. For some, the initial response may be warm and excited, but they become hostile when their expectations are not met. For others, they are less than enthusiastic, but come to embrace the idea.

Anderson notes that his people are giving the work a chance. He has taken deliberate steps from the pulpit to speak from Scripture about issues the church will face with regard to unity and division. For instance, preaching out of James, he has addressed the sin of partiality, giving an example of some of the younger generation urbanites who "were biased against the suburbanites."

Chinn concurs with Hartt on the difficulty of keeping a merged congregation together. Of the churches he studied, most of the churches that merged do not exist or failed to retain more than a third of one of the parent congregations (Chinn 2009, 178–79).

The Work Is Worth It

While the effort to have a successful, happy united congregation is difficult, the work is worthwhile and rewarding. Many congregants want to do and finish well what God has set on their heart. They appreciate getting to know the brethren they had not known before (Chinn 2009, 95).

Terry Crist, pastor of City of Grace in Phoenix, Arizona, reflected on how things have gone with their merge: "I would say that as challenging as the process has been, I wouldn't trade it for anything because we have come through it wiser and stronger and we are emerging more efficient, and most importantly, better positioned for the future. Our staff reductions have been more about right-sizing than downsizing and it has positioned us to seize God-ordained opportunities for the future" (Church Executive 2011).

At Redemption, Anderson notes that people are very excited about the merge and significant intergenerational relationships are being built. The older generation has "embraced their, kind of ... almost fatherly, motherly roles in the larger Redemption Church. They've seen the part they can play in it, as older, more established people in campuses that are a little younger. That's a huge blessing."

With these nuggets of wisdom in mind, what is next?

Welcome to the Neighborhood—How Does a Church Merge with Another?

If merging congregations is a way to keep church facilities an available resource for God and his people, how could it be advanced? How does a church start moving in this direction?

Consider Merging as a Viable Option

As noted earlier, merging congregations is a significant, high-commitment decision and often one of last resort. An interim step that can expose or prepare a church to elements of merging congregations is sharing a church building (Curtin 2002, 13–18). Creating one congregation out of two or more churches may not happen, but the experience can still yield kingdom-advancing results.

There are a number of resources (books, websites, Internet forums, and church consultants) available concerning mergers between churches. There are far fewer resources that discuss the challenges of merging churches between ethnic/racial congregations.[9]

---

9   There are two resources the author knows about. Mariko Yanagihara's work, "A Process for Church Mergers: Asian American Churches and White Churches Becoming a New Creation in Christ," and the author's dissertation, "1+1=1: The Challenges of Creating a Multiracial Church from Single Race Congregations."

Seek Advice from Those Who Have Done It

Because this option has become more frequent, there are churches that have gained wisdom through the process and navigated the difficulties likely to be encountered. Find someone who has been through the adventure and can give perspective on the endeavor.

Be Open to What God Might Do to Make It Happen

The original campus of The Table was more the result of a gift than a merge. One congregation gave the other the building, or as Hartt described it, "let's just turn it over and give 'em the keys." A few merges this author has encountered have benefited from the generosity of an older congregation with a building giving their assets to the younger congregation and taking diminished "power" roles.

Be Realistic and Have Eyes Wide Open

Church consultant Tom Bandy advises careful consideration. He comments, "Careful study of the ten keys to success reveals how stressful mergers can actually be. The remnants of Christendom thinking continue to undermine even the most faithfully conceived mergers" (Bandy 2006). Bandy's list rests on the foundations of vision, strategic planning, awareness of the expectations of all involved, and circumspection.

The work is challenging, and leading with a God-inspired vision is crucial. Hartt comments that you "need to have a really strong leadership team because of the struggles you will have."

These are some key things to be alert to if a church is going to merge with another. Based on research for multiracial church mergers (Chinn 2009, 159), there are four critical components to have in place:

1. Vision—it is clear, God-given, and Christocentric.
2. Leadership—they are courageous, have a conviction about what they are doing, and committed to getting the merge done.
3. Communication—it must be clear, consistent, and frequent.

Change and conflict management—leadership anticipates and manages transition and conflict.

Lyle Schaller observes that the following factors hinder the success of merging congregations (Schaller 1989, 142–43):

- The new congregation's culture does not change. The church does not organizationally plan for growth, so the numerically larger church still functions as its smaller predecessors did.
- Doctrinal and theological views of the parent congregations differ.
- Substantial ethnic or nationality differences are present.
- Crossing social class lines.
- Philosophies of ministry are disparate.
- Leadership abilities differ and there is a jockeying for power.
- Disagreement over what holds and keeps the congregation together relationally (i.e., personality of pastor, ministry program, cultural heritage, role in church, spiritual experience).

Conclusion

There are compelling, biblical reasons for merging churches. It can be proactive—a ministry anticipates where the local community is headed and has a vision for addressing needs. It may be reactive, when a church realizes that unless internal change takes place it will cease to exist.

It is difficult to get people to compromise, change, and develop new relationships. Yet, a God-inspired vision and call can inspire and keep congregants on track when things get crazy.

Ultimately, merging congregations is to advance the gospel. The relationships created are not limited to the edification of the believers, but are also evangelistic. The church resulting from merging congregations should be able to increase its ability to connect with the local community. By being a "living" testimony to what Christ can do, the new church can inspire redemptive conversations with its neighbors. As White notes, "Transformational relationships bring change to both parties, opening our eyes to new dimensions of faith, opening doors of opportunity, giving birth to new prospects for community partnerships" (White 2006, 148–49).

There are various reasons churches might consider merging. Some are financial, while others see a strategic opportunity to enhance their ministry. This author thinks one significant reason is age. Across the country, aging congregations in urban communities face decisions concerning their viability. Older congregants are worried about what will become of their church when they die. Merging with a younger congregation is sound stewardship—it builds on the investment of the older generation.

Memorial Baptist Church and Calvary Revival Church Peninsula in Newport News, Virginia, are examples of the direction some older congregations will head (Paitsel 2010). Memorial, a 107-year-old white congregation, was aging and only saw closing in its future. It entered into a partnership with the younger black congregation of Calvary. They are considering merging but in the "dating" stage now. They are doing ministry together and learning about one another.

One African-American congregant is hopeful about their future. As she puts it, "'I grew up at the tail end of 'separate but equal,' and it's just amazing if you look at the whole picture here. You have an older white congregation coming together with young African Americans. We can change the city'" (Paitsel 2010).

Church mergers are a unique opportunity to utilize the resources God has given to his people. More important, it offers a significant, tangible example of how God the Father reconciles himself and others through Jesus, God the Son. Not only is there conciliation between believers, but the success of merging depends on congregants recognizing that they need their "new" brethren to facilitate their personal growth in Christ. As a testimony to the Living God, joining congregations together can be a powerful witness.

A city may change the Church, but the church can change a city.

References

Angrosino, M. V. (2001). *Talking about cultural diversity in your church: Gifts and challenges*. Walnut Creek: AltaMira Press.

Baker, J. B. (2011, January 20). Lincoln, Cumberland churches may merge. *The Woonsocket Call*. Retrieved from http://www.woonsocketcall.com/node/1609.

Bakke, R. (1997). The challenge of world evangelization to mission strategy. In H. M. Conn (Ed.), *Planting and growing urban churches: From dream to reality* (79–93). Grand Rapids: Baker Books.

Bandy, T. (2006).Top ten things you see in a merger. Easum Bandy Associates. Retrieved from http://servicerealtypresents.com/blog/top-ten-things-you-see-in-a-church-merger.

Carnes, T. (2010). The "mixed veggies" of Sunset Park, Brooklyn, religion in ethnic flavors, Part 2: the Fujianese. *New York Religion.* Retrieved from http://www.nycreligion.info/?p=359.

Chinn, D. (2009). 1+1=1: The challenges of creating a multiracial church from single race congregations. (Doctoral dissertation). Western Seminary.

Church Executive. (2011, February 1). Churches still choose multi-campus approach, but mergers keep popping up. *Church Executive.* Retrieved from http://churchexecutive.com/archives/churches-still-choose-multi-campus-approach-but-mergers-keep-popping-up.

Curtin, R. D. (2002). *Sharing your church building.* Grand Rapids: Baker Books.

Dolnick, S. (2010, December 28). Brooklyn immigrant congregations clash. *New York Times.* Retrieved from http://www.nytimes.com/2010/12/29/nyregion/29church.html?_r=1&hp.

Emerson, M. O., & Woo, R. M. (2006). *People of the dream.* Princeton: Princeton University Press.

Haught, N. (2011, June 26). Church's fourth life: Zen temple. *The Oregonian,* O5.

Jacobs, J. (1993). *The death and life of great American cities.* New York: Modern Library.

Linthicum, R. C. (2005). *Building a people of power: Equipping churches to transform their communities.* Waynesboro, GA: Authentic Media.

Macaulay Honors College at City University of New York. (2010). Fourth Avenue United Methodist Church and Tian Fu. *Faiths and Freedom.* http://macaulay.cuny.edu/eportfolios/drabik10website/neighborhoods-2/sunset-park/houses-of-worship/united-methodist-church-and-tian-fu/.

National Geographic Expeditions Archive. (n.d.). Migration: Reasons to move. *National Geographic.* Retrieved from http://www.nationalgeographic.com/xpeditions/lessons/09/g35/Migrations.html.

Paitsel, N. (2010, October 13). Church partnership defies age, race and denomination barriers. *Daily Press.* Retrieved from http://articles.dailypress.com/2010-10-13/news/dp-nws-church-merger-20101013_1_black-congregation-zoe-community-church-church-partnership.

Pasquariello, R. D., Shriver Jr. D. W., & Geyer, A. (1982). *Redeeming the city: Theology, politics & urban policy.* New York: The Pilgrim Press.

Schaller, L. E. (1989). *Reflections of a contrarian: Second thoughts on the parish ministry*. Nashville: Abingdon.

White, R. (2006). *Encounter God in the city: Onramps to personal and community transformation*. Downers Grove: InterVarsity Press.

From Niche to Parish: A Qualitative Study of Congregations Engaging Transitional Neighborhoods

Kathryn Lewis Mowry
kmowry@trevecca.edu

Across North America, neighborhoods are in constant flux. My colleagues at a church in Los Angeles used to joke that if someone took his shirt to the dry cleaners on Monday, he might return on Wednesday to find it was a Thai restaurant. This is not far from reality. The market down the street has just put up all new signs in Spanish. The homeless have chosen the church steps as a sleeping place, and their bedtime routine includes shattering the church security lights. Dozens of houses in the once-proud neighborhood sit vacant. Crime is on the increase. The major industrial plant has moved out of the neighborhood, taking its workers with it. Neighborhoods are emptied of entrepreneurial spirit and leadership, as those with the means move to the suburbs. Seemingly overnight the community where the white congregation sits becomes 70 percent African-American. The community of the African-American church is suddenly filled with Hispanics. New, expensive high-rise condominiums appear where the government projects have been. The poor displaced from the gentrifying area move into another. Bhutanese refugees begin to fill the nearby apartment complexes. Dozens of languages are spoken in the elementary school. Neighborhoods, both urban and rural, are changed and changing. This change presents real challenges for congregations.

It would be much less complex if we could mark the date when change would be completed and a new normal would come to the neighborhood. Then we could catch our breath, figure out the new dynamics, adjust our ministries, and settle back into some semblance of order. The reality is that the only continuous dynamic of the neighborhood is change. Congregations in these neighborhoods often feel like they are aiming at moving targets.

Ron Benefiel (1996, 38) pointed out that churches in such transitional neighborhoods have five choices. They can "hold out" and continue to do business as usual, hoping the change might go away. They can "keep out" and build literal and figurative fences around themselves, also opening themselves to a slow demise. They can "move out," a strategy which has been chosen often by those with the means to do so. However, where churches have moved, they have often been met with a surprise. They have moved to be in a neighborhood with which they had greater congruence, only to find (sometimes before they have completed their building project) that the new neighborhood is also changing. They can "close out," say their good-byes, and possibly turn the building over to another group. Finally, they can choose to "reach out" and embrace their changing neighborhood.

There is, however, another common response of congregations in changing neighborhoods that might be added to Benefiel's list of options. We might call it "expand out." The congregation moves from trying to engage the immediate neighborhood to an expanded focus that stretches across a wide geographical area. They begin to try to appeal to a certain group of people within that broad area who might be attracted to the programming and population of their congregation. Nancy Ammerman (1997, 30) calls this a niche congregation. The congregation has found a niche in the market and hopes to cater to that niche in order to survive. Congregations in transitional neighborhoods almost always try to implement such a strategy at some point. What happens, however, when the targeted group of people will not drive in to be part of this congregation?

The focus of this study has been on congregations in transitional neighborhoods who are attempting to move from a niche focus to a parish focus[1]—congregations

---

1   I am using the parish concept to speak of a return to commitment to place. An inadequate theology of place has allowed the church in many cases to abandon neighborhoods. I am aware, however, that the concept of parish is not without baggage. The origins of the parish concept were in a European setting and were part of the Christendom model. I am also aware that cities are about networks, and that there is no way to focus completely on parish without also being involved in these networks. In light of these two observations, "parish" must be redefined for ministry in contemporary settings.

who are opening themselves to radical change in order to embody the gospel in the actual neighborhoods where they are located.

Such a move is not easy. Churches struggle to envision what this move will look like and how to get there. At the core of the issue is the way the congregation thinks about what it means to be the church. Thought patterns that have been shaped over many years are hard to break, and people often feel as if *they* will break if forced to change. Churches that have been homogeneous, whether because for a period of time they matched their neighborhood or because they tried to reach people like themselves from a wider area, struggle to know how to truly engage a changing neighborhood.

Definitions

Congregations in Transitional Neighborhoods (CTNs) are congregations with a long history in a community, which at one point was congruent with the congregation (see the definition of congruence below). At least some of the congregation's members have a memory of the "glory days" when the church was full of "our kind of people." CTNs have, however, experienced a period of decline that correlates with changes in and progressive disconnection from the surrounding community.

David Britt (1991, 33) introduced the concept of *congruence* between the congregation and its community. The church growth movement had made popular the concept of homogeneity or match of people within the congregation. Britt introduced congruence as a term to describe a match between the congregation and its context. How well do congregational demographics reflect neighborhood demographics? Congruence between the congregation and its surrounding neighborhood has been a basic assumption of most church growth theory, but it is far from reality in the situation of the CTN. With nowhere left to move to attain congruence, the church must begin to learn to be the church where there is not congruence.

CTNs have been known by other names. Ray Bakke and Samuel Roberts (1986) wrote about these congregations as Old First churches. I have abandoned this terminology because the CTN phenomenon now goes far beyond typical Old Firsts. Charles Van Engen (1989, 15) first called these congregations Older Churches in Transitional Neighborhoods (OCTNs). In my interaction with pastors and regional leadership, however, I have found that the term "older" presented confusion or too great a focus on elderly members. I have, therefore, adapted Van Engen's terminology to discuss CTNs rather than OCTNs.

CTNs have not been a major focus of congregational research. The earlier works mentioned are some of the only studies of such congregations, and some of these are already decades old. The lack of literature and research on CTNs may reveal a general hopelessness that such congregations hold promise or the possibility of change. In referring to this kind of church, C. Peter Wagner is often quoted as saying, "It is easier to have babies than to raise the dead" (1990, 19). The current study of CTNs is based on the premise that doing what is easier has never been a good determination of faithfulness.

Why Study These Congregations?

The prevalence of congregations in transitional neighborhoods should be enough to draw our attention to them. A survey of district leadership in the Church of the Nazarene in 2007 (Mowry 2011, 252–54)[2] revealed that 56 percent of church closures over the last five years had been directly related to the phenomenon of congregations in transitional neighborhoods. In the estimation of these same district superintendents, 726 churches of 2,347 or 31 percent of the congregations over which they had oversight were congregations in transitional neighborhoods. The percentage rises even more if new church starts that are not fully organized are not included.

Even if the prevalence of these congregations was not a compelling reason, the study of these congregations would still be vital because, in actuality, they are on the cutting edge. The issues with which these congregations deal are the issues with which all churches across North America will deal in the years to come. The CTN can expose to us the folk ecclesiology that prevents us from being viable in changing neighborhoods. The CTN also serves as a microcosm, revealing the issues in a specific neighborhood context with which denominations and the church-at-large struggle in the global church context. I would propose that the same issues that hinder in the changing neighborhood are a hindrance to churches and denominations in the process of internationalization.

---

2   These statistics are based on those districts who responded. With thirty-three North American districts responding, the survey had a response rate of forty percent.

Finally, these churches must be studied because engaging context is vital to participating in the incarnational work of Jesus Christ. Where we have ignored immediate context or abandoned that context, we have hindered our witness.

Methodology

The purpose of this study was to explore patterns in the interaction of congregations with their changing neighborhoods in order to name and describe the phenomenon of the CTN and to make conscious the unconscious assumptions and struggles of congregations in changing neighborhoods.

In the summer of 2009, I selected five congregations, who self-identified as moving from a niche focus to a parish focus in a changing neighborhood. I studied these congregations using ethnographic observation in each community, participant observation in congregational life, and active interviews with a cross-section of the congregation. The design was intentionally multidimensional and sought to balance particularity and comparison by thick description of five congregations in their contexts (within-case analysis) and comparative study of the findings by grounded theory (cross-case analysis).

Grounded theory is an established method for determining patterns in qualitative data. In qualitative research, patterns that are found in the data constitute theory (Auerbach and Silverstein 2003, 31). Grounded theory methodology had great value for my study, allowing me to determine the categories being used by congregants in thinking about their congregation's situation and mission. It has allowed patterns to emerge, not only within congregations, but also across congregations. Its systematic approach helped me to uncover codes and constructs that were not obvious through reading transcriptions alone or through the lens with which I was viewing the project.[3]

The five CTNs in this study had remarkable similarities even though their contexts differed greatly. I did not set out to find five remarkably different congregations, but neither did I set out to find five so similar to each other. The similarities, I

---

[3] It is important to note that this paper describes only the qualitative research portion of a larger work (Mowry 2011). An understanding of these qualitative findings as merely a partial treatment of the subject is necessary in order to avoid a pitfall which has occurred often in congregational research—that of turning sociological description into congregational prescription without biblical and theological reflection. Because my intent here has been to raise the question of "what is faithful" rather than "what works" in the changing neighborhood, biblical and theological reflection on these findings is essential.

believe, point to the fact that the CTN is actually an identifiable phenomenon in North America.

The themes uncovered in this study fell into three clusters: Anxiety themes, Themes of Trust in Resurrection, and Decision Points about Acceptable Degree of Displacement. A crucial dividing line can be identified between motivations and decisions focused on present outcomes and those based on a promised future when the reign of God comes in its fullness.

Common Characteristics

In all five CTNs studied, the congregation at the time of commitment or recommitment to the neighborhood had some degree of incongruence with neighborhood demographics. This incongruence may have been cultural, socioeconomic, generational, or all three. In most of the cases examined here, the neighborhood was made up of older whites with long ties in the community and newer residents who were younger and of other ethnic groups, usually also of a lower socioeconomic level. The congregations at the time of recommitment to the neighborhood were made up mostly of older whites with past ties in the community.

The churches in the study, during the period of incongruence, focused their efforts, at least to some degree, on trying to determine a niche and to attract people who fit that niche from a wider geographical area.

Most of the current members of the CTNs, even those in the core group of these congregations, drive in to attend church in this area to which they have recommitted. Many of these drive-in members used to live in the community where the church is and are attending now out of loyalty, not because they discovered a niche church that was really what they needed. As one church member said, "People who built the church, grew the church, loved the church moved to different parts of the community, and there is no one from the neighborhood that is keeping the church alive."

The decision to recommit to a parish model of ministry, emphasizing the immediate neighborhood, was, in all cases, pastor-initiated or at least pastor-reinitiated if there had been effort in the past to reach out to the neighborhood.

As a church moved toward a recommitment to the neighborhood, this was in all cases accompanied by a mass exodus of members who moved for various reasons, but one of those reasons seems to have been a preference for the former model of targeting a niche of people like themselves from across a wider area.

The exodus, while painful to current members, left the smaller core largely unified in mission. This unity enables the congregation to move forward and is viewed as the rainbow after the storm by most CTNs.

> We have lost some people, but the way we see it and the way I think it has really panned out … is that truly God was involved in doing the Gideon thing all over again. In reducing the troops to those who really want to engage this community and do what we need to do.
>
> God knew what he was doing and filtered the right people out and left the right people in.

****

> That's (mass exodus) what has been our salvation. I hate to use the word "cleansing," but we've had to come to a point where we believe in the mission of the church to reach our community.

****

> When we came in, there were probably 120 people roughly in attendance on Sunday morning, but within a couple of years, it had dwindled and kept dwindling as God kept filtering out people that just wouldn't fully grab hold.

Following the mass exodus, CTNs have a very high participation rate of members involved in community ministries.

For longer term members there is the experience of compounded change, which can lead to fatigue. Multiple layers of transition include transition in the neighborhood, adjustments to different cultures, adjustments to new pastors, changes in the focus of the congregation, and changes in the building or in cherished traditions. Longer term members of CTNs experience a sense of loss in response to this compounded change.

In every case, in the changing neighborhood, the congregation is experiencing new security issues. Carjacking in the church parking lot, intruders in the building, robberies, graffiti, and other vandalism are all stories told by members.

The mass exodus phenomenon, the aging and lessened mobility of members, and the vast need for services in the neighborhood all form an equation which equals a chronic shortage of volunteer labor. All of the churches in the study expressed this need for more people to help carry out the mission.

No matter how committed the congregation they all expressed, at least at some level, frustration over lack of results to their efforts. The congregations were pleased to serve their neighborhoods, but baffled that those they served never came to worship.

> There was just activity after activity ... and there was no sense of reaping any benefit for what we are doing. We are doing all this work. There was no visible evidence of success so there was this great sense of frustration.

> The people we have been giving bread to and walking the neighborhood and canvassing and talking to—none of them showed up.

> ****

> That is what I think is disappointing to everybody here that I know who is a core person. ... We are frustrated because we do not know how to minister to them. We would like them to come to the church.

> We are just frustrated because we are spinning our wheels.

All five congregations are agreed that the congregation needs to become multicultural or to reflect the demographics of the community. There is some difference over how they plan to get there and as to whether this is understood as a desirable goal or a mandate for those living under the reign of God.

Finances are a major issue in all five cases. Three of the churches or 60 percent have bi-vocational pastors. Some of the churches struggle under high mortgages. Most struggle to pay denominational budgets. Many of the churches described themselves as "giving," but many of those who are so giving have little to give. This creates a situation in which there is no money in the community and no money in the church seeking to serve that community. One pastor said, "We are literally a heartbeat away from closing." A member of another congregation voiced the same:

> There's still a couple families that are on the edge of leaving. Once they go, the financial support is gone. That's got me concerned, because once it's gone … a couple more families go, and … we're really stretching it. I don't know how we'll keep the doors open.

All five congregations have at least some "deferred maintenance." Building issues weigh heavily on the minds of those who have invested in those buildings, either in their construction or their upkeep. Comments about property maintenance were frequent in all five congregations. A proprietary attitude toward buildings and their longevity was offered as justification for several instances of minimizing welcome to others.

In grounded theory, themes are grouped and regrouped to form constructs. There are probably several ways that the themes in these five congregations would be grouped by different researchers. I would like to propose three major constructs at work in the CTN. Two clusters of motivational themes arise in the data. I will refer to these as Anxiety themes and Trusting in Resurrection themes. In addition, there are several decision points which all five CTNs faced. The various decision points of the CTN all have at their core a decision about Acceptable Degree of Displacement. Together these three concepts provide one way to organize nearly all of the major themes in the data.

Anxiety Themes

Several motivational themes for the CTN all center around anxiety over the survival or success of the congregation. Some of these are contextual realities and some are institutional realities. Several of the items in this cluster were mentioned by all those interviewed. There is a general sense in talking with many CTNs that the cup of anxiety is full and that the congregation perceives that they teeter on the brink of extinction. If just one more person leaves or one more person ceases to tithe or one more break-in happens, the church might not make it. Anxiety motivations include departure of friends and members, compounded loss, security issues, declining finances, deferred maintenance of buildings, shortage of volunteers, inability to get people from the neighborhood to attend Sunday morning worship, and fear of death of the congregation.

Figure 10.1 Motivational Themes I: Anxiety themes

The major focus of these anxiety themes is on the present. Even when this is discussed in terms of fear of not leaving a legacy, the desire to know one is leaving a legacy is a present tense need for the person or group who will leave it. The CTN is anxious that with all these strikes against them, they will be unable to preserve their contribution. The need to escape from such overwhelming anxiety probably motivates most who leave the congregation.

Themes of Trusting in Resurrection

There are several instances in the five congregations in which the curtain of anxiety is lifted and people begin to connect the mission of the CTN with the reign of God.[4] Congregations who were able to break out of anxiety did so because their hope was

---

4   While members of congregations in the study generally used "kingdom" language, I am using "reign of God" here in order to avoid the Christendom, masculine, and static associations of kingdom language. Reign of God better indicates the activity associated with the coming of the kingdom.

not placed merely in present results. They saw the reign of God breaking into the present age and were able to offer up various church forms as an offering, knowing that even as they died to these things, they could trust in the Lord of Resurrection to bring their efforts and their offerings into the coming age.

Three themes are of great significance in the data. Members of CTNs at times are able to articulate a willingness to make difficult changes when they are tied clearly to the reign of God, to demonstrate an ability to abandon present scorecards when they have a vivid picture of the reign of God that is coming, and to grasp the idea that their survival as a congregation is not essential to the growth of the reign of God in the neighborhood.

Figure 10.2 Motivational Themes II: Trusting in Resurrection

A common assumption about CTNs is that they are full of older people who cannot make changes. In several beautiful exchanges during interviews, older members of CTNs made huge changes to cherished ideas and traditions. In every case, they made these changes because they had seen the connection to the reign of God. An older man led the way for change in the congregation when he realized that the reign of God comes in Africa without the trappings he was so afraid of losing. Another older man was able to accept the sale of the pews, with all of their symbolism and history, because giving up the pews might assist the congregation to live into the reign of God.

While congregations have sought confirmation of their identity and success through various scorecards, those who are able to talk about serving faithfully without a scorecard always connect this to the fact that the ends they are seeking are not in the present age. It is not that there is no goal, but the goal is not one we will necessarily see met with our own eyes during our lifetime.

Finally, CTNs demonstrate trust in resurrection when they are able to squarely face the possibility of their own mortality and invest faithfully in the neighborhood anyway. It is significant that this kind of language of release from anxiety over the church's survival only occurs in the data coupled with proclamations about the reign of God. One pastor tells of a turning point:

> I waited about eight months before I did this, but we sat down on a Sunday afternoon upstairs ... and I told them that we're dying and that ... if we don't do things dramatically differently we will die. Then I told them even if we do things dramatically differently we may still die, but we've got the opportunity to trust that we serve the Lord of the Resurrection. ... There's this powerful temptation to say, "Everything's going to be fine and God's just going to swoop in here and bless us," and the reality is that you've got to be truthful and that is the hardest thing. But once you take that step, it's as if you've lifted a huge burden off of everyone's shoulders and people can begin to flourish again.

The examples of all three of these themes of Trusting in Resurrection from both pastors and lay people are beautiful indicators of a focus which has shifted from the present tense (*chronos*) concerns to the in-breaking (*kairos*) reign of God. This is one of the central findings of this study.

Acceptable Degree of Displacement

There are several decision points each CTN has had to address. Four of these decision points are highlighted here. Each of these is primarily a struggle with the degree to which a congregation finds it acceptable to be displaced.

The Scorecard Decision

A major decision point is the standard by which a congregation will measure success or faithfulness. Three options presented themselves with regularity. First, the CTN members may still live by the attendance scorecard that has been most prevalent in church growth thinking and need to go elsewhere to experience success by that scorecard. This may at least partially be the story behind the mass exodus in each of the case studies. When this scorecard does not promote departures, it promotes a sense of defeat or failure in the CTN. One parishioner in a CTN said it this way:

> There are some of the older folks that are still struggling with that. They're just so used to, you know, if you're going do it on Saturday, they're going to be there on Sunday morning. Or, if you do it on Thursday night, they're going to be there on Sunday morning. Sunday morning becomes the criteria for, of performance—job well done! You know, and everything is graded on that Sunday morning attendance. So that's been hard.

A second option for a CTN is to change the scorecard and begin to count new things to validate their success: numbers of meals served, numbers of families helped, etc. They may begin to collect stories of people who came back and showed gratitude. In another interview, a church member said:

> For the last four or five years, (congregation's community outreach) has grown. And I think, like Saturday, they said they had 400 people pass through the door. And that's outrageous! That's wonderful! You know, where did it come from? The word is getting out that we're here. That, and the other issue of the congregation itself not growing, being a part of that, fills that void a little bit, you know. You see something happen, and you feel a part of (it) … and that's encouraging.

Finally, they may redefine the entire issue entirely in terms of the coming reign of God. If they are successful in this redefinition, no scorecard for the church will matter as the church is only in service of the reign of God. This is a shift from doing what we do because it works to doing what we do because we trust in a promised future that is not limited to the present. To choose to measure faithfulness to the reign of God is difficult because of its lack of concrete measurability, and those who expressed this third option in the interview usually also expressed things in terms of one or both of the other scorecards at least once in the same interview.

> Not every one of those people that come through that door are going to become a part of this congregation. But every person that comes through that door is taking a part of us back out with them. That is what it's about—I am kingdom building. We're doing what God has mandated all of the churches to do—to reach out and just help people. Just love them, just help them, he'll take care of the rest.

The Parish/Niche Decision

One aspect of my research methodology in each congregation was to ask the pastor to drive me around his/her target neighborhood and teach me what was going on there. In addition, I asked each of the interviewees to tell me what community they were talking about before we talked about reengaging that community. The answers from the various congregations and members within those congregations suggest a pattern. It may very well be that clarity on defining the immediate neighborhood as "parish" may say something subtle but profound about commitment to that neighborhood and may impact our relationships in that community. In the congregations where the pastor drove me around the immediate neighborhood and gave me actual boundaries to the target population, the people also could tell me the boundaries of that target neighborhood. Those who clearly defined their neighborhood and expressed commitment to that neighborhood were actively engaging people from that neighborhood.

In those congregations in which the pastor could not clearly define the neighborhood or defined it very broadly to encompass a large area of a city, the people also could not define the target area. The people, and sometimes the pastor, were still talking in terms of the niche model, "reaching our networks" wherever we live and work, or they talked in terms of "reaching the whole world," or "going wherever anyone has a need". Those promoting either a whole world mentality or a niche mentality were frustrated that they were not adding any neighborhood adults to their fellowship. When the pastor is still trying to reach a niche of people far from the immediate neighborhood, it is no surprise that the congregation reflects this ambivalence about commitment to becoming a neighborhood church.

The Diversity Option/Mandate Decision

All of the churches in the study wish to become multicultural. They see this as good and desirable. However, some of the churches use qualitatively different language when speaking of diversity. They believe diversity is not an option, but a mandate. They believe that reflecting the demographics of the immediate neighborhood is absolutely essential for the congregation to have any kind of credible witness. Does the quality of determination behind this commitment to multiculturalism shape the result?

The distinction here is a fine one, but a profound one. Is it, "We'd really like to get some African-Americans to come" or, "We can't do it without them"? That question makes the difference between, "We'll do what we can" and "We must do this." The distinction surfaces clearly not only in the words of the pastors but in the ethos of their congregations.

The Church/Nonprofit Decision

Most of the congregations in the study are still talking primarily in terms of congregational ministry as they discuss their presence in their neighborhood. For one church, all of their community outreach was increasingly focused in a developing nonprofit organization through which they reach out to the neighborhood. The separateness from the congregation with which they view this is significant. It is remotely possible, in the case of this church, that the worshipping body might disappear and be replaced by a 501c3. This study suggests that a 501c3 may allow a church to feel they are engaging the neighborhood while maintaining the status quo in the congregation. The decision of whether or not to work through a 501c3 is an extremely complex one for the church in the city. This is an area where much further discussion and research is needed. On the one hand, the ability of a 501c3 to attract and leverage resources to cover costs of ministry makes it seem an attractive route and, in some situations, a route which enables a certain kind of survival. On the other hand, the entire discussion begs the question of whether or not a church seeking to bear witness to the reign of God would be in the business of leveraging outside resources. When confronted with overwhelming need in the community, how does a congregation discern when a 501c3 is a faithful response?

In each of the decision points highlighted here, the congregation must choose between maintaining the status quo, being displaced in selected ways, or being radically displaced for the sake of embodying the coming reign of God in the neighborhood.

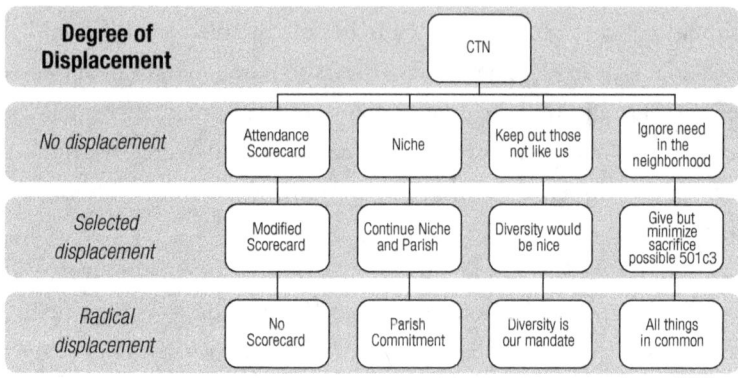

Figure 10.3 Decision points about acceptable degree of displacement

Figure 10.3 demonstrates how in each decision, the congregation must choose between preserving the status quo, changing moderately so as to somehow engage the neighborhood without the need for painful change to the congregation, or being radically displaced, investing all, and embracing internal change at a profound level. Each of the decision points faced by CTNs can be seen in terms of this decision about how much change, displacement, or dispossession of cherished forms is acceptable. From the data, I could easily add others here that follow the same pattern. For instance, a homogeneous unit requires no displacement by its members. If that church decides to reach the community without changing their own worship, facility ownership, or power structures, they could allow a renter congregation to share their space. If, however, a congregation embraces radical displacement in order to embody the reign of God, a shared multi-congregational model or even a multicultural congregation becomes a way of emptying themselves of power, control of the facilities, and comfort. Such a move may also mean the English-speaking congregation becomes intentionally displaced by learning Spanish or Cambodian in order to minister in the neighborhood. The radical level of displacement is only made possible when motivation is being drawn from trust in resurrection rather than from anxiety over survival.

Summary

CTNs in vastly different changing contexts have very similar experiences. The experience of the CTN involves loss, compounded change, security issues, and fear. It involves stepping out into a world for which we have no technical expertise. It is a bewildering experience for Americans who so value competence.

Motivation for mission is a key issue for the CTN. In the CTN, anxiety is often the theme that shapes their engagement or lack of engagement with the neighborhood. Anxiety is crippling to the imagination of the CTN. However, there are hopeful signs of other motivations that show up in unexpected times and places and from the mouths of unexpected people. These people accept profound change when they can articulate motivational themes centered on the in-breaking reign of God. The line between these two sets of factors is the line between a present-focus and a focus on a promised hope that goes well beyond what the congregations may see in their lifetimes or in the lifetime of the congregation. Trusting in resurrection allows the congregation to lay down cherished forms.

The CTN wishing to reengage its neighborhood must make several choices, all of which center around the acceptable degree of displacement or dispossession. Will we completely abandon our dream of the niche in favor of the parish, or will we continue to try for both? Will we live for rewards in the present (scorecards) or displace ourselves for the reign of God that is coming? Will we practice hospitality as fellow guests with our neighbors (with God as host), or will we try to maintain the role of host? Will we aim for deep level transformation, being completely remade by this journey to covenant faithfulness in the transitioning neighborhood, or will we short-circuit this work with quick fixes such as charitable handouts? Do we consider relationships with those different from ourselves nice, or do we consider them necessary? Where will the boundaries be?

Anxiety issues and struggle over acceptable degree of dispossession for the sake of the neighborhood are front-burner issues for the CTN, but they also reflect ecclesial understandings that go well beyond the CTN in North America. Christendom ecclesiology with its focus on preservation of church forms cannot help the church address changing neighborhoods. The CTN calls for an ecclesiology which provides resources for breaking out of the captivity to anxiety that has paralyzed the church and helps us to embody the reign of God in fresh and imaginative ways in the places to which we have been sent into exile. Rather than waiting for CTNs to die, the church in North America should begin to understand that these churches are the very congregations which can lead us into the future by teaching us how to move from anxiety motivations to living the reign of God and trusting in resurrection in the neighborhoods we have been given.

References

Ammerman, N. T. (1997). *Congregation and community.* New Brunswick, NJ: Rutgers University Press.

Auerbach, C. & Silverstein, L. (2003). *Qualitative data: An introduction to coding and analysis.* New York: New York University Press.

Bakke, R. J., & Roberts, S. K. (1986). *The expanded mission of "old first churches."* Valley Forge, PA: Judson Press.

Benefiel, R. (1996). Transitional communities and multi-congregational ministry. *Urban Mission* 13, 38–47.

Britt, D. T. (1991). From homogeneity to congruence: achurch-community model. *Urban Mission* 8(3), 27–41.

Mowry, K. L. (2011). Trusting in resurrection: eschatological imagination for congregations engaging transitional neighborhoods. (Doctoral dissertation). Fuller Theological Seminary.

Van Engen, C. (1989). Can older churches grow in the city? *Global Church Growth* 26(1), 15–16.

Wagner, C. P. (1990). *Church planting for a greater harvest: a comprehensive guide.* Ventura, CA: Regal.

Immigrant Communities in America—Objects of Mission or Missional Agents? The Case of the Church of Pentecost (Ghana) in Urban America

Birgit Herppich
bherppich@fuller.edu

Introduction

In recent years increasing attention has been drawn to the growing mission field "at our doorstep" in form of the rapidly increasing numbers of "people on the move"—international migrants who come to settle or study in Western countries, often from places and people groups which have been described as "unreached" (Appleby 1986; Phillips, Norsworthy, and Whalin 1997; Wan 1995). This increased attention perhaps has less to do with a sudden surge of interest in displaced peoples than with the fact that Western countries, and in particular, the United States, have seen an exponential rise of immigrant influx over the past few decades.

The World Bank reported for 2010 globally 215.8 million international migrants or 3.2 percent of the world's population (Ratha, Mohapatra, and Silwal 2011). International migrants in the United States numbered almost 43 million or 13.5 percent of the US population, which means that 20 percent of all international migrants live in this country. The major cities of North America have become a prime destination for East to West and South to North migration as great numbers of people from Asia, Latin America, and Africa seek economic and educational opportunities often in the desire to escape the hopelessness of oppressive and destructive economic and political environments. Urban ministry has become a ministry that involves a large percentage of immigrants.

Reflection on the missiological implications of these realities is indeed needed—in particular a recognition of the de-centeredness and de-professionalization of mission is long overdue—away from the entrenched idea that mission only happens "out there" in foreign lands and is done by specially trained individuals from the West to the rest. Enoch Wan, president of the Evangelical Missiological Society (EMS) and professor of Intercultural Studies at Western Seminary, Portland, is one of the main proponents of the emerging discipline of "Diaspora Missiology," which seeks to overlap migration studies with biblical, theological, and missiological studies and heralds the call to introduce missiological reflection on the growing population of international migrants into the curricula of seminaries across the country and the world.

While this is a highly commendable initiative, the prevalent focus on and perception of immigrant communities in the West as a mission field that God has brought to our doorstep needs to be challenged. Although it is true for a portion of recent immigrants that they originate from areas and people groups where few know Christ, many of them are in fact Christians; they bring their expressions of the faith with them and establish numerous churches, and they articulate and carry out a missionary calling to Western countries where Christianity is declining.

With no other group is this more obvious than the thriving African churches in America's cities which have been founded in the past twenty years by recent African immigrants. A case study of the Church of Pentecost, which is the largest and fastest growing Protestant church in Ghana, and its exponential growth in the United States will serve in this article as illustration for the contention that any relevant missiological reflection on "people on the move" has to take into account the fact that a majority of the migrant communities in urban centers throughout the Western world originate from the new Christian heartlands in the South and East and have to be considered as agents of mission rather than "objects" of missionary endeavor.

The following exposition calls attention to two key characteristics of immigrants in the United States—namely, their concentration in urban areas and majority Christian background—and then explores the missionary orientation and practice of the Church of Pentecost, its expansion and missionary vision in America, as well as some of the challenges and opportunities its leaders identify in this Western urban context.

"Diaspora Missiology" and Immigrants in America

The emerging field that has been termed "Diaspora Missiology" is concerned with the missiological study of people on the move. Enoch Wan first introduced a framework for Diaspora Missiology in 2007, emphasizing its interdisciplinary character and contrasting its focus, conceptualization, perspective, paradigm, ministry patterns, and ministry styles with "Traditional Missiology" represented by associations like the American Society of Missiology (ASM) and the EMS (Wan 2007). Various consultations and articles developed the approach further, resulting in the Seoul Declaration on Diaspora Missiology from November 14, 2009, which defines diaspora missiology as "a missiological framework for understanding and participating in God's redemptive mission among people living outside their place of origin" (LCWE Diaspora Educators Consultation 2009).

The understanding of "diaspora" in this construct is unhelpfully broad, and more importantly, it limits mission to a one-way activity aimed at migrant communities as objects of Christian mission. In 2010 Wan and Joy Tira articulated a more detailed outline of the new discipline in which they emphasize its supplementary character to traditional missiology and define "diaspora missions" as the threefold ministry of ministering to, through, and beyond the diaspora. This involves evangelism and service directed toward migrant groups, motivation and mobilization of migrant Christian communities to reach out to their own people and beyond cross-culturally to other people respectively (Tira and Wan 2010).[1] While the presence of Christian communities among immigrants is acknowledged in this expansion of the framework, the dominant focus remains outreach to migrant communities and a call to churches and Christian organizations to get involved in it, either directly or "through" Christian immigrants.

Diaspora Missiology is informed by the understanding that the "mission field" out there has now come to our doorsteps and one-sidedly emphasizes calls for outreach to the people who have moved into our neighborhood. In this it misses

---
1 See also the conversation on "Ministering to Scattered Peoples" at the Lausanne III conference in Cape Town in October 2010, http://conversation.lausanne.org/en/conversations/detail/10999 (accessed April 9, 2012).

crucial attributes of the recent arrivals. First, this approach assumes that immigrant communities are either not believers or if they are, they need to be motivated and mobilized to reach out to their own people and beyond. Second, it reduces the Christians among them to passive participants in strategies and programs others devise rather than independent, self-motivated actors in Christian mission. Both are highly problematic and ignore the significant fact that the majority of immigrants in the United States have established churches among their people which are growing exponentially; and, most importantly, that many have a missionary vision and lifestyle of outreach which is generally not in need of outside help but that declining Western churches could rather learn from.

For example, immigrant Christians live on a daily basis with and minister to people on the margins, they help other immigrants cope with the trauma, displacement, and practical challenges of living in a foreign land, and they espouse values and social structures that provide the supportive community through which immigrants can adapt in the new environment. Immigrant churches model religious commitment in the context of an individualistic, increasingly secular, and materialistically focused society, and they are applying the Christian faith directly and in practical ways to the daily pressures of life. In this way they are the most effective instruments of God's mission among migrant and other marginalized communities and beyond.

Many Immigrants in America are Christians

Several scholars and analysts of US Census data have pointed out that in the case of the United States, a large percentage of the "foreign-born population" are in fact Christians.[2] Sociologist Stephen Warner called attention to the disproportionately high representation of Christians among many immigrant communities because "people who leave their country represent a biased, not a representative, sample of their compatriots" (Warner 2004, 20). For example, Christians in Korea represent 25% of the population, whereas about half of Korean migrants to America are Christians. In addition, there is a high conversion rate of non-Christian Koreans in the US resulting in about 75% of Korean Americans being Christians. Other examples Warner cites are Catholic Vietnamese, Arab Christians from Palestine, and Christian nurses from India.

---

2   The US Census data define "foreign-born" as those in the population who were not American citizens at birth. This includes naturalized citizens, lawful permanent residents, refugees and asylees, persons on certain temporary visas, and the unauthorized.

The "New Immigrant Survey" shows that almost two-thirds (64.7%) of the overall "foreign-born" population are self-identified Christians (Jasso et al. 2003). Not surprisingly, many are Catholic Christians from Latin-American countries, especially Mexico, as well as the Philippines, Poland, the Dominican Republic, and Vietnam. The largest proportion of Protestants also originates from Mexico, followed by the former Soviet Union, the Philippines, and Ghana. The data of this study are from 1996, but they are not likely to have changed significantly since, if anything, as most of the source countries of immigrants in America are predominantly Christian, the numbers of Christians among immigrants in America have probably increased.

The 2007 Pew Research Center report "Changing Faiths" on Latino immigrants in the United States reveals that 68% of Hispanics are Roman Catholics and 15% are evangelical Protestants (Pew Research Center 2007). More significantly, the report challenges the common tendency of evangelical Christians to dismiss Catholic Christians as objects of outreach rather than agents of mission. Of these Latino Christians, 40% describe themselves as "born again" or "evangelical," which includes 28% of Catholics and 70% of non-Catholic Christians. The vitality and actual practice of the religion by members of Hispanic predominantly Catholic immigrant communities typically exceeds the US average. They pray daily (70%), attend church at least once a week (44%), read Scripture (38% at least weekly), and share their faith at least monthly (42%).

Among African immigrants, too, Christians constitute a considerable percentage. Statistics are lacking partly because of the paucity of scholarly attention to recent African immigrants in America and their religious life. However, the growing proportion of Christians on the continent, especially in West Africa where the majority of African immigrants in America originate from, is reflected among African international migrants, and the mounting number of African churches springing up in the urban centers of the country gives evidence to this fact. Most significantly for the present argument, many African Christians in America "see their relocation as part of a divine plan that allows them to move with their faith and plant churches in the West" (Olupona and Gemignani 2007, 107). Olupona and Gemingani's groundbreaking volume on "African Immigrant Religions" shows the missionary vision and engagement of African congregations in America, and Hanciles' *Beyond Christendom* (2008) provides a comprehensive analysis of the potential impact of African Christian immigrants on American religious life.

It is of paramount importance that a missiology of "people on the move" takes account of the fact that a goodly proportion of immigrants in America are Christians with a vibrant and missionary faith. As Jehu Hanciles, professor of World Christianity at Candler School of Theology, Emory University, asserts, "every Christian migrant is a potential missionary" and as far as Christians are concerned, the South-North migrant movement is also a missionary movement (Hanciles 2008, 297). From this follows the call to a different framework of Diaspora Missiology which reflects the realities more accurately. Missiological study of migrant communities needs to consider the missiological implications of ministry by Christian migrants and their communities. A different tripartite approach which is more true to the facts ought to consider ministry by and with Christians on the move as well as ministry to non-Christian migrants.

Immigrants in America Settle in the Cities

Data suggests that ministry to, with, and by migrants and their congregations, certainly in the American context, is urban ministry. The vast majority of immigrants to America settle in the major metropolitan areas of the country. But even before they ever came here, these people were on the move; international relocation typically is not the first step for many global migrants. John Arthur has coined the term "chain migration" to describe the fact that African immigrants "typically reach the United States in stepwise fashion, sometimes living in several other countries before managing to secure a visa for the ultimate destination in the Unites States" (Arthur 2000, 2–3). This chain migration often begins with rural to urban migration within and between developing countries and continues with international migration to Western European and North American cities.

For the United States, data from the US Census Bureau provide a very clear picture of the fact that the typical migrant communities are located in the major metropolitan areas. The foreign-born population in the top twenty metropolitan areas comprises almost 65% of the total immigrant population in the country with each one of these metros exceeding the national average in percent of immigrants. The following graph of the immigrant population in American metropolitan areas by numbers is derived from the 2009 American Community Survey (ACS) data (Florida 2010).

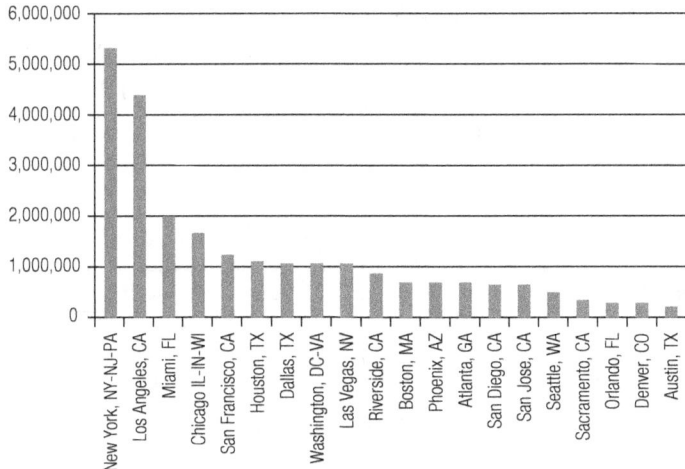

Figure 11.1 Top 20 metropolitan areas in the US, immigrant populations by numbers

The conclusion from these basic facts is that thinking and strategizing about urban mission cannot ignore the fact that large sections of the population in American cities are international migrants. Missiological reflection on "people on the move" is, to a large extent, missiological reflection on urban ministry—diaspora mission is urban mission. This also holds true for the growing and missiologically significant proportion of Africans among international migrants in America.

African Immigrants— A Growing Minority of Missiological Significance

African emigration from the continent escalated in the final two decades of the twentieth century when the economic decline, political repression, and social chaos of the post-independence period reached its peak in many African nations. On the American side changes in immigration legislation provided the "pull factor" in form of the Immigration and Nationality Act (1965) that eliminated national origin, race, or ancestry as a basis for immigration to the US. The Immigration Reform and Control Act (IRCA, 1986) which offered a major amnesty, and—most important for Africans—the 1990 Immigration Act that launched the "Diversity Immigrant" visa program.[3] Since the 1990s the USA has been the chief destination

---

3   Africans continue to be the main beneficiaries of the diversity program with Nigeria (7,145), Ghana (7,040), Ethiopia (6,353) and Kenya (5,721) being the top four of a recent list (NationMaster) and Ghanaians receiving a record number of 8,752 of the 2010 allotment (USAFIS 2011).

country for African international migrants, and by 2005, it had the largest African foreign-born population of all industrialized nations. This trend persists as the 2010 American Community Survey confirmed that the absolute numbers as well as the percentage of Africans among foreign-born residents in the US continues to grow exponentially (Grieco and Trevelyan 2010).

	1990	2000	2009	2010
Number	36,3819	881,300	1,502,163	1,606,914
Percent of foreign-born population	1.84%	2.80%	3.90%	4.02%

Figure 11.2 African-born population in the United States (Grieco & Trevelyan 2010)

There is a small but rapidly growing body of research on this "new African diaspora" in America. Most are collections of articles by various authors, usually social scientists (Konadu-Agyemang, Takyi, and Arthur 2006; Koser 2003; Okpewho and Nzegwu 2009). Insightful analyses with a focus on Ghanaian migration to America are provided by John Arthur and Ian Yeboah, who are African immigrants themselves (Arthur 2008; Yeboah 2008). Here I will only present a summary of the most significant characteristics of this immigrant group.

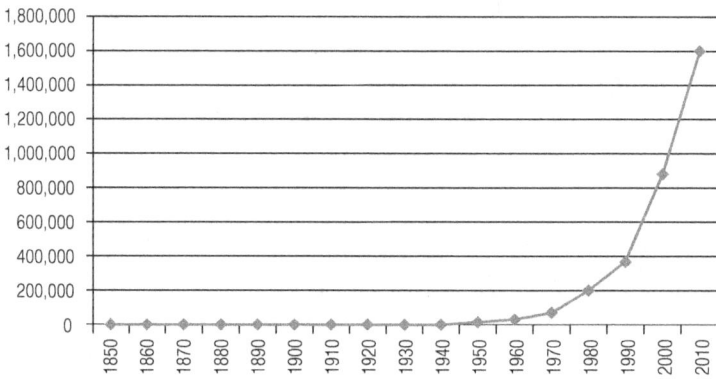

Figure 11.3 African-born in the United States (US Census, ACS 2010)

More than 75% of the new African migrants arrived in America after 1990. Most come from West Africa (37%) with Nigeria and Ghana the dominant countries of origin, followed by East Africa (24.2%) with Ethiopia, Kenya, and Somalia as the main source countries. The majority are from Anglophone countries and have high proficiency in English (65.8%), and almost nine out of ten have at least high school education (86.4%) with 42.8% holding a bachelor's degree or higher. These educational attainments of African immigrants are among the highest of all foreign-born and exceed that of the native American population. This is also reflected in higher medium earnings, lower likelihood of unemployment, a concentration in management or professional and sales or office-related occupations and about a third being owners of their own home (Dixon 2006; McCabe 2011).

The exponential growth rates of Christianity that the continent has seen since most countries gained independence in the mid twentieth century have made it a major heartland of the faith. Moreover, it is the same well educated and upwardly mobile middle class of African societies that predominantly responds to the vibrant African initiated, often charismatic new church movements, which feels the need to seek better opportunities outside the continent and has the means to migrate to the industrialized nations of the West. The most important study on Christian African immigrants so far was done by Hanciles, who compiled data from seventy-one African founded churches in six major metropolitan centers across the United States. He concludes that "African immigrant churches are among the fastest growing in America's cities, where they increasingly exhibit a strong missionary consciousness" (Hanciles 2008, 381).

Contrary to scholars who emphasize the support function of religious communities for their immigrant ethnic group (Arthur 2000; Ebaugh and Chafetz 2000), various recent studies confirm the missionary orientation of African immigrant churches in the American context (Akinade 2007; Biney 2011; Bongmba 2007; Hanciles 2008). In 1998, Gerrie Ter Haar observed that Ghanaian Christians in the Netherlands exhibited a strong missionary consciousness (ter Haar 1998). More recently, Claudia Währisch-Oblau's study of African church leaders in Europe, which is based on extensive participant observation and interviews over a period of almost ten years, clearly showed the "missionary self-perception of Pentecostal/Charismatic church leaders from the Global South" in the West (Währisch-Oblau 2009). In what follows, I will use one of these African initiated churches in America, the Ghana-based Church of Pentecost, as an illustration for the ministry by Christian migrant communities that needs to be reflected upon missiologically to evaluate present realities accurately. The insights are based on a research project which included participant observation and surveys in a cross-section of local congregations and interviews with leaders of the Church of Pentecost across the United States.

The Church of Pentecost (Ghana)— An Example of Immigrant Missionary Engagement

The Church of Pentecost (CoP) traces its beginnings back to the ministry of the African Apostle Peter Newman Anim (1890–1984), who is recognized as the "Father of Ghanaian Pentecostalism" because three of the classical Pentecostal churches in Ghana originated in his ministry beginnings in the second quarter of the twentieth century. Upon Anim's invitation, Irish missionaries Sophia and James McKeown (1900–1989) arrived in the then Gold Coast in 1937. It is to this date that the CoP refers back as their beginning because it developed through McKeown's ministry after he parted company with Apostle Anim in 1939. The church is characterized by African cultural forms and styles of worship; indigenous evangelism, ministry, and leadership; and charismatic emphases on the work of the Holy Spirit, prayer and faith healing, holiness and church discipline. Since the 1960s the CoP has seen exponential growth through active evangelism by its leaders and church members. It is now the largest and most rapidly expanding Protestant church in Ghana, with a total membership of 1,980,843 at the end of 2010 (The Church of Pentecost 2011).[4]

A Missionary Vision from the Beginning

Missionary vision and evangelistic expansion has been a foundational characteristic of the CoP from its inception. The mission statement of the church, which can be found in every document and on every website of various regions and local assemblies, outlines the global and holistic vision:

> The Church of Pentecost is a worldwide, non-profit-making Pentecostal church with its headquarters in Accra, Ghana. It exists to bring all people everywhere to the saving knowledge of our Lord Jesus Christ through the proclamation of the gospel, the planting of churches and the equipping of believers for every God-glorifying

---

4   The Chairman, Dr. Opoku Onyinah, accounted for a membership of 20,000 in 1962, over 170,000 in 1987, and 1,882,156 in 2009 in his state-of-the-church address in May 2010 (Onyinah 2004, 226; Amegah 2010).

service. It demonstrates the love of God through the provision of social services in partnership with governments, communities and other like-minded organizations. (The Church of Pentecost 2011)

The streamer on the Headquarters' website summarizes the Church of Pentecost's global missionary outlook: "Bringing the world to the saving knowledge of Christ." Foundational for this confident missionary self-perception is the belief that the church has a unique identity and global calling, which is grounded in past prophecies, especially in what is known as "God's First Covenant" with the church. It was prophesied in 1931 that God would raise a "great international Pentecostal Church which would send out missionaries from the Gold Coast to all parts of Africa and the world as a whole" (Larbi 2001, 250–52; The Church of Pentecost 2000, 147–49; 2009, 16–20).

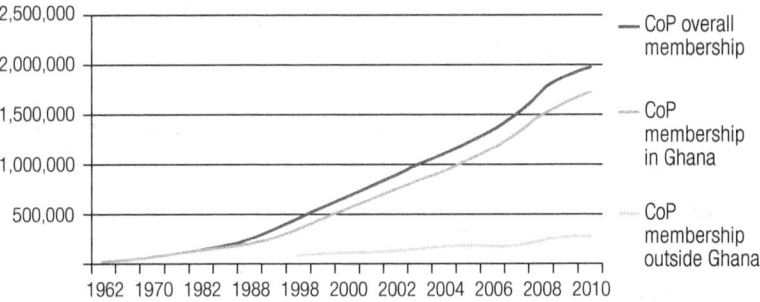

Figure 11.4 Membership of the Church of Pentecost in urban America

A combination of migration movements and the enthusiastic missionary engagement of leaders and members resulted in the establishment and rapid growth of the CoP in other countries on the African continent and beyond, as the annual reports by the International Missions Director, Apostle Dr. S. K. Baidoo, indicate. In 2004 the CoP had "International Missions" in 55 countries worldwide with an overall membership of 168,102 in 2,079 assemblies (Baidoo 2005). By the end of 2007 these numbers had increased to 189,118 members outside Ghana in 2,307 congregations in 57 countries (Church of Pentecost 2007) and by 2010 to 277,258 members outside Ghana in 83 nations (The Church of Pentecost 2011). These statistics show the significance of the CoP as an African church with a missionary vision, which is why it represents an astute illustration for the missionary engagement of immigrant Christian communities in the Western context.

Like other West Africans, members of the CoP started arriving in America as international migrants in the early 1980s. New York was and still is the main gateway city for Ghanaian arrivals, but they are represented in all the major metropolitan areas of the United States. Initially these African immigrants attempted to join local American churches, but soon they realized that their needs of community and spirituality were not met in the way they had hoped. Lack of understanding for the needs specific to immigrants and African (Ghanaian) culture, the experience of rejection and marginalization as immigrants and as Africans in particular, and a lack of recognition of their maturity as Christians and leaders of their churches and communities, were among the reasons for the disconnect with homegrown American churches. The African leaders are gracious in their comments, but the American context is not a welcoming one for African immigrants. As one of the pastors put it, "Somewhere we realized that, for the cultural differences our people were not so much into the [name of the church they attended] setup, and so we decided to come up with a Church of Pentecost branch."

	Members	Percent of membership
New York Region	6,095	37.4%
Washington Region	4,692	28.8%
Chicago Region	3,024	18.5%
Western Region	2,480	15.3%

Figure 11.5 The Church of Pentecost, U.S.A., Inc. membership in 2009

In 1984 a small group in New York started meeting for prayer and mutual support, and this cell quickly grew and soon called for pastoral leadership from their mother church in Ghana. It was sent in the form of the first "Resident Missionary," Apostle Alfred K. Awuah (US Head of the church, 1989–1992). On January 29, 1989, The Church of Pentecost, U.S.A., Inc. was registered with the State of New York. The church has spread to all major areas of Ghanaian immigration in the twenty years since, and by the end of 2009 had 105 assemblies in the US with a membership of 16,297. They are led by 1,434 presbyters (467 elders, 408 deacons, and 559 deaconesses) and 33 employed ministers, and the church's administrative structure now encompasses four regions or areas divided into 28 districts (The Church of Pentecost U.S.A. Inc. 2010).

The CoP has three basic ways of starting new local congregations in America. One of the most common ways new assemblies are established is when members move to a new place because of jobs, educational opportunities, and business or other reasons such as family issues and connections. They are likely to soon begin a prayer group in somebody's home, invite others, grow, and eventually ask for pastoral oversight from the church leadership. Kingsley Larbi, who wrote the most extensive account of the history and characteristics of the church, confirms that this is the dominant pattern of growth in Ghana and beyond (Larbi 2001, 252). A second pattern in the United States is to begin a new congregation with a core of members that live in one general vicinity, so that they do not have to continue to travel the long distance to an existing assembly. Finally, the church uses a pattern of sending missionaries to pioneer new areas. The latter strategy is particularly followed for international outreach to new countries.

Missionary Functions of an African Immigrant Church

In urban America the majority of CoP outreach is among the Ghanaian and other African immigrant communities. Almost 88% of the members originate from Ghana and another 8% from other African countries. But that does not imply a lack of vision for the native population. A significant proportion of the membership feels the church needs to do more to reach out to non-Africans (82.8%), and almost half of them (46.8%) have actually invited a non-African to their church. Among the leaders, too, there is a strong desire to reach out to anybody and everybody in the society, and they reject a perception of the Church of Pentecost as an exclusively African church. While they feel strongly about meeting the physical and spiritual needs of African, especially Ghanaian immigrants who find living in America a challenging experience, they express a passionate missionary vision for this context where they identify a lack of Christian fervor, spirituality, morality, and community.

In the United States most of the local churches use the Akan language as the majority of members originate from this dominant ethnic group in Ghana. However, about 30 of their 105 congregations are "Pentecost International Worship Centers" (PIWCs); these are English-speaking churches which are established with the expressed goal to reach out to "the un-churched, non-Akan speaking Ghanaians, non-Ghanaians, College students, professionals" of any cultural background (The Church of Pentecost U.S.A. Inc. 2010). Ghanaian membership in Akan-speaking assemblies in the US is predictably about 99%, but in the PIWCs it is 77%, which represents a marked increase in non-Ghanaian members. While this is progress, the desire to reach out more effectively to the surrounding culture is tangible. The current leadership puts much of their hope for this in the second generation, the young people who understand the culture because they have grown up in America and speak the language without accent. The future will reveal the impact and developments of this still emerging generation of leaders in the church. There is much need for further research into this area in which Wan and Edu-Bekoe offered a first exploration that identifies some of the challenges faced by the generational and cultural gap between "overseas born Ghanaians" and "local born Ghanaians" in the US (Edu-Bekoe and Wan 2011).

In addition the pastors point to the opportunities afforded them to utilize the economic advantages they gain in America to support the mission work of the church back in Ghana, in other African countries, and the world. The chief example of the latter is the outreach to Latin America and the Caribbean which The Church of Pentecost, U.S.A. has spearheaded in recent years. In 2006 Evangelist Omane Yeboah was appointed as "Missionary Attaché" to Latin America, and his report of 2009 listed 19 churches in 5 countries (Dominican Republic, El Salvador, Trinidad and Tobago, Haiti, Costa Rica) with 1,652 members (The Church of Pentecost U.S.A. Inc. 2010, 33–37). By and large it is Districts comprising several local churches in the United States that "adopt" the work in specific overseas countries, providing significant support from the tithes and offerings of their members.

These data challenge the prevalent notion that immigrant congregations are primarily "reproducing ethnicity" for their own constituency (Ebaugh and Chafetz 2000) and rather confirm the missionary functions of immigrant churches suggested by Jehu Hanciles. He maintains that

- Immigrant Christians and their descendants have a striking record when it comes to winning converts among immigrants.
- They encounter a society in which Christianity is experiencing decline in numbers and influence (and therefore more obviously a "mission field").
- They represent the face of Christianity to a goodly proportion of the nation's disadvantaged and marginalized population.
- They are far more attuned than American Christians to religious plurality, an area of increasing challenge for American Christianity (Hanciles 2008, 379–80).

The final argument points to the fact that African immigrants typically come from a context of religious plurality. This holds true for the CoP as well. At home in Ghana, neighbors, colleagues, and family members are often Muslims or practitioners of traditional religions, and Ghanaian Christians self-evidently and confidently communicate their faith without feeling threatened by people of other convictions. They have grown up with, and in a very foundational way, understand religious plurality that gives them a head start in reaching out in the hugely diverse context of urban America.

A further missionary function of immigrant churches Hanciles identifies relates to the salience and impact of transnationalism. African migrants, arguably more than others, maintain strong ties with the homeland and live in the "transnational" mode of existence in which migrants are socially active, both in the society of adoption and the society of origination. Their congregations function as centers of change and transitions, and the "forces of transnationalism greatly enhance their capacity for sustained missionary engagement not only with American society but also within the wider global context" (Hanciles 2008, 299). The Church of Pentecost in the United States exemplifies this transnational existence and illustrates how it becomes a missionary function with their engagement and support of missionary outreach back in Ghana and in other African countries that lack material resources, including the Latin American outreach mentioned earlier.

Conclusion

This brief investigation of the CoP in America showed that while there is a percentage of non-Christian immigrants in America that represent an opportunity of outreach that is often greater than in their home context, a sizeable proportion of Christian immigrants in American cities establish vibrant churches with a strong missionary vision both among their own people and beyond. They are in fact the most effective agents of mission to migrants as they are living alongside them, sharing the challenges and struggles of their marginalization in American society. Immigrant churches provide the support and practical help, the community and spiritual nurture other immigrants are longing for; they are in a much better position to reach out with the gospel than mainstream American churches. Therefore, any missional engagement by homegrown churches and organizations reaching out to immigrants can, in my view, only be in partnership and collaboration with these immigrant Christian communities, not using them as a means through which to reach our missional goals and targets. American congregations and missions organizations can join them and come alongside them in their missionary vision and practice.

Contrary to an understanding of diaspora mission in which migrant communities are reduced to objects of Christian mission, a very large percentage of these communities are actually Christian and exercise exceptionally vibrant expressions of the faith. They also view the West and America specifically as in need of the gospel and the Savior they know as well as the revitalization that their spirituality represents. These immigrant Christian communities are active agents of missional engagement in the American context. Thus any missiological reflection on the realities of global urban migration today has to consider the great significance of the ministry by these Christian immigrants and their communities as vital to mission in the twenty-first century.

References

Akinade, A. E. (2007). Non-Western Christianity in the Western world: African immigrant churches in the diaspora. In J. K. Olupona & R. Gemignani (Eds.), *African immigrant religions in America* (89–101). New York: New York University Press.

Amegah, S. K. (2010). *Pentecost chalks successes*. Retrieved from http://www.thecophq.org.

Appleby, J. L. (1986). *Missions have come home to America: The church's cross-cultural ministry to ethnics*. Kansas City, MO: Beacon Hill Press.

Arthur, J. A. (2000). *Invisible sojourners: African immigrant diaspora in the United States*. Westport, CT: Praeger.

_____. (2008). *The African diaspora in the United States and Europe: The Ghanaian experience*. Research in Migration and Ethnic Relations Series. Burlington, VT: Ashgate.

Baidoo, S. K. (2005). The Church of Pentecost 2004 International Missions Board end-of-year report. Sowutuom, Accra: The 35th Session of the General Council Meetings.

Biney, M. O. (2011). *From Africa to America: Religion and adaptation among Ghanaian immigrants in New York, religion, race, and ethnicity*. New York: New York University Press.

Bongmba, E. K. (2007). Portable faith: The global mission of African initiated churches. In J. K. Olupona & R. Gemigani (Eds.), *African immigrant religions in America* (102–129). New York: New York University Press.

Church of Pentecost, Ghana. (2008). *The Church of Pentecost worldwide—Summary statistics 2007*. Retrieved from http://www.thecophq.org.

Dixon, D. (2006). *Characteristics of the African born in the United States*. Migration Policy Institute. Retrieved from http://www.migrationinformation.org/USFocus/display.cfm?ID=366.

Ebaugh, H. R. F., & Chafetz, J. S. (2000). *Religion and the new immigrants: Continuities and adaptations in immigrant congregations*. Walnut Creek, CA: AltaMira Press.

Edu-Bekoe, Y. A., & Wan, E. (2011). Diversity of Ghanaian diaspora in the US: Ministering to the Ghanaian communities through Ghanaian congregations. In S. Moreau & B. Snodderly (Eds.), *Reflecting God's glory together: Diversity in evangelical mission* (35–62). Pasadena, CA: William Carey Library.

Florida, R. (2010, July 29). 20 U.S. cities with the most immigrants. *The Daily Beast*. Retrieved from http://www.thedailybeast.com/blogs-and-stories/2010-07-29/us-cities-with-the-most-immigrants/#.

Grieco, E. M., & Trevelyan, E. N. (2010). Place of birth of the foreign-born population: 2009. American Community Survey Briefs. U.S. Census Bureau. Retrieved from http://www.census.gov/prod/2010pubs/acsbr09-15.pdf

Hanciles, J. J. (2008). *Beyond Christendom: Globalization, African migration, and the transformation of the West*. Maryknoll, NY: Orbis Books.

Jasso, G., Massey, D. S., Rosenzweig, M. R., & Smith, J. P. (2003). Exploring the religious preferences of recent immigrants to the United States: Evidence from the New Immigrant Survey Pilot. In Y. Y. Haddad, J. I. Smith, & J. L. Esposito (Eds.), *Religion and immigration: Christian, Jewish, and Muslim experiences in the United States* (217–53). Walnut Creek, CA: AltaMira Press.

Konadu-Agyemang, K., Takyi, B. K., & Arthur, J. A. (Eds.). (2006). *The new African diaspora in North America: Trends, community building, and adaption*. Lanham, MD: Lexington Books.

Koser, K. (Ed.). (2003). *New African diasporas, global diasporas*. New York: Routledge.

Larbi, E. K. (2001). *Pentecostalism: The eddies of Ghanaian Christianity, studies in African Pentecostal Christianity*. Dansoman, Ghana: Centre for Pentecostal and Charismatic Studies.

LCWE Diaspora Educators Consultation. (2010). The Seoul declaration on diaspora missiology. The Lausanne Movement 2009. Retrieved from http://www.lausanne.org/documents/seoul-declaration-on-diaspora-missiology.html.

McCabe, K. (2011). African immigrants in the United States. Migration Policy Institute. Retrieved from http://www.migrationinformation.org/USfocus/display.cfm?id=847#23.

NationMaster. (2011). US Visa Lottery Winners (most recent) by Country. NationMaster, http://www.nationmaster.com/graph/imm_us_vis_lot_win-immigration-us-visa-lottery-winners.

Okpewho, I., & Nzegwu, N. (Eds.). (2009). *The new African diaspora*. Bloomington, IN: Indiana University Press.

Olupona, J. O. K., & Gemignani, R. (2007). *African immigrant religions in America*. New York/London: New York University Press.

Onyinah, O. (2004). Pentecostalism and the African diaspora: An examination of the missions activities of the Church of Pentecost. *Pneuma* 26(2), 216–41.

Pew Research Center. (2007). Changing faiths: Latinos and the transformation of American religion. The Pew Forum on Religion and Public Life and The Pew Hispanic Center. Retrieved from http://pewhispanic.org/files/reports/75.pdf.

Phillips, T., Norsworthy, B., & Whalin, T. (1997). *The world at your door*. Minneapolis, MN: Bethany House.

Ratha, D., Mohapatra, S., & Silwal, A. (2011). The migration and remittances factbook 2011: The World Bank Group. Retrived from http://siteresources.worldbank.org/INTLAC/Resources/Factbook2011-Ebook.pdf.

ter Haar, G. (1998). *Halfway to paradise: African Christians in Europe*. Fairwater, Cardiff: Cardiff Academic Press.

The Church of Pentecost. (2000). *Songs: Compiled for council meetings, retreats, conferences, etc. English and Twi*. Accra: The Literature Committee, The National Music Committee.

———. (2009). *Missions handbook*. Dansoman, Ghana: The Church of Pentecost Missions Board.

———. (2011). Annual statistics 2010. The Church of Pentecost 2011. Retrieved from http://thecophq.org.

———. (2011). Mission statement. The Church of Pentecost 2011. Retrieved from http://thecophq.org.

The Church of Pentecost U.S.A. Inc. (2010). 2009 Annual report. New York: The Church of Pentecost.

_____. (2010). *Pentecost International Worship Centers: Guidelines Drafting Committee Report*. New York: The P.I.W.C. Guidelines Drafting Committee.

Tira, S. J., & Wan, E. (2010). Diaspora missiology and missions in the context of the 21st century. *Global Missiology* 1(8). Retrieved from http://ojs.globalmissiology.org/index.php/english/article/view/383.

United Nations Department of Economic and Social Affairs Population Division. (2011). Trends in international migrant stock: The 2008 revision, UN database. United Nations Department of Economic and Social Affairs, Population Division 2009. http://esa.un.org/migration.

USAFIS. (2011). US program of Green Card lottery—Year 2012. Retrieved from http://www.usafis.org/green_card/prev_years.asp.

Währisch-Oblau, C. (2009). *The missionary self-perception of Pentecostal/Charismatic church leaders from the Global South in Europe: Bringing back the gospel*. Vol. 2. Global Pentecostal and Charismatic Studies. Leiden: Boston.

Wan, E. (1995). *Missions within reach: Intercultural ministries in Canada*. Hong Kong: China Alliance Press.

_____. (2007). Diaspora missiology. *Occasional Bulletin* 2, 3–7. Retrieved from http://www.emsweb.org/images/stories/docs/bulletins/OB_20_2.pdf.

Warner, S. R. (2004). Coming to America: Immigrants and the faith they bring. *Christian Century* 121 (3), 20–23.

Yeboah, I. E. A. (2008). *Black African neo-diaspora: Ghanian immigrant experiences in greater Cincinnati, Ohio area*. Lanham: Lexington Books.

Appropriating Faith within the City: An Examination of Urban Youth Ministry in Immigrant Churches[1]

Janice A. McLean
janice@cityseminaryny.org

Introduction

For many religious communities, one of the main priorities they grapple with on a continual basis is how to overcome the real and/or perceived generational tensions and cultural dynamics, in order to pass on and nurture within the next generation a meaningful and mature faith.[2] The significance of this transference, as it relates to the future and proliferation of these communities, is visible in the great emphasis being placed on youth groups, Christian education classes, Christ-oriented retreats,

---
1   In this paper, I define youth ministry in an inclusive manner—to incorporate the various ways that ministry to the youth is performed within the churches studied, and not limited specifically to the youth group. I contend that what is seen in the youth group forms an extension of the overall ethos that a congregation has toward their youth and their development. The young people described in this paper range in ages from ten to approximately thirty-five. One reason for this range is to ensure that adequate space was given to those in their thirties to speak about their experiences during their teenage and early twenties and how that in turn impacts how they lead and interact with those who are currently pre-teens, teenagers, and in their twenties.
2   See also the admonition in Deuteronomy 6:1–9; 11:1–7. According to Gary Parrett, J. I. Packer, and S. Steve Kang, these passages demonstrate that "Israel was commanded to keep the instruction and formation of their children as a chief priority." However, this focus on the religious instruction and formation of children was not limited to the Israelites and the Old Testament, as evidence in the Gospels and the pastoral epistles also highlights these activities as priorities of believers (Parrett, Packer, and Kang, 2009, 310–11). See also Dean, 2010; Carroll and Roof, 2002; Dawn, 1997.

and other programs that are led by adults who seem able to bridge the generational and cultural divide and produce this specific kind of youth. However, when an urban immigrant religious community is added to this equation, the issue of the development of faith takes on added complexity.

As various studies indicate, the religious communities in which many immigrants participate play a prominent role in their lives—one that enables them to creatively navigate and interact with the host context and live out their faith (Foley and Hoge, 2007; Olupona and Gemignani, 2007; ter Haar, 1998; Adogame and Weissköppel, 2005). This is accomplished by providing a space where "members of an ethnic group can come together around cultural symbols and practices that resonate with them" (Foley and Hoge, 2007, 10). Within urban communities, some of which are marked by issues of poverty, crime, and socioeconomic and political disempowerment, the social, cultural, and religious capital that immigrant congregations provide for their members are particularly meaningful.

As a generation, the youth constitute the front line in terms of cultural and social change. Given the liminal position that second-generation youth inhabit between the urban context and the immigrant church communities, they provide us with a significant window through which we can examine the terrains of urban youth ministry and some of the complexity that accompanies the transference of faith in an urban immigrant context. The vision gained from this type of analysis is vital, for in their engagement with Christianity (its ideas and institutions) within an urban context, immigrant youth reveal not only what could be the future of religious beliefs and practices, but also the extent to which Christianity will need to be resilient, innovative, and responsive to several local, global, social, and cultural developments.

In this chapter I seek to examine the characteristics of and challenges associated with urban youth ministry among second-generation West Indian immigrants. Some of the questions that will be considered are: What are some of the religious practices and beliefs being nurtured among the youth within immigrant religious communities? How are these beliefs and practices facilitated in formal and informal ways? How are the religious lives of second-generation immigrants assisting them to navigate the urban context and the social malaise they encounter? Using data obtained from qualitative research conducted among West Indian second-generation youth in New York City and London, I will seek to answer the above questions and ascertain what are some of the features that constitute the religious lives of urban young people.

Characteristics of Urban Youth Ministry

In answering these specific questions, I begin with a brief analysis of what is seen as foundational for the congregations in which these youth ministries occur—namely their beliefs. As Pentecostals, these congregations are a part of a global movement that places particular emphasis on a direct personal encounter with God, the indispensable role of the Holy Spirit as power-for-mission, and the importance of the miraculous and numinous (Pomerville 1985, xi). There is also a strong belief in the Trinity—which forms the basis for their baptismal formula, and in their soteriology, these congregations adhere to a three-stage process—justification, sanctification, and the baptism of the Holy Spirit.

Formally Nurturing the Faith of Urban Youths

Having briefly discussed what constitutes some of the basic doctrines of the wider Pentecostal movement, I give particular attention to some of the specific beliefs being nurtured amongst the youth in two West Indian Pentecostal churches in New York City and London. For these churches, one of the most fundamental beliefs is that of salvation and having a relationship with Jesus. Through the sermons, liturgy, midweek services, Sunday school curriculum, youth group meetings, printed bulletins, and online resources, the young people are continuously confronted with humanity's depravity because of sin, the sacrificial redemption of Jesus on the cross, and the invitation to have a relationship with Jesus. In these formal ways, the youth are simultaneously called into and encouraged to remain within the community of those who have a relationship with Jesus. One prominent part of the liturgy that expresses the significance of having such a relationship is the "altar call." As one of the concluding features of the liturgy, the altar call gives the preacher a final opportunity to appeal to nonbelievers and encourage believers in their faith. In giving the appeal, the preacher invites nonbelievers to come to the altar, then leads them in the "sinner's prayer." This is followed by a time of celebration and counseling—where the new converts are taken into another room to receive counseling while the rest of the church praises God for their salvation. Oftentimes, this section of the altar call may also be followed by a second invitation—one directed at believers who may need prayer because of some difficulty they are experiencing, or as means of encouraging the faithful to remain steadfast in their relationship with Christ.[3]

A second belief that is given a place of significance within these immigrant Pentecostal churches is the baptism of the Holy Spirit. For many of the members, this baptism indicates that an individual is both set apart and equipped with gifts by the Holy Spirit, which in turn enables them to fulfill a divine task or ministry (McGee 1998, 46). In various formal settings—Sunday services, official printed documentation, prayer meetings, etc., this belief is used as a means of communicating to the youth that ministry is linked to the work of the Holy Spirit in their lives and not their education or age. As a result, different areas of service are made available for the youth to function as God's instrument of blessing for his people. One area of ministry in which the participation of youth is particularly noticeable is in the area of music. In both congregations, young people were numbered amongst the leaders of the praise and worship team, and the members of the band. In the church in Brooklyn, a boy of about thirteen was one of the primary musicians—the keyboard player.[4] In this role, he played a vital and significant role in the worship life of his church, by collaborating with the praise and worship team and those leading the service to create and maintain an atmosphere in which the people of God could both commune with and hear from the Lord.

Intricately linked with the baptism of the Holy Spirit is another belief—that of sanctification. It is believed that as a result of the Holy Spirit's presence in a person, he can illuminate that individual "because, [by] dwelling within, he can get to the very center of one's thinking and emotions, and lead one into all truth" (Erickson 2002, 889). In terms of the development of the Christian life, it is the Holy Spirit who "guides the believers from spiritual birth to maturity" (Erickson 2002, 880). An integral part of this development is the sanctification process, in which the Holy Spirit facilitates the ongoing changing of the believer's heart and the renewing of his or her mind to seek after the things that are righteous in God's sight. One consequence associated with this ongoing change is the acquisition of a new identity—that of a "saint," and an accompanying lifestyle marked by holiness.

How then is this belief reflected within the formal features of the churches? In the months that I conducted ethnographic research within these two churches, there was the regular affirmation of the "saint" identity, by active engagement in renewing

---

3 It is necessary to note, however, that one aspect of this encouragement may be the confession of sins and recommitting of oneself to Jesus.
4 The other was the organist who played while the hymns were being sung.

one's mind to seek after the things that please the Lord. An excerpt from a sermon on February 11, 2007, highlights these realities within the churches. Speaking on Psalm 5:12, "Surely, Lord, you bless the righteous; you surround them with your favor as with a shield," the pastor says:

> You see that in your Bible? ... [The Lord] will bless who? The righteous. Are you righteous? [Response from the congregation: "yes!"] Why are you going to accept the foolishness the devil sends your way when God says the favor of the Lord is yours as a seal? ... Because I know the devil messes first of all in our minds and if he can get your mind, he can get your body to stop coming to prayer meeting; he can get your body to stop wanting to read the Word; he can get your body to start compromising.

Nurturing the Faith of Urban Youths in Informal Ways

Having discussed how the beliefs about salvation and having a relationship with Jesus, the baptism of the Holy Spirit, and sanctification are being communicated and nurtured in immigrant youth in formal ways, we will now examine how these same beliefs were also being fostered in informal ways. The primary informal means in which these beliefs are engendered among the second-generation youth in West Indian immigrant Pentecostal churches is through relationships. In these congregations the youth are surrounded by several adults who love them, have their best interests at heart, and are able to guide and encourage them in matters of faith. What was notable about these adults is that many of them have known these young people since they were born and as a result have formed very close bonds with them—even to the extent that the adults may become additional parents for the youth. I should state here that I have chosen to use the term "additional" instead of "surrogate" or even "spiritual" to describe these parent-like relationships because these adults do not take the place of the youth's biological parents. They function in a greater capacity than just spiritual in the life of the youth, by also providing emotional, financial, and emotional support. According to one young man, he called older women in the church mother "not out of disrespect, it's not [because] they're old but just the fact that they have proven to be a mother to me. Even sister [name] ... I call her mom. When everybody hear me call her mom, they're like, 'She's not old enough to be your mom!' But she's always been like a mother to me from since I was a kid, since I was like six years old. She's always been like a mother to me."[5] In this family-like context, the youth are encouraged through phone calls and face-to-face conversations to make a profession of faith or to work at maintaining a relationship with Jesus.

In terms of the relationship between the baptism of the Holy Spirit and ministry, the adults first model what this looks like in practice, while simultaneously communicating its interrelation to the youth and by initially providing them with occasions to minister to the church through such avenues as Sunday school presentations and the youth choir. As these youth continue to grow in their faith, additional opportunities are provided to participate in ministry—this may take the form of moderating youth group meetings, or moderating/preaching during the youth and Sunday worship services. Throughout this entire process the youth are accompanied by various adults—their additional parents and the youth group leaders in particular—who come alongside them to aid in discerning their call to ministry.

During a group interview with several young people, one teenager in Brooklyn related that the discovery of his call came in the context of being asked by one of the youth group leaders to serve as a praise and worship leader. He stated: "I [am] called [as a] praise and worship leader, and if I wasn't asked to do that, I would not go up there and do it." In response to his statement, he was told by the vice president of the youth group leader that: "she's [the youth group leader] the one who is around you all, she's the one who can point out certain things and say okay, [name], your calling is going to do praise and worship." This statement elicited the following response from one of his peers: "I understand what he's saying, [it takes] a leader to recognize who can do what—the mission and [calling]."[6] In the second generation's embracing of the "saint" identity and the accompanying process of sanctification, modeling also comes into play. As a result some of these adults become the standard for a committed Christian and therefore a person who lives an imitable life.

Religious Practices of Urban Youths

So how are the beliefs discussed above seen in practice? Here I define practices not in terms of techniques or instructions on how to do something. Instead as Craig Dykstra and Dorothy Bass explain, they are "things Christian people do together over

---
5   Interview with second-generation male in Brooklyn, April 2, 2007.
6   Group interview, April 11, 2007.

time to address fundamental human needs in response to and in light of God's active presence for the life of the world" (Dykstra and Bass 2002, 15). As such, Christian practices are part of the whole way of life.[7] What, therefore, are the features of the way of life for these young people in Brooklyn and London?

The way of life of most of the young people that I interviewed was oriented around their relationship with Christ and service to others. For many of these young people, such an orientation was visible in the disciplines of daily reading the Scripture and praying, periodically fasting, and confession. For some, these disciplines were linked with a focus on holiness and wanting to remain apart from what they consider to be worldly influences such as hip-hop and rap music, drinking, partying, having sex, etc. In the cases where a young person was struggling with these areas or had engaged in any of these activities, that individual would choose to limit involvement in ministry within the church until reaching a point where these issues had been addressed. In their daily lives, many of the young people spoke about behaving in a manner that was respectful—not cursing out people in public, being loud on public transportation, or gossiping or wasting time at work. In these ways, these young people are intentionally marking themselves as "the other" with the objective that such a lifestyle will provide them with an opportunity to tell their peers and or colleagues about Jesus.

Flowing out of their relationship with Jesus was a focus on serving the church and the wider community. According to a young man in London, a serious commitment to Christ at the age of sixteen became not only his inauguration into the life of the church but placed him in a position where the church's involvement within the community became a catalyst for his later involvement within the community. He stated: "I've always been very interested in the community and applying myself to the community. Being here is just like a natural progression."[8] For several young people, however, serving their church and the wider community not only entailed being involved in programs like Saturday schools, mentorship, food pantry, evangelistic services, etc. It also necessitated a process of reexamining various religious and cultural traditions so that the church could be a place where the community was present and its ongoing work of nurturing faith was conducted in manner that

---

7   I am indebted to Mark Gornik for his assistance in framing my thoughts on Christian practice in this manner. See Mark Gornik, "Practices of Ministry in the City," a presentation made at City Seminary of New York February 2, 2011.
8   Second-generation male, July 12, 2007.

resonates with the emerging generations while calling them to a "way of life that is deeply responsive to God's grace" (Dykstra and Bass 2002, 15).

One young woman in London expressed her views in following manner:

> I feel that we believe that we would like that when you come into this church it would reflect the community. … And I don't think we're going to achieve this multicultural congregation unless we actually strategically look at the community, actually identify who is in our community, actually look at ways of bringing in, and we have to make changes. So, therefore, language would have to change and not necessarily our belief but our tradition in this sense of expectation.[9]

Navigating the Urban Context

Having incorporated both the beliefs and practices described above, how are the religious lives of second-generation immigrants assisting them in navigating the urban context and the social malaise they encounter? In answering this question, however, we have to first discuss the terrain of that urban context. What are the stories being told or images being depicted about urban youth, and what are the implications for immigrant youths? According to Jennifer Tilton, in America urban "youth of color, particularly black boys and girls, have long been linked with other symbolic associations—criminality or sexuality" (Tilton 2010, 10). As a result, the majority of the stories being told about urban youth of color focus on them being delinquent, thugs, or involved in gangs, i.e., they are so dangerous that they need to be quarantined so as not to damage the rest of society; or they are viewed as being sexually irresponsible—normally represented in the media and other sectors as having several children and living on welfare.

In the United Kingdom, not only are similar stories being told, but also they are being expressed in a manner that continues to conform to the systematic manifestations of racism toward blacks.[10] As one second-generation male in London states:

---

9   Second-generation female, July 9, 2007.
10   One factor enabling the pervasiveness of racism in the lives of blacks has been location, i.e., they reside and work in close proximity to whites. In many of these interactions they are treated with suspicion, or in a manner that gives credence to the various stereotypes that have emerged about West Indian youth. See also the discussions on racism in Beckford, 2004; Graham, 2007.

> I think for me at times it's been very frustrating. You encounter racism at every level of society, [in] every institution. And when you say what you see, you're deemed to have a chip on your shoulder in many different cases. And it seems to be a very common chip on the shoulder because a lot of people who look like me have the same experiences.[11]

How then do the religious lives of the immigrant youth in Brooklyn and London assist them in navigating the terrains of these urban contexts? First the religious life of the West Indian immigrant youth provides them with an alternative context in which they are able to reconstruct the stories about themselves and the possible trajectory of their lives. In Brooklyn, the religious community gives "adolescents access to adults other than their parents … [and also provides] a sense of identity and belonging to the adolescents" (Waters 1999, 202). More fundamental, however, is that it enables the young people to lay claim to a particular West Indian identity—Christ-loving "saints," hardworking, excelling academically, law-abiding members of the society—that provides an avenue that helps to foster their upward socioeconomic and educational mobilities. For the young men, this particular West Indian identity is linked with a construction of masculinity that admonishes men to be responsible, financially able to provide for one's family, and take the lead in decisions concerning their household and family.

In London, the religious community has provided many members of the second generation with certain skills that they have used in their secular jobs and a place where they were challenged not to conform to the low expectations the society had of them but instead to live up to their full potential. The composition of this script was particularly important for the young men, who were continually labeled as underachievers. According to one second-generation male:

> In terms of my school life I left school without any qualifications and I think for me school hadn't been a positive experience overall. … I was not really taking any qualifications when I left school. … When I first left school my teachers … were suggesting that I'd be a grave-digger. So I don't think the expectations were high of me in terms of just the school environment. And at one point I was considering that as a career. … She [the informant's mother and a

---

11   Second-generation male, dated July 12, 2008.

pastor's wife] felt that I could do better than that if I keep pushing myself more. And when I went to college ... I was surprised when I actually got my qualifications.[12]

Thus as a result of his mother's encouragement and various opportunities to lead and minister in the church, this young man and many like him discovered that they had the ability to excel academically and acquire the necessary qualifications and employment that would enable them to provide financially for their families and be responsible men within the society.

Challenges of Urban Youth Ministry

So far in this paper, I have discussed in some detail some of the characteristics of urban youth ministry in two West Indian Pentecostal Churches in Brooklyn and London. In what remains I will examine some of the challenges associated with this ministry. In both congregations, the members are predominantly female. In this manner, they are representative of a phenomenon that is mirrored throughout Christian congregations around the globe. As a result, within Christianity at large and these two churches in particular, there are several ways in which they may be seen as emphasizing a feminine spirituality, i.e., having a receptivity to and the call to surrender one's life to Christ. In the act of worship, this receptivity and surrender is manifested in different members crying during the service, holding hands with fellow congregants during prayer, dancing, etc. As a result of engaging in these practices, the church may be regarded as a place that is not conducive to male development. Addressing this perception is critical especially in an urban context where young men are being socialized to embrace a heightened masculinity constructed around aggression, violence, the denigration of women, and "gangsta" culture. In such a context, it is therefore very critical for these churches to provide an alternative construction of masculinity that enables the young men to embrace their manhood and Christ without becoming feminized in the process. One vital element in facilitating such a construction is the need for strong, responsible, caring Christian men to accompany these young men on their journey of faith, and helping them to deconstruct and challenge the societal views about black masculinity.

---

12   Second-generation male, dated July 8, 2007.

Another challenge for conducting urban youth ministry is creating a space for engaging with young people about the issues they encounter in the wider community—sex, racial issues, etc. For the two churches I studied, the creation of space may mean coming to terms with the parts of the liturgy or the cultural and religious traditions that may serve to further alienate and marginalize the young people. Is the use of hymns and lecture style sermon the most effective way in which to communicate to a generation whose learning style is dominated by sound bites and video clips? Will room be made for their perspectives, especially those that may call for major changes in the structure of the church? For these churches in particular the challenges posed by the immigrant youth are significant, in that they will determine the future of the church's existence. For unless Christianity is perceived as relevant and spaces of belonging continue to be created, many immigrant youth may not find it worthwhile to remain in these churches. The prophetic nature embedded in this statement finds fulfillment in the British context, in which the failure of several black-majority churches to be relevant and provide spaces of belonging for many of the second generation resulted in many leaving the church. Therefore, as the third generation comes of age in London, their presence and absence are forcing many church leaders to grapple with matters of belief and practice. With both the first and second generations having experienced the exodus of their children and their peers from the church these leaders see a major part of their duty is to ensure that the church strives to remain relevant to the third generation. A second-generation woman describes the issue of relevance in the following manner:

> So growing up I knew that I had separate clothes. You have your church clothes, you had your house clothes, you had your school clothes, and you wore the very best to come to church and I feel that [it places] pressure on people coming through the doors. If we were flexible in our appearance, i.e., if a person wants to come in their jeans and a T-shirt and trainers on a Sunday, they can worship just as well as somebody who has got on a hat, that long frock, and high-heel shoes, or even better sometimes. And I think that we have to accept changes especially our appearance even from as basic as our hair to our dress as well. If we want to reach and keep the youth you have to look at our services. And our service needs to promote that.[13]

---

13   Second-generation female, July 9, 2007.

The final challenge that urban youth ministry poses is one of leadership. As these churches work on being places of belonging for the second-generation young people in their midst, they will also need to provide space for them to become more involved in leadership of the churches. Creating such a space not only allows the youth to have a say in how the church's future evolves, but it communicates to the youth that they are vital members of the church, and not immature believers who cannot make any contribution or be entrusted with the faith.

Conclusion

Nurturing faith in young people is one of the primary tasks of the church, and without it a congregation may not have a future. As the two immigrant churches in this paper reveal, passing on of the faith is a priority in which various adults and leaders are actively engaged. Through various formal (sermons, liturgy, bulletins, etc.) and informal (modeling and relationships) avenues, the church passes on fundamental beliefs in salvation and having a relationship with Jesus, the baptism of the Holy Spirit, and sanctification to their second-generation youth. In accepting these beliefs as their own, many of the second-generation youth have developed a way of life oriented around their relationship with Christ and service to others. It is necessary to note that such an orientation is not dormant because it forms the platform from which they engage with the urban context that surrounds them. In the process, these young people discover that their religious lives provide an alternative context in which to reconstruct the stories about themselves and the possible trajectory of the lives. However, as this paper has also highlighted, urban youth ministry also has three particular challenges: 1) providing an alternative construction of masculinity that enables the young men to embrace their manhood and Christ without becoming feminized in the process; 2) creating a space for engaging with the issues young people encounter in the wider community—sex, racial issues, etc.; and 3) carving out spaces where the youth are involved in the leadership structures of the church. As the churches in this paper are faithful in nurturing faith in their urban youth ministries while addressing the challenges that arise, they will be providing their children, grandchildren, and the generations to come with a place of belonging where they can appropriate faith in the city.

References

Adogame, A., & Weissköppel, C. (Eds.). (2005). *Religion in the context of African migration.* Bayreuth: Pia Thielmann & Eckhard Breitinger.

Anderson, A. (2004). *An introduction to Pentecostalism.* Cambridge: Cambridge University Press.

Beckford, R. (2004). *God and the gangs.* London: Darton, Longman & Todd.

Carroll, J. W., & Roof, W.C. (2002). *Bridging divided worlds: Generational cultures in congregations.* San Francisco: Jossey-Bass.

Dawn, M. (1997). *Is it a lost cause?: Having the heart of God for the church's children.* Grand Rapids: Eerdmans.

Dean, K.C. (2010). *Almost Christian: What the faith of our teenagers is telling the American Church.* New York: Oxford University Press.

Dykstra, C., & Bass, D.C. (2002). A theological understanding of Christian practices. In M. Volf & Bass, D.C. (Eds.), *Practicing theology: Beliefs and practices in Christian life* (13–32). Grand Rapids: Eerdmans.

Erickson, M. J. (2002). *Christian theology* (2nd ed.). Grand Rapids: Baker Books.

Foley, M. W., & Hoge, D. R. (2007). *Religion and the new immigrants: How faith communities form our newest citizens.* New York: Oxford University Press.

Graham, M. (2007). *Black issues in social work and social care.* Bristol: Policy Press.

Hollenweger, W. J. (1972). *The Pentecostals: The charismatic movement in the churches.* Minneapolis: Augsburg Publishing House.

McGee, G. B. (1998). Pentecostal and charismatic missions. In J. M. Philips and R. T. Coote (Eds.), *Toward the 21st century in Christian mission* (41–53). Grand Rapids: Eerdmans.

Olupona, J. K., & Gemignani, R. (Eds.). (2007). *African immigrant religions in America.* New York: New York University Press.

Parrett, G., Packer, J. I., & Kang, S.S. (2009). *Reaching the faith, forming the faithful: A biblical vision for education in the church.* Downers Grove: IVP Academic.

Pomerville, P.A. (1985). *The third force in missions.* Peabody: Hendrickson Publishers.

ter Haar, G. (Ed.). (1998). *Strangers and sojourners: Religious communities in the diaspora.* Leuven: Peeters.

Tilton, J. (2010). *Dangerous or endangered? Race and the politics of youth in urban America.* New York: New York University Press.

Waters, M. (1999). *Black identities: West Indian immigrant dreams and American realities.* Cambridge: Harvard University Press.

Interviews:

Second-generation male, Brooklyn, April 2, 2007.

Group interview with 1.5 and second-generation youth and young adults, Brooklyn, April 11, 2007.

Second-generation male, London, July 12, 2007.

Second-generation female, London, July 9, 2007.

Second-generation male, London, July 8, 2007.

A New Day Dawning in the Old Country? Twenty-first-century Urban Trends in Germany and Their Implications for Urban Church Planting

Stephen Beck
stephen.beck@fthgiessen.de

Germany is known as the land of the sixteenth-century Reformation, the land of Martin Luther. But "used-to-be's" don't count anymore: That the great majority of the 80 million residents do not think of God as a mighty fortress but as either nonexistent or not relevant to the intelligent is seen in the fact that less than 2 percent of the population claim an evangelical faith. Since the Enlightenment secularism, the de-sacralization or removal of "God" from all things, has swept Western Europe and has turned Germany into a functionally atheistic, spiritual wasteland.

> The nation's spiritual health is failing. ... The church is widely perceived as irrelevant, and open hostility to anything Christian is increasing. ... In northeastern Germany (former communist East Germany) possibly only 0.5% are evangelicals. ... It is often difficult for born-again ministers in the EKD[1] to openly minister in their own churches! ... The Free Churches have a higher proportion of evangelicals, but they constitute only 1% of Germany's population. (Mandryk 2010, 361)

---
1 Evangelische Kirche Deutschlands, the Protestant state church, includes twenty-three different ecclesiastical groupings organized into a federation.

This is the case in a country resistant to breaking from historical norms and established institutions and suspicious toward innovation and new forms.

The purpose of this paper is to analyze the effects of as well as opportunities resulting from urbanization and to consequently propose a contextualized approach to church planting needed to infiltrate the urban settings of the old country.

Trends in German Urban Development

For the sake of researching economic trends in Germany, the federal government decided in 1998 to divide Germany into eleven metropolitan regions. Urbanologists know them as the eleven Metropolregionen, while the more common designation is Ballungsräume (literally, balled-up spaces). The boundaries for each of the Metropolregionen are come by fairly naturally, each region following its own unique history and cultural development. We list the eleven urban centers in order of importance:[2]

1. Rhein-Ruhr: 10.2 million inhabitants. This is divided into 2 major urban sprawls. Metropole Ruhr: With a population of 6 million, this metroplex runs from Duisburg and Moers (on the west) to Dortmund (on the east), Hamm (northeast of Dortmund), and Witten (southwest of Dortmund). Metropolregion Köln/Bonn is the vertical line-up of Düsseldorf, Köln, and Bonn.
2. Frankfurt Rhein-Main: 5.8 million. This covers the area of Giessen in the north to Darmstadt in the south, with major urban centers Wiesbaden, Mainz, and Frankfurt in-between.
3. Munich: 2.6 million
4. Berlin-Brandenburg: 4.2 million
5. Middle Germany or Sachsendreieck: Dresden-Leipzig-Chemnitz: 3.2 million
6. Stuttgart: 2.7 million
7. Hamburg: 4.2 million
8. Hannover-Braunschweig-Göttingen-Wolfsburg: 3.9 million
9. Nürnberg: 2.5 million
10. Rhein-Neckar-Dreieck: Mannheim-Heidelberg-Saarbrücken: 2.4 million
11. Bremen-Oldenburg: 2.3 million

---

2 Ranking numbers taken from Regionales Monitoring 2010.

A Summary Analysis of Germany's Metro Regions

1. The total population of these eleven metro regions is 44 million, slightly over 50 percent of Germany's total population. This means that 36 million, or slightly under 50 percent of Germany's population, live outside of the metropolitan regions. That includes vast regions, such as the North Sea and Baltic Sea regions, the central-west region that surrounds the Rhein-Ruhr, the southwestern area touching on the borders of France and Switzerland, and the southeast area that touches on Austria and the Czech Republic. This indicates that vast areas of Germany have remained nonurban, but the centers of power and influence are in the metro regions.

2. Every metro region consists of multiple circles (Ringe): 1) The inner circle is the center of the city. Often, this inner circle was the original city and may still display portions of a wall or an outlook tower. Generally, a German city is constructed to house the main train station at its heart, making it easily accessible. While this center includes residences, hotels, and businesses, it generally also includes the red-light district with its prostitution, brothels, and drug trafficking. Often a major street will circle around the inner ring of the city. 2) The second and larger circle consists of dense residential areas, sometimes with shops lining the first floors of the high-rises built to accommodate residents. Usually a highway runs around the second ring, separating it from the third. 3) The third ring is generally the outskirts of the city. Most often these are towns that have been annexed to the city within the last century. Many have an original village feel, with their own sense of identity and community pride, but are serviced by and pay taxes to the central city government. 4) Separated from the third ring by vast green spaces are smaller and larger towns[3] and villages.[4] This fourth ring is the "green belt." Many small villages have been amalgamated in the past thirty years into small towns, but many tiny and self-contained villages still decorate the green belt.

As is generally the case with European villages, each German village prides itself on its own distinct history and traditions. Thus the mentality prevails that only families with ancestries several generations back are considered by the insiders to truly "belong." New residents, no matter how much good they bring to the village, will always remain "outsiders" in the villagers' minds.

---

3   Germans call them cities and differentiate between large cities, population of 100,000 and over, and small cities, population between 10,000 and 100,000.
4   Populations under 10,000.

3. Portions of urban populations work and shop inside a city's circles during the day but live nights and weekends in the green space. Frankfurt proper, for example, is 1 million people by day, 660,000 inhabitants by night. This means a mixing and fusion of cultures throughout an entire region, with cultural continuity between inner city and far-away villages.

4. Of the eleven metro regions, four clearly impact the nation more than the others:

- Rhein-Ruhr: Its significance to Germany lies mostly in the area of cultural development and economic impact. With its many autobahns and two notable airports (Köln-Bonn and Düsseldorf) the Rhein-Ruhr ranks high for its interconnectivity to the rest of Germany and Europe.
- Frankfurt-Rhein-Main: Though Wiesbaden and Mainz are the capitals of two connecting provinces, the power-city of this metroplex is Frankfurt. Next to London it is the banking capital of Europe, called by many the Europecity. With the river Main coursing its way through the downtown of Germany's only skyline, Frankfurt is also nicknamed "Mainhattan." The Frankfurt airport makes Frankfurt-Rhein-Main the leading transportation center in Germany. That 51 million people make their way through the Frankfurt airport annually contributes to the city being the crime capital of Germany.
- Berlin-Brandenburg: Berlin is the largest city-proper in Germany (3.3 million). As Germany's capital, it is the political center of Germany. It also ranks as a cultural gathering place for many artists, journalists, musicians, and entertainers.
- The Greater Munich area: especially in the area of education and science, Munich is the nation's leader. Bavaria is historically a Roman Catholic province, and Munich is the seat of the Roman Catholic Church in Germany.

How Immigration Affects Germany's Urbanization and the Religious Landscape

There are 15.3 million immigrants in Germany (Bundesamt für Migration und Flüchtlinge). That means 19% or one in every five persons have an immigrant background. Nearly 33% of children under age five are from migratory origin (Mandryk 2010, 359). The ethnic breakdown is as follows:

- 14.2% from Turkey
- 9.4% from Russia
- 6.9% from Poland
- 4.2% from Italy
- 3.0% from Rumania
- 3.0% from Serbia
- 2.6% from Montenegro and Croatia
- 2.3% from Herzegovina and Bosnia
- 2.2% from Greece (BAMF).

According to the Amt für Multikulturelle Angelegenheiten [Bureau for Multicultural Opportunities] (AMKA 2009, 36), five developments have influenced migration and immigration policies in the past few years:

- The fall of the Berlin wall and the reuniting of the two Germanies in 1989/90, along with the collapse of the Soviet empire. This caused a strong surge of immigration from the east.
- Civil war in Yugoslavia in the early 1990s caused a strong migration to Germany, particularly to Frankfurt.
- A new law for citizenship in 2000 (called Optionsregelung): Children born since 2000 in Germany, whose parents fulfill certain residency requirements, automatically have not only the citizenship of their parents but also German citizenship. When they are eighteen, they have to choose between the two citizenships.
- EU expansion since 2004 has increased the number of people from Estonia, Latvia, Lithuania, Poland, Czech Republic, Slovakia, Hungary, Slovenia, Malta, and Cyprus.
- A new immigration law in 2005 confirmed Germany as an Einwanderungsland (immigration land). New immigrants are required to take German classes.

If we look at Frankfurt, the most international city percentage-wise, we learn the following: 24.3% are immigrants (but the whole Frankfurt-Rhein-Main metro is 33% immigrant). Approximately 170 different nations have gathered in Frankfurt and over 200 different languages are spoken. People from other EU countries comprise 35% of the immigrants, 19% are from Turkey, and 18% are from the Balkan countries. One of approximately every thirty Frankfurters originates from

Asia; one of approximately every fifty Frankfurters comes from one of the African countries (ibid., 39).

Meanwhile, Germany's birth-rate of 1.3 is among the lowest in the world. Between 1965 and 2009 the number of births in Germany decreased by 50%, and by 2050 is projected to halve again. The fact is that the number of German children born since 1965 sank by a whopping 65%, but the higher number of births in the immigrant population offset this to 50% total decline (Sarrazin 2010, 53, 60). It is especially in the area of marriage and family that the impact of rising immigration figures in the face of declining German population figures is felt most keenly. In 1999, in 74% of couples who married, both had German citizenship. By 2002, that number had decreased to 58% of couples being both German and 32% making up the constellation of German/non-German. Today, two-thirds of newborns have at least one non-German parent; over 90% of newborns in 2008 had German citizenship plus a second or third citizenship from one of the parents. Urbanologists conclude: "It is anticipated, that in the near future a majority of the population of Frankfurt will have a multicultural background" (ibid., 36).

Tentative Conclusions for Urban Church Planting

1. The division into eleven metropolitan regions is of recent enough origin that generally Germans lend little significance to the country's urban trends. This explains why, in our experience, not only the concept of church planting is considered to be strange,[5] but "urban church planting" in particular. But, in terms of impacting the nation holistically, to the cities we must go!

2. The makeup of a metro region calls for multiple church planting approaches. As one metro region consists of city rings, large/small towns, and isolated villages, reaching the region will consist of several and diverse methodologies.

3. If we speak of and strategize for "urban church planting movements," we should follow the inside-out movement of culture. This means:

---

5   This reality is expressed poignantly by Matthias Barthels in Barthels and Reppenhagen, 2006: "Such considerations and intentions are met with opposition and fear: How can something like that work when, in fact, our help and finances and personnel is declining constantly? . . . . Such considerations and intentions are also met with misunderstanding and rejection. We recently experienced just that: As we suggested such a church planting project to our congregation here in Pommern, the first reaction was: 'What are you talking about, this is not Brazil!'" (author's translation).

- We must focus on an entire metropolitan area, planning a movement from city center to village.
- An anchor church or "cathedral congregation" should be planted in the inner ring, being the main catalyst for a movement, analyst of the developing culture, and a training ground for future planters.
- We do best to recruit long-standing residents of any given village and then train, assess, and send them back into their village to plant a church that is part of and supported by the greater movement.

4. For maximum national impact, denominations and mission organizations should plant parallel movements in all eleven metropolitan regions, giving priority to the "the Big Four" and those with the fewest number of evangelical churches per million residents.

5. As immigration continues and the population decreases, Germany will become 50/50 in the ratio of German/non-German within the next twenty years. The church of the future is one that is neither ethnic nor German but intercultural. This is in the German context countercultural, but will prove the gospel's transcultural power to reconcile all peoples to Christ.

Studies on (Urban) Church Planting in Germany

Since 1995, over 1,000 churches have been planted (Mandryk 2010, 361), which amounts to an average of sixty-six per year in a country in which 98 percent of the 80 million people have no living faith in Christ. Our interest in this section is the research done on church planting in the last twenty years in Germany, and the conclusions we may draw from this research for the mission of church multiplication in the eleven metropolitan areas.

We are particularly interested in research by those in and deeply connected to the German context. We have found several non-German studies that—though highly regarded by many—have superimposed their findings on Germany's unique history and context. For example, David Garrison's research (Garrison 2004) is suspect at one particular point: He establishes ten factors of church planting movements from God's work outside of Europe. One of those factors is "house churches" or home-based cell groups. He then asks: "Where are the house churches? Only after we've addressed these questions are we likely to find Church Planting Movements" (ibid.,

140). This is improper research methodology. It presupposes an end result and seeks to fit Western Europe into it. Studies below will show, in fact, that Garrison's house church characteristic does not quite fit into Germany's culture.

The same can be said of emerging/emergent church authors. This movement out of the English-speaking world makes a strong distinction between modernity and postmodernity, the latter becoming the movement's point of departure. For the German situation this distinction is exaggerated.[6] That is not to say that postmodernism has not touched the German way of thinking and living. But German culture is steeped in a built-in reverence for institutions. Science and philosophy are still valued as the centers of authority. The true force of contention in Germany is not postmodernism but secularism. Not only is Germany's brand of secularism unique, but one must even make a distinction between the secularism of West and East Germany. West Germany's secularism is such that the West German thinks he knows what Christianity teaches and has decided it has no relevance for him. East German secularism is such that the individual does not engage with Christianity because he does not know anything about it. The secular West German has liberated himself from the God-concept, but is still open to religious questions. The secular East German has learned life without God and sees no need to ask religious questions (see Schroeder 2007, 251).

What light, then, has been shed on church planting in the German urban situation?

Michael Herbst and the Institut zur Erforschung von Evangelisation und Gemeindeentwicklung

Michael Herbst, professor of practical theology in University Greifswald and state church pastor in that East German town, leads the Institute for Research on Evangelization and Church Development (Institut zur Erforschung von Evangelisation und Gemeindeentwicklung). The value of the institute's publications does not lie in

---

6   Cf. Ralph Kunz in Reppenhagen and Herbst 2008, 171: "The confessional contexts, the differing degrees of secularization, the political situations, and the economic conditions all differ from person to person. The 'post' in postmodernism implies a discontinuity that actually does not exist" (author's translation). In a footnote Kunz explains: "I favor an interpretation of postmodernity that does not see in that concept the end but the extension, increase, and radicalization of modernity" (author's translation). See also Andreas Feldtkeller's chapter, *Kontextuelle Missionstheologie*, in Reppenhagen and Herbst 2008, 49: "In the 20th century, modernism developed an understanding of reality, whose pillars were empirical observation and rationalism. It connected strongly to the Aristotelian stream of European thinking. The protestant church [of Germany] attempted in the second half of the 20th century, with its program of 'religionless Christianity,' an adaptation to modernity, in which she followed modernity's own narrowness and misunderstanding of reality" (author's translation).

research of particular church plants, but in their call to the German church to be the carrier (Träger) of the missio Dei, accompanied by research on the particular DNA required. Of particular interest to the institute is the English Anglican Church's "Fresh Expressions of Church" as a model for German state church renewal. Herbst's call to be missional/conversional is not new; others before him have trumpeted the call to the state church: Johann Hinrich Wichern in a famous speech in 1848; Dietrich Bonhoeffer in the first part of the twentieth century before being executed in 1945; Georg Vicedom's insistence that the German church be responsible to carry out the missio Dei, a phrase coined at the 1952 world missions conference in Willingen, Germany; Fritz Schwarz and his son, Christian Schwarz, in the 1980s, as well as the calls by pastor Manfred Seitz.[7]

For the most part, these calls have fallen on deaf ears in the state church. Herbst's colleague in the institute, Johannes Zimmerman, comments, "Regretfully, it is still rather the exception than the rule for 'church growth in Germany' to be a topic in the university theology faculties" (Herbst et. al. 2004, 47). Similarly, Volker Roschke laments how difficult it has been for the vision of a missional church to take root in German church soil:

> The vision for church planting—despite all attempts—could not be communicated adequately. In addition, the realization, how this vision translates into reality has been missing. Consequently, we in Germany have to continue teaching the A,B,Cs laboriously, when we want to explain what church planting even is. We are at the very beginning of a path of experience! (Barthels and Reppenhagen 2006, 106)

Especially illuminating is Roschke's reasoning for the state church's reluctance to become missional: "Rebuilding an existing church succeeds seldom or never! ... In our analysis of why church planting has gained with only great reluctance any kind of footing in Germany, it has also become clear that there is a culture of resistance to innovation in our church" (ibid.,113).

---

7   For detailed accounts and assessment of impact, see Herbst 2010.

Bernd Rother

Bernd Rother's published 2004 doctoral dissertation from the University Erlangen, Kirche in der Stadt (Church in the City), analyzed urban congregations that started within European state churches, yet developed separate worship services and infrastructure from that of the parish state church (Rother 2004). These congregations are called "Gemeinschaften" (fellowships), where several degrees of independence are recognized in the state church. Like Herbst, Rother examined the English Anglican Church Planting Movement as an exemplary backdrop to the continental scene; in addition, the Basileia Vineyard Church in Bern, Switzerland; the Communauté Saint Nicholas in Strasbourg, France; and the German church plants Oase in Giengen, Christliche Gemeinschaft in Fürth, and the Hosanna-Dienst Gemeinschaft in Heidelberg were examined. Every one of these church communities within the state churches experienced numerical growth. From Rother's descriptions, we may summarize the following common characteristics:

- all operate from the theological basis that every person is in need of a personal conversion to Jesus Christ, the church operating, consequently, with a missional ecclesiology;
- all appeared to have a charismatic emphasis;
- all were goal-oriented from the very beginning;
- all used the worship service as the main point of attraction;
- all were led by a strong and visionary leader, who served as the leading planter; and
- all oriented themselves to particular target groups.

Wilfried Härle, Jörg Augstein, Sibylle Rolf, Anja Siebert

In the study, *Wachsen gegen den Trend: Analysen von Gemeinden, mit denen es aufwärts geht [Growing against the Trend: Analysis of Churches that are Moving Forward]*, conducted between 2003 and 2006 within the German state church (Haerle et al. 2008), thirty-two growing congregations, all from the "green belt" of metropolitan regions, were analyzed.[8]

---

8   Originally 120 congregations were given the opportunity, but only 32 fulfilled the criteria required for analysis.

These churches reached mainly young families, the financially stable, and the well-educated. In effect, they reached their own kind. We list in summary the pertinent growth factors according to the study:

- A desire and intentionality of the congregation to open themselves to people estranged from the church, offering Alpha groups, basic Christianity groups, special evangelistic events, and special outreach worship services.
- The worship service (Gottesdienst) is the main attraction point and the heart of congregational life. It is characterized with vitality (Lebendigkeit), congregational participation (intensive Beteiligung), celebratory liturgy, the pastor's use of priestly garments, and the Lord's Supper in a prominent position and celebrated every Sunday.
- Next to the Gottesdienst, cell groups with trained leadership are the most important element.
- High priority is placed on pastoral care and counseling (Seelsorge). Having trained pastoral care workers changes the congregational climate, as members feel cared for.
- Lay involvement (Mitarbeiterschaft) and training was found to be a precondition for growth.

Sabine Schroeder, Konfessionslose Erreichen: Gemeindegründungen von freikirchlichen Initiativen seit der Wende 1989 in Ostdeutschland (Reaching the Non-Churched: Church Planting from Free Church Initiatives in East Germany since the Fall of the Berlin Wall in 1989)

Sabine Schroeder's 2007 doctoral dissertation for the University of Greifswald and Michael Herbst focused on the planting of Free Churches in East Germany during the first fourteen years after the fall of the wall (1989). She studied exactly 100 church plants over 14 denominations (Schroeder 2007, 167), covering the 6 East German provinces (ibid., 168). Of the 100 church plants, 49 are located in large cities, i.e. a population over 100,000; 40 in smaller cities with a population between 10,000 and 100,000; and 11 in villages.

We summarize Schroeder's findings as follows:

- Church growth initiatives between 1989 and 1993 grew on average by 33 people; church plants started between 1994 and 1998 by 22.5 persons; church plants begun between 1999 and 2002 by 12.75 people. Fifty percent of the total numerical growth came from conversion to Christ. Schroeder estimates this growth positively: "Even if the churches are small and only few unconfessing ["Konfessionslose" is a word used for those who confess no faith, i.e., stand outside the church] are reached, we find (in these statistics) a glimmer of hope that should not go unnoticed" (ibid., 219). The author is careful to point out that the conversions happened as non-Christians experienced congregational life over a longer process of time.
- More women were reached than men (ibid., 177).
- In most cases, the congregation did not operate with a "target group" (ibid., 178).
- Of the one hundred congregations, not a single one developed a concept or strategy to reach their particular part of Eastern Germany (ibid., 220).

From her analysis, Schroeder offers the following recommendations:

- Contextualization: Church planters must develop a concept that understands and deals with the unique East German situation and history.[9] The flip side of this contextualization principle is the refusal to import any foreign methods, no matter how well they worked elsewhere (ibid., 225). We must understand the sociological background of the people that are to be reached, and we must find a church planter whose sociological background is in harmony with the target culture (ibid., 216).
- Perseverance: Schroeder speaks of the need to be mentally and spiritually prepared for the long and arduous road. As statistics show, planting free churches in Eastern Germany is costly, with noticeable results coming only after significant time has elapsed and great amounts of energy have been expended (ibid., 217).
- Missional pro-activism: In his first year, the church planter should spend 50 percent of his time in evangelism, outreach, networking, and connecting with people (ibid., 227). The planter and his team

---

9   Ibid., 238: "Empirical analysis brought us to the conclusion that the East German mentality was being reflected in only few church plants" (author's translation).

must live where the target people are. Church planting must take the incarnational approach: "In this way, the people do not come to the church but the church goes to the people and is integrated into the town life" (ibid., 248).
- Vision and motivation: The vision and values of the church plant must be carefully considered and written down. The planter must be able to explain it and inspire others with it (ibid., 241).

Tentative Conclusions[10]

To our knowledge, there exists no study of church planting in Germany as it relates specifically to the eleven metropolitan regions. But the above analyses allow us to conclude that church plants will impact Germany's eleven metropolitan regions if:

- The Holy Spirit causes a deep change of heart in vast portions of the German population. German secularism and its love affair with its own brand of intellectualism, science, and philosophy calls for churches that operate out of an intelligent theological/apologetic base; emphasize the Bible's authority and reliability, Jesus' divinity, the Holy Spirit's experiential work in a person, the importance of the church (organism) and church structure (organization), and every person's personal need for conversion from sin and self to faith in Christ.
- They place great emphasis on the worship service as the central gathering point to attract people. German postmodernism is not anti-institutional. The role of the institution in German history and the German's historical respect for institutions translates into the Sunday worship service being a sign of a church's legitimacy. From the New Testament, we know that the church is much more than gatherings for worship. But in the mainstream German's mind, this is where it begins.
- They will create a worship experience that respects the German values of order, efficiency, and quietness, while allowing for flexibility and charismatic touches.
- They will put an emphasis on home groups. To be sure, hospitality is not a German virtue. It is part of the culture to remain formal and distant. In our assessment, home groups as the central gathering

---

10 Space does not allow for interaction with other recent studies. We only mention here the 360-page analysis by several practical theologians and sociologists in Block, J. and Mildenberger, I. (eds.), *Herausforderung: missionarischer Gottesdienst* (Leipzig: Evangelische Verlagsanstalt, 2007).

mode of the congregation will remain un-German for a long time to come. But it is a sign of the gospel's breakthrough power when Germans gather in one another's homes, offering hospitality, generosity, and informal relationships to one another.
- They will have strong leadership that charts the course for the church plant, without appearing "out front" or top-down. Strong authority is suspect in the German setting; consensus is the German way. But church planting that can develop into a movement needs transformational leadership that will simultaneously invest in and empower the laity.
- They will identify a target group, fashioning style, atmosphere, and teaching level around the group, while being open and welcoming to all people.
- They will be missional-incarnational in orientation. The church planter will be "out" making contacts, visiting, and networking at least 50 percent of his time. The church as a whole will be engaged in the community through actions of loving service and a friendly presence. It will not be involved in aggressive evangelistic efforts or showy approaches, yet it will find ways to abundantly sow the gospel into its surroundings through friendship evangelism, evangelistic groups, and special events.
- They will be multiplicational in their intention. This requires a careful strategy. The gospel will not multiply through family lines. Germans speak of valuing the family, but the horrendously low birth rate reveals that valuing family has not translated into a family culture, except among immigrants. Instead, individualism, work, health, and wellness are values that truly drive German society. Multiplication will happen through proactive daughter church planting.

Case Study:
The Beginnings of an Urban Church Planting Movement

What Happened?

Out of a church planting DNA that reflects the eight summary points listed above,[11] churches of various denominations have started to focus in recent years on Germany's metropolitan regions. Here is how it happened:

---

11 See the Appendix at the end of this chapter for the ten DNA factors of CMP.

Landau (Rhein-Neckar-Dreieck) is a university town of 40,000 people. In 1998, Harald Nikesch planted a church there, which would become a training ground for future church planters.

Two graduates of the Giessen School of Theology interned in North America for a year before moving to Berlin to start the Berlinprojekt in January 2005. Their carefully selected start-team consisted of eleven people and grew to forty by the fall of 2005, when the team decided to begin late-afternoon worship services.

In October 2005, I began to teach practical theology (including church planting as well as urban theology and ministry) at the Giessen School of Theology and began coaching recent graduates and several seminary students in planting Frankfurt CityChurch. In January 2006, we began biweekly Sunday evening gatherings in Frankfurt.

In the spring of 2006, another graduate of the seminary approached me with the request to be mentored in urban church planting. Sensing this might be the beginning of a work of God, I developed a mentoring strategy, dividing the process into three phases: Phase 1 would be group sessions to study the first eight chapters of the *Redeemer Church Planter Manual*, written in 2002 by Allan Thompson and Tim Keller. This would be followed by Phase 2, an internship in a church representing the "DNA." During Phase 2, the intern would experience all necessary church planter practices such as networking, leading discovery groups, developing relationships with non-Christians, preaching, etc., and meet with his mentor to cover theological, apologetic, homiletic, and leadership principles and study the rest of the church planter manual. Phase 3 would be the actual church planting project, with a mentor accompanying in the first two years. This City Mentoring Program (CMP) was offered to several free church denominations.

The mentoring process continued to develop: in the fall of 2006, we started regular Phase 1 groups in our home, all of which have ranged from eight to twenty-one participants. Over the next year, some of these initial "mentorees" began internships in Landau, Berlinprojekt, and Frankfurt CityChurch, and have "graduated" to plant additional churches.

Additional existing churches have joined the City Mentoring Program with a commitment to the ten DNA factors and the desire to train interns for daughter church planting, including churches in Bremen, Neubrandenburg, Berlin, and Ruhr-Stadt.

In late 2010, I began encouraging seminary students to join me in planting Church for All Nations (Frankfurt-Rhein-Main), a multicultural, multilingual church plant. This church plant has the goals of 1) being part of the state church; 2) bringing multiethnic, self-supported missionary-pastors who wish to reach their people groups on staff;[12] 3) focusing missional and diaconal efforts on the plight of the immigrants; and 4) planting at least nine anchor churches throughout the metropolitan region.

Two major components of CMP have enriched the mentoring process:

- The development of an assessment center for church planters, enabling us to measure giftedness and suitability for church planting, conduct personality profiling, and evaluate spiritual-emotional-marital maturity.
- The development of the European Institute for Church Planting & Church Growth (EICC), offering a fifteen-course curriculum of weekend courses dealing with issues surrounding urban church planting. Internet course offerings, research, and publications will round out the work of this department of the City Mentoring Program.

Summary

- Seventeen churches and current church plants shaped themselves around a certain philosophy of ministry.[13] These 17 churches cover 6 of the 11 eleven metro regions.
- The metropolitan regions where CMP has no presence to date are München,[14] Nürnberg, Sachsendreieck, Hannover-Braunschweig-Wolfsburg, and Stuttgart.
- With the exception of 4 recent start-ups (Frankfurt-Bornheim, Church for All Nations Frankfurt-Rhein-Main, Berlin-Kreuzberg, Düsseldorf), the other 13 of these 17 churches report the following picture:
    - Number of people currently attending worship service, including children: 1,475
    - Number of those currently attending who are non-Christians: 245

---

12   Similar to the hybrid method used in France; see Baker 2009.
13   CMP has been working with churches in Austria, where especially in Innsbruck numerous conversions are happening in several churches. This is not reflected in these statistics. Most recently, CMP has been invited to give guidance and teaching to missionaries and pastors in France.
14   A church plant is scheduled for 2012, led by Steffen Müller.

- Number of disillusioned Christians who made their way back to the church: 413
- Number of conversions since beginning the churches: 265
- Number of baptisms since beginning the churches: 261

An Indigenous, Grassroots Movement

The three-phase program offers, in our assessment, the following strengths:

- Through Phase 1 groups, people are given an opportunity to investigate the theory of urban church planting. Having the Redeemer Church Planter Manual translated into German in the past year has greatly increased the viability of these groups.
- CMP is connecting with additional theological institutions. We believe this is the key to more missional church planters in Germany. Recruiting, teaching, and motivating students through Phase 1 groups on or near campuses are ways to call more workers into the harvest.
- The CMP assessment program provides qualified church planters with helpful and needed self-knowledge and prevents unqualified couples from becoming casualties of church planting.
- The assessed and approved mentorees raise their financial support from their circles of friends and congregations. The German church mentality is not one of sending and supporting Germans to go to German cities to plant missional churches. CMP has encouraged its mentorees to seek prayer and financial support from German sources, in order to awaken in the German church a missional zeal for Germany's cities. This has proven successful.
- Through donations to CMP, we are able to grant many interns some financial support. The conditions are that in Phase 3—regardless of denomination—they plant churches with the DNA, that the church plants give 1 percent of their budgets back to CMP for the support of future church plants, and that the church planters be willing to mentor interns and participate in CMP's ongoing mentoring seminars.
- The mentorees move to CMP church plants for Phase 2 at no cost to the church plants, while benefiting the church plant with their gifts and benefiting from the experience they gain in the church plant. An addition, we encourage each intern to take (free of charge) at least ten courses in the EICC.

- When the interns graduate from Phase 2, the church plants in which they interned commission to plant their daughter churches (Phase 3). This celebration helps infuse into the sending church the DNA of multiplication.[15]
- A mentor works and walks with the mentoree in each of the phases. This allows experience, perspective, and wisdom to accompany the intern/church planter.

Conclusion

Is a new day dawning in the old country of Germany? We think it is too early to tell if we are truly dealing with the beginnings of a church planting movement "German style." But our study of urban trends in Germany and our analysis of the research done in church planting in German state and free churches suggest we may be on the brink of a new day and that we are called to fan the Spirit's flame. Therefore:

We need to emphasize church planting movements of many denominations in the "Big 4" metropolitan regions, as these have the greatest influence on the nation as a whole.

We need to be intentional in planting movement churches in those metropolitan regions where no churches with the CMP DNA exist.

CMP needs to become a viable partner with all evangelical theological institutions in Germany, offering EICC courses and Phase 1 groups with mentors in place at those institutions.

A proactive recruiting and training of mentors is crucial to the spread of this "movement."

Appendix

The ten DNA factors of CMP

1. *Gospel-driven:* Given Germany's past Lutheran pietism and present atheistic secularism, it is crucial that we begin here. To be a Christian means identifying yourself not by church affiliation, cultural background, or self-righteous moralism, but by the gospel of Jesus.

---

15   For example, the *Berlinprojekt* considers supportively the *Hamburgprojekt* as its daughter church, like Frankfurt CityChurch considers Kirche für Potsdam as its daughter church.

2. *Reformational-theological:* the same theological emphases of the first Reformation will lead to a second reformation: sola scriptura, sola gratia, sola fide, sola Christi, soli deo gloria. An intelligent commitment to and a non-authoritarian handling of a Christ-centered theology, the preaching of God's Word as front and center of the church, a God-centerd worship service as the attractional gathering point, and the frequent celebration of the Lord's Supper. A reclaiming of culture to the glory of God's holiness, a re-sacralizing and de-secularizing of all things, is part of the church's reformational mission.
3. *Prayer-driven but intentional in planning:* We do not initiate anything without prayer for God's leading, but we do not move on anything without vision, goal-setting, and strategic planning.
4. *City-centered:* We focus on the eleven metropolitan regions of the nation, spreading the gospel in word and deed.
5. *Contextualized:* Each church's culture and methodology must reflect the culture and mentality of the target group.
6. *Multi-cultural:* Following Christ, we value every nationality and social background and seek racial reconciliation in our congregations, including integration of Germans with all ethnic groups.
7. *Multiplying:* Each church is part of an indigenous multiplication movement from its city ring to the green belt.
8. *Missional:* We are incarnational-"attractional." As we build up Christians in obedient, faithful, and persevering love for Jesus, we reach out and gather non-Christians into the life of the church.
9. *Decentralized into cell groups:* Cell groups throughout the city, led by trained believers, are the basic units of the church.
10. *Transdenominational:* Every church functions supportively toward other churches, networks, and denominations, thereby expressing the unity of the body of Christ to the city.

References

Baker, S. (Ed.). (2009). *Globalization and its effects on urban ministry in the 21st century*. Pasadena, CA: William Carey Library.

Barthels, M., & Reppenhagen, M. (Eds.). (2006). *Gemeindepflanzung–ein Modell für die Kirche der Zukunft? [Church Planting—A model for the church of the future?]* Neukirchen: Neukirchener Verlag.

Bundesamt für Migration und Flüchtlinge [Government Office for Migration and Asylum-Seekers]. Information retrieved from www.bamf.de.

Garrison, D. (2004). *Church planting movements: How God is redeeming a lost world.* Midlothian, VA: WIGTake Resources.

Härle, W., Augstein, J., Rolf, S., & Siebert, A. (2008). *Wachsen gegen den Trend: Analysen von Gemeinden, mit denen es aufwärts geht [Growing against the trend: Analysis of churches in which it is moving forward].* Leipzig: Evangelische Verlagsanstalt GmbH.

Herbst, M. (2010). *Missionarischer Gemeindeaufbau in der Volkskirche [Missional church renewal in the state church].* Neukirchen-Vluyn: Neukirchener Verlag.

Herbst, M., Ohlemacher, J., & Zimmermann, J. (2005). *Missionarische Perspektiven für eine Kirche der Zukunft [Missional perspectives for a church of the future].* Neukirchen: Neukirchener Verlag.

Mandryk, J. (2010). *Operation world.* Colorado Springs, CO: Biblica Publishing.

Geschäftsstelle des IKM. (2010). Regionales Monitoring 2010: Daten und Karten zu den Europäischen Metropolregionen in Deutschland [Regional Monitoring 2010: Information and Maps for the European Metropolitan Regions of Germany]. Verband Region Rhein-Neckar. Retrieved from http://www.region-frankfurt.de/media/custom/1169_3593_1.PDF?1291884601.

Reppenhagen, M., & Herbst, M. (Eds.). (2008). *Kirche in der Postmoderne [Church in Postmodernity].* Neukirchen: Neukirchener Verlag.

Rother, B. (2005). *Kirche in der Stadt: Herausbildung und Chancen von Urbanen Profilgemeinschaften [Church in the city: Development and opportunities in urban fellowships].* Neukirchen: Neukirchener Verlag.

Sarrazin, T. (2010). Deutschland Schafft Sich Ab: wie wir unser Land aufs Spiel setze [Germany is self-destructing: How we're playing with our destiny]. Deutsche Verlags-Anstalt.

Schroeder, S. (2007). *Konfessionslose Erreichen: Gemeindegründungen von freikirchlichen Initiativen seit der Wende 1989 in Ostdeutschland [Reaching the unchurched: Church planting from free church initiatives since the fall of the Wall 1989 in East Germany].* Neukirchen-Vluyn: Neukirchener.

Stadt Frankfurt am Main. Amt für Multikulturelle Angelengenheiten. (2009). *20 Jahre AmkA: 1989–2009 Amt für Multikulturelle Angelegenheiten.* Frankfurt: Central-Druck, Heusenstamm.

Islam in Urban America: Developing Strategy to Reach Diaspora Muslims through the Local Church

Mark Hausfeld
mh1focus@gmail.com

Introduction

The purpose of this essay is to reflect on one ministry and its efforts to touch the lives of *diaspora* Muslims from Pakistan and India. The missional helix process will be the template to assist a case study reflection on South Asian Friendship Center's (SAFC) efforts to reach diaspora Muslims in the urban setting of the West Rogers Park neighborhood in Chicago. From SAFC's example, the local church can apprehend the value that theological foundation, historical perspective, and cultural analysis all have on strategic formation and, ultimately, on the mission to reach diaspora Muslims in America with the gospel of Jesus Christ.

SAFC was birthed in prayer meetings. For thirteen years, a group of diaspora Indian believers sought God for Chicago's burgeoning community of South Asian immigrants who were settling in this West Rogers Park neighborhood. Dr. Samuel Naaman, cofounder of SAFC, said "their prayers brought the pieces of SAFC together" (Interview with author, January 11, 2008). He shared that others joined this diaspora group's prayer effort; *Women's Aglow*, the *Prayer Furnace*, Moody Bible Institute, various city and suburban churches, as well as numerous individuals strategically and consistently prayer-walked the West Rogers Park neighborhood. Dr. Naaman recalls that "SAFC began with prayer penetration into the Muslim community" (ibid.). This humble, Spirit-led beginning in 1997 effectively anchored the SAFC in the market and residential heart of the West Rogers Park neighborhood. The "Center," as it is referred to by those who minister there, claims the following mission statement:

> The South Asian Friendship Center is a bookstore, *chai* (tea) and Internet cafe and welcoming space where tutoring, ESL, youth and kids clubs, women's lunches, cricket World Cup showings, citizenship classes and fellowship happen. We extend our hand in friendship to the Devon community in the name of the Lord Jesus Christ, and we love people of all ethnicities and creeds. ("South Asian Friendship Center," n.d.)

Three of SAFC's staff are native-born South Asians. Dr. Samuel Naaman and Pastor Faisal were born and raised in Pakistan and immigrated to the States. Urdu is their first language, but they are completely fluent in English as well. Dave Echols and his wife, Kathy, were missionaries in Pakistan twelve years before coming to SAFC, so they too are fluent in Urdu and very familiar with Pakistani culture. This brilliant staff is also comprised of men and women who have backgrounds at Moody Bible Institute, Trinity University, and Trinity Evangelical Divinity School. Mark Engle, director of SAFC, is a former businessman who became a missionary to South Asians in West Rogers Park. These full-time missionaries have said that knowing the language and culture certainly helps one relate to the Muslim community, but not being fluent speakers of the target community's language must not hinder the local church's determination to reach diaspora Muslims in America. If we purpose to receive them like they receive us in our foreign mission endeavors, we will accomplish much for the kingdom among them here.

The SAFC is a glocal mission, a ministry paradigm that incorporates local and global target and tactic. Its basis is that mission is to be done at home and abroad, and the strategies most effective abroad are also the most effective in local contexts. SAFC operates within this glocal paradigm to touch the percentage of Chicagoland's South Asian diaspora Muslim population living in their own neighborhood, a number estimated to hover at 400,000 (Samuel Naaman, interview with author, January 11, 2008). They recognize that if this diaspora population, now reaching its fifth decade of rapid rootedness in American urban centers, is going to be reached for Christ, the established, ubiquitous American church must welcome them with missional intent and strategy. The challenge remains that for the most part, "the amazing growth of Islam in North America during the last few decades has gone largely unnoticed by the evangelical church. Many people still think that mission is only done overseas, and that unreached people do not live here in North America" (McDowell and Zaka, 1999). Biblically, missions is not dichotomized into "home" and "world" definitions. People are unreached if they do not have an adequate witness of the gospel (Rom 10:14–15) no matter who they are or where they live. Prior to his ascension, Jesus said, "you will be my witnesses in Jerusalem, and in all Judea and Samaria, and to the ends of the earth" (Acts 1:8b). With the "ends of the earth" having planted themselves in our own communities, the church now has ample opportunity and every responsibility to reach hundreds of thousands of diaspora Muslims who may otherwise never be exposed to the gospel. This does not preclude Christ's call to foreign lands, but it extends the call to a glocalized context.

When, at his ascension, Jesus left his disciples with these inspired words, the gospel was nestled in Palestine and the majority of believers were Jewish converts. They were primarily located in a very urban Jerusalem. Jesus needed his disciples and apostles to understand the geographic trajectory his gospel would take through them. He made them world ambassadors, and their mission was to share his good news with everyone, everywhere.

From its early days, America's immigration laws have facilitated cross-cultural missions. In a visit to Stockholm, Sweden, I visited the Philadelphia Church, which was responsible for the planting of numerous American East Coast congregations at the turn of the nineteenth century. Mission comes full circle when the planted church plants churches, and the church in America has been a missions sending body from its early beginnings. The Assemblies of God started as a missions sending organization. As a denomination, we have always prioritized mission outreach, and as God would have it, we have arrived at a place where missions to the unreached can take place among them in their home countries and in our own.

Our call to missions in America entered a new dimension in the twentieth century with the influx of what was to us a new group of immigrants. President Lyndon B. Johnson's signing of the 1965 Immigration Law literally changed the face of America (Ludden, 2006) and what our own Jerusalem would look like. Previous immigration had favored northern and southern Europeans. The 1965 Immigration Law opened the ports of the United States to immigrants from Asia and the Middle

East. "Today, 14 percent of legal immigrants to the U.S. each year are Muslims" (McDowell and Zaka, 1999). Most of America's Muslim population increase is settling in the cities. Four-fifths of all mosques are located in metropolitan (urban or suburban) areas, most often city neighborhoods (Bagby, Perl, and Froehle, 2001). "They [diaspora Muslims] expect to continue their religious commitments here and even work to expand their spiritual movements. But, in the United States, they live in neighborhoods with many Christian families, something that would not be the case in their home countries" (Pocock and Henriques, 2002). Today, our urban Jerusalems are the dwelling places of Muslims who have come from the "ends of the earth." Part of the local church's challenge to reach them is her need to become acquainted with their places of origin, which, historically, is deeply rooted in the context of Islam's urban origins.

Islam's Urban Ethos: Background Insights for the Local Church

The Prophet Mohammad was the world's first Muslim, and he indicated such in the Qur'an, Sura 6:14:

> Say: "Shall I take for my protector any other God, the Maker of the heavens and the earth? And He it is that feedeth but is not fed." Say: "Nay! But I am commanded to be the first of those who bow to God, and be not thou of the company of those who join gods with God." (Qur'an 6:14)

This apostle of Islam was not born in a backwater, barren place in the deserts of Arabia. He was born in AD 570 in the city of Mecca, Arabia's urban commercial trading hub and "stopping place for merchants and businessmen of all races, religions, and countries. In general, it was open to the world" (Watt 1953). In this Meccan context, Mohammed worked as a merchant and traveled with trading caravans to other cities of the Arabian Peninsula. From his youth, he was known for his contemplative nature (McCurry 2001), and at age forty (AD 610), he had an ecstatic experience that caused him to believe he was possessed by a *jinn* (Arabic for evil spirit). His wife Khadijah and her Christian relative persuaded him that his revelations came from *Allah* (Arabic for God) through the angel Gabriel. For three years, he kept the revelations relatively secret, but in AD 613 Mohammed felt he received the command to begin public preaching. He preached for six years without being seriously challenged (ibid., 41). His emphasis on the oneness of Allah countered Mecca's polytheistic religious context and societies. Eventually, this hindered the economies of those who profited from the polytheistic pilgrims who traveled to Mecca to worship the gods and spend their money while there. A power struggle ensued, and the angry Quraysh ruling elders decided to assassinate the prophet (also a native of the Quraysh tribe). Warned by friends that his life was in danger, Mohammed accepted "the invitation to serve as a leader-arbitrator to the warring Arab tribes in the city of Yathrib, later called Medina, about two hundred miles to the north of Mecca" (Barton 1918).

Not only was Mohammed the first Muslim, but with his family and followers, the prophet became a member of the first diaspora community of Muslims. They were pushed out of Mecca under duress and, at the same time, were pulled to Medina to take advantage of business and political opportunities. Medina became the launching pad of Islam as Mohammed's people and business skills helped him to gain ascendancy among the warring tribes he mediated. He successfully united them as an Islamic *ummah* (Arabic for community) and led them to challenge the Meccans. In AD 630, a very powerful Mohammed led an army of 10,000 men to Mecca, where he gained control without a fight. By the time of his death in AD 632, Islam had spread to most of the Arabian Peninsula. By AD 633, Islamic armies had conquered Jerusalem, Damascus, and Antioch where nearly 600 years earlier, disciples of Jesus Christ were first called "Christians" (Acts 11:26b). By AD 641, disciples of Islam's prophet controlled Cairo and Alexandria. The decades that followed saw the following urban centers fall to the rule of Islam: Tripoli (Libya) by AD 644; Baghdad (Iraq) and Herat (Afghanistan) by AD 646; Salamis (the hometown of Barnabas) and Paphos (Cyprus) by AD 650; and Ordoba, Granada (Spain) and Bukhara (Uzbekistan) by AD 750. In just over one hundred years after Mohammed's death, the Islamic Empire had spread from the Arabian Peninsula to the modern nations of Pakistan to the east and Spain to the west. The major cities of the conquest became financial resources and launching points for further conquests in the name of Allah and the "apostle of Islam." From Islam's inception, the religion has had an urban ethos that is mirrored today in Muslim and non-Muslim cities around the world.

Since Islam's first-century urban advances in the region, "North Africa and the Middle East have been a Muslim world ... and that world has been predominately urban" (Conn and Ortiz 2001). Currently, the largest populations of Muslim people groups live outside the Middle East and North Africa. In Central Eurasia, there are eleven cities of over one million people ("The 100 Gateway Cities," 1999). In Bangladesh and India, there are cities that host tens of millions of Muslims (ibid.). Indonesia, a nation with the largest Muslim population in the world, hosts four cities with over one million people on the island of Java alone (Cities and Urban Areas 2002). A staggering "51 of the 100 'gateway cities' [in] the 10/40 window are predominantly Muslim" (Bethel University Heart and Mind).

Diaspora Muslims with this predominant urban ethos are immigrating to the United States. The ports of entry are urban neighborhoods and communities like Los Angeles, Houston, New York, and Chicago. This study focuses on one Chicago neighborhood's Muslim population and the local church's efforts to reach them with the gospel. Vital to this local church's ability to strategize for the task of Muslim outreach is an understanding of the foundation the church has for mission to Muslims in the city.

Theological Foundation: An Urban Guide to Reach Urban Muslims

There is a broad tendency for people to perceive the Bible as text set primarily in rural or pastoral settings. The Scriptures begin in a garden (Gen 2:8), and images forged by the telling of the parables, shepherd, harvest, and fisherman stories dominate our perception of the setting in which most of Scripture takes place. Artistic renditions of village scenes look much like their rendition of urban scenes, and with our mind's eye we see the whole of Scripture as a book written against an often rural or pastoral setting. The truth is that the context of Scripture is largely urban.

The same book that begins in a garden setting quickly moves toward an urban one with the mention of a city named Enoch in Genesis 4:17. It ends powerfully with reference to the New Jerusalem in Revelation 22:3, a city whose builder is God himself (Rev 21:2). Between the first pages of Genesis and the final pages of Revelation, the basic Hebrew and Greek words for city in the Bible are "mentioned some 1,200 times and refer to 119 different cities" (Bakke 1987). After Cain's naming of Scripture's first city, the Bible's pages turn time and again on the hinges of the rise and fall of great cities like the pompous Babel (Babylon) who sought to build a great city and a tower to reach heaven (Gen 11:1–9). Nineveh of Assyria numbered at least 120,000 people (Jonah 4:11). Old Testament cities like Jerusalem of Israel,

Babylonia of Babylon, and Susa of Persia were the hubs of empires. These bastions of power were also population centers that drew people to them both voluntarily and, as were Judah's and Israel's respective diaspora experiences, involuntarily.

The urban world of the Bible extends to the New Testament (Bakke 1987). The Gospels are rarely perceived to be urban, but Matthew and Mark write that Jesus went about all the cities and villages of Galilee (Matt 9:35–11:1; Mark 6:6, 56). Some may think that Jesus entered urban ministry from the rural surroundings of Nazareth. However, Jesus may have been more experientially prepared for city settings than previously thought because of Nazareth's proximity (four miles north) to Sepphoris, the regional capital of Galilee. James F. Strange, of the University of South Florida, writes:

> Flavius Josephus described the rebuilt Sepphoris as the "ornament of all Galilee," which suggests that this small city was beautifully laid out and rebuilt under Herod Antipas. Josephus also claims that Sepphoris was the "strongest city in Galilee," an observation of a military man and, therefore, to be taken seriously. Excavations in Sepphoris tend to confirm these lofty words of Josephus. Sepphoris was laid out in a grid or blocks with streets paved with crushed limestone. A Roman theater stood partially cut into the hillside. Citizens of Sepphoris could retire to the theatre for an evening's entertainment, probably of mimes, light comedy, or other fashionable amusements. Ordinary residences and elegant mansions stood here and there within the city blocks. Since Sepphoris was built on a hill, it was visible for miles. This may be the city that Jesus spoke of when he said, "A city set on a hill cannot be hidden." (Strange 2001)

Richard A. Batey's published research, *Jesus and the Forgotten City: New Light on Sepphoris and the Urban World of Jesus,* opens with a foreword by Paul Maier. Here, Maier states that Batey's research "pushes beyond the rural-redeemer image to the city-savior image of Jesus as well" (Strange 2001). Maier writes:

> The city not only edged dramatically into Jesus' life and ministry but subsequently became central to the future expansion of Christianity. It was from such metropolises as Antioch, Alexandria, Ephesus, Athens, Corinth, and Rome that the gospel was carried to the

countryside, where the rural sorts—the *pagani* (hence the term *pagan)*—were the last to convert. This Christianity which began in hamlets like Bethlehem and Nazareth in the person of Jesus finally came full circle through the mediation of urban culture. (Batey 1991)

The urban ethos of the New Testament apostolic efforts began with Jesus' ministry, but the Apostle Paul is the ultimate example of an urban missionary. The book of Acts begins in the monotheistic and fundamentalist urban environment of Jerusalem (Acts 1:4) and ends in the pluralistic and polytheistic city of Rome (Acts 28:30). The text gloriously relates the work of the Holy Spirit as it manifests itself through the urban church. The Word of God and the Spirit of Jesus collaborate with an urban fellowship of believers in Acts to demonstrate theology in action or what the early twentieth-century Pentecostals termed "Orthodoxy set on fire!" It is written, "the Jesus movement quickly spread to the Greco-Roman cities, especially to those of the eastern Hellenic end of the empire" (Stark 2006).

The centrality of the message of the person and work of Christ did not change in either context, whether from the lips of Peter in Jerusalem or of Paul in Rome. Paul's ministry was characterized by his visitation as a missionary to establish, nurture, and encourage the urban church. His epistles of the New Testament are titled today by the names of the urban centers he visited. The Bible, and particularly the context found therein for the message and methods of the New Testament church, are urban. The New Testament authors and practitioners were also, in many respects, diaspora Jews and Gentiles immigrating to the cities, either pushed as slaves or pulled by opportunity. The missiology that develops from the New Testament is ambitiously urban because "if the goal is to make disciples of all nations, missionaries need to go where there are many potential converts, which is precisely what Paul did. His missionary journeys took him to major cities such as Antioch, Corinth, and Athens, with only occasional visits to smaller communities such as Iconium and Laodicea. No mention is made of him preaching in the countryside" (Stark 2006).

This theological foundation is vital for evangelistic outreach to diaspora South Asian Muslims in Chicago's West Rogers Park neighborhood. Its theological pylons are the moorings for contemporary urban missiology. "This principle seems clear: the further one goes into the avant-garde frontier of creative ministry, the more important it becomes that we be deeply rooted in the biblical, theological and historical tradition. We need deep roots to survive in urban ministry" (Bakke 1997). South Asian Friendship Center's missionaries and staff hold fast to this conviction by making it the foundational impetus for what they aspire to accomplish, and how they accomplish it. Interviews with at least three staff members uncovered yet another foundational principal that cannot be disregarded. Each person interviewed passionately referred to Acts 17:26–27 (NIV) when he spoke of the mission's scriptural basis for ministry. The scripture follows:

> From one man he made every nation of men, that they should inhabit the whole earth; and he determined the times set for them and the exact places where they should live. God did this so that men would seek him and perhaps reach out for him and find him, though he is not far from each of us.

David Echols, former missionary to Pakistan, cofounder of and missionary with SAFC expresses it this way:

> The uttermost parts of the earth are here. Our calling is to people, not geography. Muslims are here by God's strategy and plan. They come to the city for work, school and opportunities to better their lives. Acts 17:26–27 is key to the center (SAFC). This is God's call. He is bringing them to us to reach them by proclaiming the message of Romans 10:14–15, "How, then, can they call on the one they have not believed in? And how can they believe in the one of whom they have not heard? And how can they hear without someone preaching to them (v.14)? And how can they preach unless they are sent? As it is written, '"How beautiful are the feet of those who bring good news!'" (Interview with author, January 11, 2008)

Dr. Samuel Naaman, cofounder of SAFC, echoes David Echols' conviction: "Muslims are moving to America and this is not by accident. This is God's doing, not man's" (Samuel Naaman, interview with author, January 11, 2008). In our conversation, he also went on to quote Acts 17:26–27 as SAFC's response to reach Muslims at this port of entry in Chicago for South Asian Muslim peoples. It is pivotal to everything Center-related: the call, the vision, and the mission it moves them to accomplish.

Historical Perspective:
The West Rogers Park Neighborhood in Transition

West Rogers Park's fascinating history is directly relevant to the current venues for ministry, and was a common thread in conversations I had with SAFC staff members. Its first inhabitants were the Pottawatomie Indians, a Native American tribe that occupied that part of what today is an urban metropolis (West Rogers Park). In the 1830s Irishmen, Englishmen, Germans, Luxembourgers, and several other immigrant groups settled the area. Philip Rogers was among those first settlers. He initiated trade with the Pottawatomie and eventually purchased 1,600 acres of land from the US government. The area became known as West Ridge in 1890 and was annexed to Chicago on April 4, 1893.

Since those early years, immigrants have invested their vitality and vision resulting in a community whose educational and cultural institutions, places of worship, and business and community organizations reflect fascinating ancestry and vast diversity. Today, West Rogers Park is home to the largest concentration of Jews in Chicago, many of whom are of Russian and Polish decent. Street signs are in Hebrew; stores and businesses identify themselves in Russian and Polish. Their numbers have declined since the l960s, when Jews comprised more than two-thirds of the total population, but to date West Rogers Park remains the city's greatest access to all things Jewish. More than twenty synagogues serve the area, the majority of which are Orthodox or Traditional. There are kosher butchers, bakers, restaurants, and food markets which carry a variety of Jewish products. Devon Avenue has remained the main street of West Rogers Park for over a century. For many years, it was the central Jewish marketplace. In recent years, other ethnic groups have moved into the area, establishing their own shopping districts on Devon. Nevertheless, its Jewish heritage immortalizes itself in the remaining synagogues, signage, and Jewish places of business (Rosen 1999). In spite of the fact that its pace of growth has decreased after the 1960s, West Rogers Park (West Ridge) has continued to be a popular destination for many ethnic groups, and today its commercial centers cater to Jews, Middle Easterners, Indians, Pakistanis, and Koreans. The 2000 census recorded that 73,199 people resided in West Rogers Park, of which approximately 46 percent were not native born (Mooney-Melvin, 2005). Currently, the growth of the Asian communities from Pakistan, Bangladesh (to a lesser degree), and India is dramatically evident on the Devon Avenue trek. Within three blocks, stores and restaurants post English signs accompanied with scripts of languages in Urdu (Pakistan and Northern India), Sanskrit (India), Dari (Afghanistan), Cyrillic (Russia), and Mkhedruli (Georgia).

A simple walk down present-day Devon Avenue transposes a person to another world. The faces of the elderly are ethnically European; they partner with area architecture to somewhat nostalgically testify to the neighborhood's ancestry which literally originated against European backdrops of the Thames, Rhine, Rhone, Po, and Danube rivers. However, in contrast to this European setting, the sights, sounds, and smells that colorfully and pungently attack the senses decry that this neighborhood is not European anymore. The faces are South Asian, and they are mostly young. The businesses are owned and operated primarily by ethnic Pakistanis and Indians. Census demographic statistics indicate that as of the early nineties Asians alone have the highest and fastest population growth rates in this community (Mooney-Melvin 2005). The South Asian Friendship Center (SAFC) finds itself strategically located to reach this unreached diaspora populace who have made and increasingly continue to make this neighborhood their home.

Cultural Analysis: Incarnational Outreach

Change has characterized the neighborhood of West Rogers Park since it was first settled. The period of the settler is gone; however, South Asian immigrants continue to make this neighborhood their home in a context broadly influenced by its early ethnic beginnings. Those beginnings characterized the forming of a nation at large, and they established a certain set of core values that immigrants today still confront when they set foot on American soil. They enter an American cultural ethos that may challenge their individual, communal, and societal values. Dr. Samuel Huntington writes:

> America's core culture has been and, at the moment, is still primarily the culture of the seventeenth- and eighteenth-century settlers who founded American society. The central elements of the culture can be defined in a variety of ways but include the Christian religion, Protestant values and moralism, a work ethic, the English language, British traditions of law, justice, and the limits of government power, and a legacy of European art, literature, philosophy, and music. Out

> of this culture the settlers developed in the eighteenth and nineteenth centuries the American creed with its principles of liberty, equality, individualism, representative government, and private property. Subsequent generations of immigrants were assimilated into the culture of the founding settlers and contributed to and modified it. But they did not change it fundamentally. This is because, at least until the late twentieth century, it was Anglo-Protestant culture and the political liberties and economic opportunities it produced that attracted them to America. (Huntington 2005)

The core cultural ethos of America, Huntington discusses, is in part what pulls the diaspora Muslim from India and Pakistan to West Rogers Park in the city of Chicago. America's pull and often the South Asian Muslim's native push toward diaspora life in the United States, in the very least, represents increased opportunity and new civil freedoms. However, it does not negate the negotiating a diaspora Muslim might find himself doing to succeed in an indisputably Western culture that is deeply rooted in Anglo-Protestant values. Part of what draws him to West Rogers Park is the security offered him by the neighborhood's existing and growing South Asian context. It is also part of what offers missional Christians the greatest venue for outreach to large numbers of people who have never had an adequate witness of the gospel. Dave Echols of the SAFC observes the following:

> This community (West Rogers Park) is a microcosm of South Asia (India and Pakistan). All that is culturally important is located here. You have Muslim culture most accessible through the Mosque. The Mosque acts as immediate and close contact to religion which reflects cultural values. When they first come here, they shy away from the Mosque because they want to make the most of the freedoms they do not have in their country of origin. However, when they are hurt in the majority culture, and/or do not relate to the host culture, they go to the Mosque. They must have community and a sense of belonging whether they like it or not. (Interview with author, January 11, 2008)

When the local church understands the Muslim's reliance on community, it is able to embrace great opportunity to touch the lives of diaspora Muslims who attempt to settle in local neighborhoods. Our ability to place ourselves where we might become the end of a diaspora Muslim's search for a place and acceptance might be compromised if we expect him to conform to our ways without struggle or sacrifice. Furthermore, we have the opportunity to be the answer to that struggle, and to replace the void left by sacrifice and change.

The South Asian Friendship Center firmly grasps this, and begins its outreach by positioning itself in the heart of this growing Muslim neighborhood. It calls itself a friendship center and sees itself as just that—a place where the gift of hospitality and intentional friendship outreach foster relationships that become conduits for the love of Christ among people who experience it for the first time.

Friendship Center outreach values the culture of Muslims as much as it values its own Western, Anglo-Protestant culture. Workers there appreciate the round-the-clock conflict diaspora Muslims face and they attempt to bridge the divide between who they have been in their own countries and who they might become in this new one. They have learned the essence of Islamic faith and culture so they can anticipate need and know how to meet it in culturally acceptable ways. They understand the value of community and honor, and they make it their goal to be the community the Muslim might return to when he faces need, whether it be for material help, cultural acclimation, or personal companionship. They are a place where the light never dims, and in everything they do, they point seekers to the way of the cross.

It is true that the events of 9/11 have compounded outreach to Muslims in American cities. It has created an atmosphere of mutual distrust which has set the church itself on its heels for the past seven years. "A majority of Muslim Americans (53 percent) say it has become more difficult to be a Muslim in the U.S. since the September 11 terror attacks. Most believe that the government singles out Muslims for increased surveillance and monitoring" (Salmans 2007). Dr. Wafaa Kaf, assistant professor of audiology at Missouri State University, affirms that "it is very difficult for Muslims in America due to profiling. There is freedom, but some has been taken" (interview with author, December 6, 2007). As the church, it is not our goal to make it easier for Muslims to be Muslims in America, but if we are going to make it easier for Muslims to become followers of Christ in America, we have to know and love the Muslim first not for what he represents, but for who he is and can become in Christ. It means having the courage to view 9/11 and current events in Afghanistan and Iraq through a slightly different lens. Regardless of how horrific the terror is, it has served to wake us up to the hazard we face if we fail to see Muslims as people

Jesus loved enough to give his life for, just as he gave his life for those of us who have already followed him.

I have said that the staff of SAFC values the culture of Muslims as much as it values its own. In this regard, they are a paradigm of biblical truth that not only calls us to reach America's diaspora Muslims with the gospel, but makes us responsible for them, whether 9/11 had taken place or not. If, as the church, we are able to believe that Muslim culture is as important as ours, we will be able to take on the responsibility for our brothers' culture (Woodley). It is what Christ did for us when "the Word became flesh and made his dwelling among us" (John 1:14). Jesus' incarnation was his intentional cross-cultural effort to understand and live among a people whose culture was the antithesis of heaven's. His journey took him to his death, which in turn became our venue for redemption—and that was Christ's supreme equalizing moment. The same sacrifice that saved me was intended for my Muslim brother. How could I not become what he needs to make that happen? It is the great challenge to the local church: Christ-like, cross-cultural self-abandonment for the sake of lost souls. The real test will be our willingness to do it. The SAFC provides an effective model for cross-cultural outreach-based biblical self-abandonment and complete regard for our brother's culture.

Strategic Formations for Mission

The South Asian Friendship Center bases all strategy for outreach on two major premises. First, the center was birthed by intercessory prayer, and to this day, it is considered the most vital element of ministry strategy in West Rogers Park. Dr. Samuel Naaman reminds us that "[the] plan is not from anything but prayer: seeking God daily and having an expectation and anticipation that God is going to move among Muslims. You go on your knees and shake the strongholds" (interview with author, January 11, 2008). Second, everything that takes place at the center is founded in community and friendship, and it is contextualized with the purpose of outreach to South Asian Muslims and Hindus. For the sake of this research, we will focus on the element of outreach to Muslims.

SAFC's strategy begins with a search. First, they find the Muslims in their community. It is very unlikely that one would find Muslim seekers sitting in a local church congregation on a Sunday morning, but Muslims will be in the mosque. It is the primary link to the community. Visits to the mosque, and interaction with the leaders and attendees, provide invaluable insight into the particular group it serves. The ethnic and social composition at the mosque gives strong indication of what Christian mission will need to be in that specific community. Though the mosque will not favor evangelism efforts, a Christian guest will generally be warmly welcomed. Friendships are often forged at mosques, and mosque leaders are generally gracious and collaborative in community and relational contexts.

South Asian Friendship Center immerses itself in the community. Frequenting local businesses; eating in local restaurants and shopping in neighborhood stores are wonderful means of engaging in meaningful acquaintances and friendships with Muslims. One meets Muslims by establishing a presence in local schools, colleges and community centers, and by simply walking the streets and visiting the neighborhood.

In the context of friendship, SAFC positions itself to meet diaspora Muslims at their places of need. Its initial draw is its contemporary, comfortably furnished bookstore and reading room which offer secular and faith-related literature for all ages. It is a place where emphasis on hospitality and relationship supersede our Western marriage to the clock. In a room adjacent to the bookstore is a coffee/*chai* (tea) café where guests have free access to WiFi.

The relatively new reading room/café approach to outreach is particularly effective with "coconuts" (Mark Engle, interview with author, January 11, 2008), or second-generation diaspora Muslims in their twenties and thirties who are more open to new ideas than their first-generation relatives. Though they are South Asian on the outside, they have been raised in America and have been steeped in Anglo culture. The tension this "coconut" status creates in them, in the context of their Asian Islamic community, becomes a place of opportunity for those in outreach to them.

This opportunity is part of a new demographic that highlights the more youthful population group in West Rogers Park. Most of their ministry in the past has been to first-generation adults in their forties and children up to thirteen years of age through their neighborhood Kids Clubs. In the past, SAFC found that the twenty- and thirty-year-olds resisted connecting with them. The local mosques have called SAFC "the *Kaffir*"—Urdu word for unbeliever—place and warned them against going there. Though this kind of pressure has hindered outreach to a point, today's twenty- to thirty-plus-year-olds hunger for the atmosphere and services the center offers. Dr. Samuel Naaman calculates that a mere 1 to 2 percent of the Muslim South Asian community is "anti-SAFC" (interview with author, January 11, 2008). In a community where the more recently arrived diaspora Muslims are more deliberate about maintaining and growing their Islamic faith and heritage, this is a powerful testimony to the effectiveness of SAFC's presence there.

The South Asian Friendship Center deliberately helps newcomers in their assimilation process by offering ESL classes and opportunities for learners to practice new language skills.

They minister in the area of counseling, and have a staff who offers contextualized help to women who seek certain refuge at the SAFC. One woman was being harassed by a man at the mosque. She did not trust the mosque's leadership, so she asked SAFC to mediate and discuss the problem with them. Healthy discussions and collaboration to resolve the problem with mosque leaders sowed good seed among them (ibid.).

SAFC also has a full-time apologist who holds discussions on the Qur'an and the Bible. He helps Muslims with misconceptions and false teachings they have about Christianity and the Scriptures. He trains and equips volunteers to address and, if needed, defend their Christian faith. Sam Shamoun is a gifted teacher who regularly guest-lectures at colleges and universities.

Dr. Samuel Naaman recalls that "in the Old Testament, the motif was 'come and see what the Lord is doing.' In the New Testament the motif is 'go and tell what the Lord has done'" (ibid.). He defends SAFC's commitment to street evangelism by acknowledging that "Muslims will not show up at church, therefore we must go to them. The church cannot be about mere attraction, but penetration" (ibid.). SAFC evangelizes up and down Devon Avenue. On seasonable days and on Pakistani and Indian national holidays, the staff of SAFC blitz the Devon Avenue sidewalks by distributing Bibles, *Jesus* DVDs in Hindi and Urdu, the Psalms sung in Urdu set to contemporary music, and other Christian literature to eager recipients.

One August I took an Intercultural Urban Ministries class from Assemblies of God Theological Seminary to SAFC. It was India's Independence Day. Indians and Pakistanis dressed in colorful national attire crowded the streets for public celebrations. The SAFC staff asked if the class would join in their street evangelism efforts. We were eager to touch the lives of the multitudes of Muslims and Hindus on the streets that day. As I handed out *Jesus* film DVDs, Christian literature, and Christian Scripture on audio to so many Muslims, I thought of living and working in Pakistan. If I had tried to do the same thing on any street in Pakistan I would have been arrested, kicked out of the country, or even killed. My eyes filled with tears as many Muslims came to me and said, "You gave my friend a movie about Jesus; do you have one for me?" From that day I realized the incredible opportunity the local church in America has to reach diaspora Muslims with the gospel.

Though it does not look like a church, SAFC is the face of the local church in West Rogers Park. Center missionaries and staff see themselves as a church and as an extension of a faithful group of local churches who collaborate with them. They have enabled the planting of a local convert-friendly church in West Rogers Park as part of this collaborative outreach effort. SAFC receives its support from an interdenominational cohort comprised of the Christian Missionary Alliance, the Evangelical Free Church, The Bible Church, the Assemblies of God, and some independent charismatic congregations. They welcome volunteers, and SAFC encourages local church involvement by providing seminars that help equip the local church to reach Muslims in their own communities.

While the purpose of my research at South Asian Friendship Center was not evaluative, I came away from my experience there rechallenged by the call to reach Muslims for Christ and encouraged by the opportunities God gives us for success among them. I saw good models of everything I expected to see, and I learned many new things about contextualized outreach to diaspora Muslims in America.

The one question I had at the end of my time with SAFC was particularly relevant to a specific premise for outreach: that to be effective among diaspora Muslims in America we have to be people of Pentecostal power. Dr. Dudley Woodberry, professor of Islamic Studies at the School of International Studies at Fuller Theological Seminary, recently wrote an article for *Christianity Today* entitled, "Why Muslims Follow Jesus: The Results of a Survey of Converts from Islam" (Woodberry 2007). In it, he records the results of a survey that tallied the responses of 750 Muslims from 30 countries and 50 ethnic groups who embraced Christ between 1990 and 2007. Ranked among their answers to the question asking why they decided to follow Christ, they listed "the power of God and answered prayers, healing, and deliverance from demonic powers" as their second most motivating factor, and "dreams and visions of Christ" as their fourth (Woodberry 2007). I inquired about the absence of the element that depends on the power of the Holy Spirit demonstrated in signs, wonders, and miracles, and Mark Engle admitted that the multidenominational constituency of workers at the Center made that a sensitive issue. He does, however, recognize the need to begin praying publicly for God to perform signs, wonders, and miracles among Muslims in the community.

Conclusion

A close friend and colleague of mine in mission to the Muslim world once shared a powerful analogy depicting the chances of unreached Muslims to hear an adequate presentation of the gospel in America as opposed to overseas. Its essence is what motivates us in our work among unreached Muslims in their homelands, and it is what must motivate the church in America to reach the lost on her own shores. The illustration follows:

> Being "lost" in America is like falling off the back of a sailboat in Lake Michigan 100 yards off Chicago's Navy Pier on July 4th at noon.
>
> Being "lost" almost anywhere in the Muslim world is like falling off the back of an ore freighter in the middle of Lake Michigan in a raging gale at midnight.
>
> In both of those scenarios, you could drown. But the probability of your being saved (hearing and having opportunity to respond to the Gospel) is vastly different in each case. (E-mail message to author, January 12, 2008)

Logic dictates that the diaspora Muslim in America has greater opportunity to accept Christ as a diaspora Muslim than he ever had while in his home country. Will the local church in America respond to this opportunity to reach Muslims on her shores by offering salvation's lifeline to them while she has the chance? Is it also possible that a church awakened to the cry of the lost Muslim on her own shores might be awakened to the critical need for workers on faraway shores? This is all doable, and I believe that God is calling us all to the task, now.

References

AD2000 and Beyond. (1999). *The 100 Gateway Cities in the 10/40 Window*. Retrieved from http://www.ad2000.org/1040city.htm.

Bagby, I., Perl, P. M., & Froehle, B. T. (2001). *The mosque in America: A national portrait*. Retrieved from http://www.allied-media.com/AM/mosque_study.htm#2.

Bakke, R. (1997). *A theology as big as the city.* Downers Grove, IL: InterVarsity Press.

_____. (1987). *The urban Christian: Effective ministry in today's urban world.* Downers Grove, IL: InterVarsity Press.

Barton, J. L. (1918). *The Christian approach to Islam.* Boston, MA: Pilgrim Press.

Batey, R. A. (1991). *Jesus and the forgotten city: New light Sepphoris and the urban world of Jesus.* Grand Rapids, MI: Baker.

Bethel University Heart and Mind. (n.d.). Retrieved from http://www.bethel.edu/alumni/HeartMind/07summer/missions.html.

Monga Bay. (2002). Cities and urban areas in Indonesia with population over 100,000. Retrieved from http://www.mongabay.com/igapo/Indonesia.htm.

Conn, H. M., & Ortiz, M. (Eds.). (2001). *Urban ministry: The kingdom of God, the city, and the people of God.* Downers Grove, IL: InterVarsity Press.

Huntington, S. P. (2005). *Who are we? America's great debate.* London: Simon & Schuster.

Ludden, J. (2006, May 9). 1965 Immigration law changed face of America. *NPR.* Retrieved from http://www.npr.org/templates/story/story.php?storyId=5391395.

McCurry, D. (2001). *Healing the broken family of Abraham: New life for muslims.* Colorado Springs, CO: Ministries to Muslims.

McDowell, B. A., & Zaka, A. (1999). *Muslims and Christians at the table: Promoting biblical understanding among North American Muslims.* Phillipsburg, NJ: P&R Publishing.

Mooney-Melvin, P. (2005). *Encyclopedia of Chicago: West Ridge.* The Electronic Encyclopedia of Chicago. Retrieved from http://www.encyclopedia.chicagohistory.org/pages/1341.html.

Pocock, M., & Henriques, J. (2002). *Cultural change and your church: Helping your church thrive in a diverse society.* Grand Rapids, MI: Baker Books.

Rosen, H. (1999). Jewish United Fund news: Neighborhood Stories. *JUF News.* Retrieved from http://www.juf.org/news/neighborhood.aspx?id=9610.

Salmans, S. (2007). Muslims in America. *Trust: The Pew Charitable Trusts.* Retrieved from http://www.pewtrusts.org/our_work_report_detail.aspx?id=32854.

South Asian Friendship Center. (n.d.). Retrieved from http://www.safcbookstore.com.

Stark, R. (2006). *Cities of God: The real story of how Christianity became an urban movement and conquered Rome.* New York: HarperCollins.

Strange, J. F. (2001). *Sepphoris was the ornament of all Galilee.* Retrieved from http://www.bibleinterp.com/articles/sepphoris.htm.

Watt, M. (1953). *Muhammad at Mecca.* London: Oxford at the Clarendon Press.

West Rogers Park/West Ridge Historical Society. History of our area. Retrieved from http://www.rpwrhs.org/index.php?option=com_content&view=section&id=8&Itemid=11.

Woodberry, J. D., Shubin, R. G., & Marks, G. (2007, October 24). Why Muslims follow Jesus: The results of a recent survey of converts from Islam. *Christianity Today.* Retrieved from http://www.christianitytoday.com/ct/2007/october/42.80.html.

Index

9/11, 265–66
10/40 window, 21, 258

A
Abimelech, 81
Abraham, 121
Adam, 88, 129
advocacy, 52–53, 64, 68–69, 73, 107
Afghanistan, 257, 263, 265
Afghani, 74
Africa, 22, 25, 38, 40, 42, 44, 191, 200, 209
    African, 200, 203–13, 238
        communities, 170
        diaspora, 44, 206
        sub-Saharan, 125
Ambrose, 62
America(n). *See* United States of America.
American Society of Missiology (ASM), 111, 201
Antioch, 36, 93, 257, 259–60
anxiety, 186, 189–90, 192, 196–97
Appadurai, 46–47, 54
Arabia, 256
Arian, 60, 62, 67, 73
    heresy, 60
Arius
    heresy, 62
Armenia, 61, 71
Arthur, John, 204, 206
asceticism, 60, 72
Asia, 19, 24–25, 32, 36, 38, 40, 42, 104–05, 125, 200, 238, 255
    Asian, 159, 170, 262–63, 267
Asia Minor, 60–62, 67, 71–72, 93

Asian Theological Seminary (ATS), 106–07
    Center for Transformational Urban Leadership (CTUL), 106
    Transformation Urban Leadership (TUL), 106–08
Assemblies of God, 255, 269
Association of Religion and Data Archives (ARDA), 141, 143
Athanasius, 62
Athens, 36, 60, 259–60
Augustine, 60, 80
Awuah, Alfred K., 210

B
Babylon, 36, 81–82, 86, 91, 93, 121, 258–59
Babylonian
    exile, 36
Bakke, Ray, 54, 120, 127, 183
Bandy, Tom, 175
Barrett, David, 21, 24, 42–43
Basil of Caesarea, 59–74
basileas, 64, 69–72, 74
Bass, Dorothy, 224
Benefiel, Ron, 182
Berachah Home for Healing, 126
Berlin Wall, 20, 237, 243
Bhutan, 151–52
    Bhutanese, 181
Bible, 21, 36, 83–84, 91, 94, 98–101, 104, 106–09, 114, 121–22, 223, 245, 258–60, 268
    biblical, 9, 20, 36–37, 45, 54, 73, 84, 90–93, 99, 102, 104, 113, 120, 124, 128, 132, 164, 176, 200, 260, 266

themes, 84, 90
college/school, 1, 97–98, 100
Scripture, 37, 39, 69, 77, 84–85, 87–89, 91–92, 122–23, 173, 203, 225, 258, 261, 268
study, 109, 132
Bonhoeffer, Dietrich, 241
border pedagogy, 102, 108
Bosch, David, 22
Bosnia, 237
Bosnian, 145
Brazil, 6, 29, 151
Bristol, 13
Britt, David, 183
Brown, Peter, 68
Burma, 151–52
Burundi, 44, 152
Bush, Luis, 21

C

Caesarea, 59–68, 70–72
Caesarean, 63, 66, 69
Cain, 36, 80–81, 83, 87, 121, 258
Canaan, 81, 121
Canada, 44, 139–44, 146, 148–54, 156
Cape Town, 21, 39
Cappadocia, 59–64, 67, 72
Carey, William, 22, 140
Caribbean, 40, 161, 212
Carthage, 69
Center for Research on Canadian Evangelicalism, 141
Central Africa, 22
Central Asia, 24, 31
Chaldeans, 121
Chambers, Robert, 105
Chan, Kim Wing, 26
Chicago, 11, 27, 30, 124, 155, 205, 210, 253–54, 258, 260–62, 264, 270
Chicago Council on Global Affairs, 11
children, 7, 13, 63–64, 67, 70, 80, 143, 226, 229–30, 236–37, 248, 267
China, 22, 24, 26–27, 40, 150
Chinese, 26–27, 50, 161, 167
China Inland Mission, 22
Christian, 9, 13, 20, 22, 29, 38–39, 42–44, 46–47, 50, 54, 59–60, 62–63, 67–68, 71–74, 89, 91, 98–100, 104, 106, 110, 112–13, 120–21, 125–27, 130, 133, 135, 164, 172, 200–04, 207, 209–14, 219, 222, 224–25, 228, 233, 244, 247–51, 256–57, 263–64, 267–68
anti-Christian, 43
non-Christian, 22, 43, 71, 126, 202, 204, 213, 244, 247–48, 251
workers, 7, 98, 100
Christian and Missionary Alliance, 13, 126, 269
Christianity, 5, 29, 37, 42–43, 62, 97, 109, 112, 120, 132, 144, 153, 200, 207, 212, 220, 228–29, 240, 243, 259–60, 268
Christianity Today, 269
Chrysostom, John, 60
church
fathers, 59
growth, 5, 183, 193, 241, 244, 248
movement, 139, 183
history, 98–99, 103, 114
immigrant. *See* immigrant.
leadership, 44–45, 184, 211, 230
local, 30, 97–98, 115, 160, 164, 211–12, 253–54, 256, 258, 264, 266, 269–70
planting, 5, 11, 29–31, 106, 112, 140, 142, 144, 154–55, 203, 233–34, 238–50, 255
modern, 5
urban. *See* urban.
city
case studies of, 43
escape of, 119, 123
negative view/stereotypes of, 2–3, 12, 87
riots, 97–98, 116
secularization of the, 38
transformation of, 90
City Mentoring Program (CMP), 247–50
class, 3, 29, 51, 103, 164–65, 167, 176, 207
Claudius, 61
Clayman, Chris, 7
communication, 10–11, 60, 65, 83, 106, 156, 172, 175
community, 1, 8, 13, 24, 29, 63, 67, 71–74, 87, 89, 99, 101, 103, 106–07, 111, 124, 131, 159, 160–61, 164, 168, 170–72, 176, 181, 183, 185–88, 193–96, 202, 210–11, 213, 220–21, 225–27, 229–30, 235, 246, 253–54, 257, 262–67, 269
development. *See* development.
compassion, 13–14, 43, 82, 87–88, 91

Congregations in Transitional Neighborhoods (CTNs), 181–87, 189–93, 196–97
Conn, Harvie, 35, 37, 39, 41–43, 45, 48, 54, 84, 88, 120
conquest, 5, 81, 257
Constantine, 60, 62, 68
Constantinople, 60–61
conversion, 88, 90, 93, 120, 125, 133, 142, 202, 241–42, 244–45, 249
convert, 9, 23, 111, 125–26, 132, 212, 221, 255, 260, 269
Corinth, 36, 93, 259–60
Council of Nicaea, 62
covenant, 87, 89, 197, 209
   new, 123
   old, 123
Cox, Harvey, 54, 127
cross-cultural, 13, 49, 108, 111, 201, 255, 266
cultural, 3, 10–11, 20, 22, 28, 31, 35, 43, 46–47, 51–53, 64, 88, 106, 108, 111, 113, 153, 170, 176, 186, 208, 210–12, 219–20, 225, 229, 234, 236, 250, 253, 262–65
   barriers, 7, 13, 113
   creativity, 50
   diversity. *See* diversity.
   ghetto, 3
   insensitivity, 43
Cultural Mandate, 88, 128–32
culture, 5, 7, 9–10, 20, 23, 31, 43, 47–50, 88, 107–08, 124, 132, 161, 167, 169–70, 176, 187, 210, 212, 228, 236, 238–41, 244–46, 251, 254, 260, 263–67
Czech Republic, 235, 237

D

da Silva, Jose, 44
Daley, Brian, 65
Damascus, 36, 257
Daniel, 36
Darfur, 44
Davey, Andrew, 43
debt, 59, 63, 66, 133, 172
development, 10, 12, 24, 42, 60, 88, 99, 105, 107, 120, 132, 144, 153, 156, 212, 220, 222, 228, 234, 236–37, 240, 248
   community, 8
   urban, 12, 234
Devil, 83, 223
   Satan, 86
Dinan, Andrew, 69, 72
discipleship, 52, 92–93, 121, 128
discourse
   prophetic, 64–65, 67, 73
diversity, 7, 10, 13, 41–43, 50, 166–67, 195–96, 205, 262
   cultural, 6, 97, 166
   ethnic, 106
Dominican Republic, 203, 212
drugs, 120, 124, 127, 129–31, 133, 135, 166, 235
Dykstra, Craig, 224

E

East Asia, 31
Ecclesiology, 184, 197, 242
   ecclesiastical calling, 60, 68
economy, 48
   capitalist, 45
Eden, 80–81
Edict of Milan, 37
Edu-Bekoe, 212
Egypt, 81, 98, 122
Elijah, 70
Ellul, Jacques, 54, 77–82, 84–94, 121–23, 126
Emerson, Michael, 160, 162, 171
Enoch, 36, 81, 258
Ephesus, 36, 93, 159
Essenes, 92
eternity, 66, 80, 93
Ethiopia, 207
ethnic, 6, 45, 50, 93, 97, 106, 161, 170, 174, 176, 236, 239, 263, 267
   conflicts, 44
   group, 31, 44, 161, 186, 207, 211, 220, 251, 262, 269
   identity, 31
   profiles, 28
ethnicity, 3, 20, 28, 106, 113, 165, 167, 212
ethnolinguistic, 20, 22–23
ethnos, 20

Europe, 37–38, 40, 42, 77, 124, 160, 207, 236, 239
European, 99, 170, 242, 255, 263

cities/villages, 204, 235
racism, 38
Eusebius of Vercellae, 60
Eustathius of Sebaste, 60, 70
evangelical, 1, 13–14, 21, 31, 53–54, 73–74, 80, 107, 109, 120, 139–49, 152, 154–56, 203, 233, 239, 250, 255
theology, 13, 77, 106
white, 1, 13–14
Evangelical Missiological Society (EMS), 111, 200–01
evangelism, 11, 13, 23, 43, 46, 52, 54, 64, 72–73, 92–93, 111–12, 141, 164, 201, 208, 244, 246, 267–68
E1, 20
E2, 20
E3, 20
evangelization
global, 1, 9, 28
world, 20, 22, 32, 54
Eve, 129
exploitation, 4, 7, 12, 86

F

faith, 9, 13–14, 22–23, 43, 62–63, 66–67, 74, 91, 121, 142, 153, 176, 200, 202–04, 207–08, 213–14, 219–21, 223–25, 228, 230, 233, 239, 244–45, 267–68
commitment, 4
Fischer, Claude, 3, 10
Foreign Policy, 11
Fortune 500, 11
France, 150–51, 235, 242
French, 121, 170
monarchy, 98
Revolution, 98
Freedman, Jonathan, 3, 10
freedom, 3–5, 264–65
Friedman, Thomas, 26
frontier missions. *See* missions.
Fuller Theological Seminary, 269

G

Galatia, 36, 93
gang, 120, 124, 127, 131, 135, 226
Garrison, David, 30, 239–40
gender, 165, 167

genocide, 44
Gentiles, 36, 93, 112–13, 260
Germany, 6, 150–51, 233–41, 243–46, 249–50
German, 234–35, 237–46, 249–51, 262
Ghana, 199–200, 203, 207–13
Ghanaian, 206–08, 210–13
Gibeon, 36
Glenmary Research Center, 141
globalization, 9, 35, 39, 42, 45–54, 97, 109
overview of, 45
Gomorrah, 121
Good Samaritan, 67
gospel, 4–5, 7, 9, 13–14, 19–23, 29–31, 43, 65, 68, 71–73, 92, 105, 112, 140, 142–45, 154, 164, 166, 168, 170, 176, 183, 208, 213–14, 239, 246, 250–51, 253, 255, 258, 264, 266, 269–70
access, 21, 31, 154
Graham, Billy, 53
Great Commandment, 90, 92, 112
Great Commission, 14, 22, 90, 112
Great Tribulation, 135
Greek, 14, 20, 63, 103–04, 258
Greenway, Roger, 13, 54, 93, 120, 127
Gregory of Nazianzus, 60, 62–65, 67, 69–70
Gregory of Nyssa, 62, 70
Guatemala, 20
Guatemala City, 20

H

Hanciles, Jehu, 203–04, 207, 212–13
Haney, Jim, 154
Hannerz, Ulf, 49–51, 54
Harvard Divinity School, 99
Hayden, Michael, 23
Hebrew, 103–04, 258, 262
Hellenism, 92, 260
Herbst, Michael, 240–43
hermeneutics, 84, 90, 93, 106–09
Hiemstra, Rick, 141
Hispanic, 165, 181, 203
Holman, Susan, 63–64
Holton, Robert, 51–53
Hong Kong, 11, 151
Horton, Arthur, 124
Hu, Ying, 26
human rights, 92

Hunter, George, 5
Hunter, Lorne, 142

I

immigrant, 7–8, 13, 23–24, 29–30, 44, 50–51, 99, 110, 155, 159–62, 165–66, 170, 199–208, 210–14, 220, 223, 226–27, 229, 236–38, 246, 248, 253, 255–56, 262–64
  churches, 9, 170, 207, 211–13, 219–20, 222–23, 230
immigration, 6, 23, 51, 205, 210, 236–39, 255
Immigration and Nationality Acts of 1965 and 1990, 110, 205
India, 22, 40, 150, 170, 202, 253, 258, 263–64, 268
  Indian, 253, 262–63, 268
Industrial Revolution, 38, 42, 48
injustice, 73, 91–92
inner city, 130, 133, 235–36
  slums, 12
International Christian Concern, 73
International Mission Board, 139, 154
  Global Research Department, 139, 152, 154
Iran, 151–52
Iraq, 151–52, 257, 265
Isaiah, 130
Islam, 253, 255–57, 268–69
Israel, 9, 36, 81, 87, 122, 163, 258–59

J

Japan, 125, 150
Jeremiah, 36
Jericho, 36, 81
Jerusalem, 36–37, 82–84, 88–89, 93, 121, 168, 255–57, 260
  New Jerusalem, 83, 93, 258
John the Baptist, 71
Johnstone, Patrick, 28–29
Jonah, 82, 87–88, 91
Joppa, 36
Joshua Project, 139, 152–54
Joseph, 66, 70, 72
Julian, 62
justice, 36, 43, 79, 91–92, 168, 263
  social, 92

K

Kai, Ying, 30
Kaiser, 85, 88
Kearney, A. T., 11
Keller, Tim, 9–10, 43, 247
Kentucky, 145–46
Kenya, 151, 207
Kingdom of God, 29, 36, 90–91, 143, 153, 161–62, 165, 167, 169, 171, 174, 194, 254
Kingswood, 13
Koetsier, C. Henk, 77
Korea, 202
  Korean, 170, 202, 262

L

Laodicea, 37, 260
Larbi, Kingsley, 211
Lasswell, H. D., 78
Latin, 37
Latin America, 31, 38, 40, 42, 161, 200, 203, 212–13
Latino, 161, 203
Latourette, Kenneth Scott, 31
Lausanne Congress on World Evangelization, 20–21, 39, 43–45, 53
linguistics, 20, 106, 113
Linthicum, Robert, 86, 89–90, 163, 168
Livingstone, David, 22
London, 11, 148, 220–21, 225–29, 236
Los Angeles, 6, 10–11, 181, 205, 258
Lot, 121
Louisville, 145
Lundy, David, 109

M

Macedonia, 19–21, 36, 93
majority world, 42, 98, 100–07, 109, 114–15
Malaysia, 125, 151
Mandryk, Jason, 141
Manhattan, 126
Manila, 106
marginalized, 13–14, 41, 107, 202, 212
Marsden, George M., 99, 101
Martin of Tours, 60
Massachusetts, 146–47
Mazaca, 61

McGavran, Donald, 5
McGuire, B. P., 71
McKinsey Global Institute, 27–28, 30
mega-regions, 35, 39, 48, 50–52, 54
megacity, 30, 50
Mexico, 8, 150, 203
Miami, 6, 205
Middle East, 24, 257–58, 262
migrants, 6, 8–9, 49, 51–52, 106, 110, 149–50, 155, 199–200, 202–06, 210, 213
migration, 6–9, 97, 109–10, 119, 139, 151, 153, 156, 200, 204, 206, 209, 214, 237
   circular migration, 8
   human mobility, 8
   repatriation, 8
missiology, 110–11, 155–56, 204, 260
   diaspora, 23, 98, 107, 109–13, 115, 153, 200–01, 204
   traditional, 111–12, 115, 201
missionary, 7, 22–24, 27–28, 30, 36, 67, 99, 113, 139–41, 154, 200–04, 207–09, 211–14, 248, 254, 260–61
   modern movement, 22, 31
missions
   agencies, 2, 7, 9, 20–21, 134
   field, 2, 14, 21, 31, 99, 199–201, 212
   frontier, 19–20
   history of, 14
   strategist, 28
   strategy, 6, 21, 31, 112, 139–41, 156, 255
   urban. *See* urban.
Mixtecas, 8
modernity, 45, 77–80, 87, 94, 240
Modestus, 67–68
Mohammad, 256
monasticism, 71
monocultural, 7
Monsma, Timothy, 54, 93
Montreal, 44, 148, 155
Moody Bible Institute, 253–54
Mubarak, 98
multicultural, 7, 108, 188, 195–96, 226, 237–38, 248
multigenerational, 108
multinational corporations (MNC), 48, 51
Muslim, 42, 213, 253–54, 256–58, 260–61, 264–70
   diaspora, 253–58, 264–67, 269–70

N

Naaman, Samuel, 253–54, 261, 266–68
nation-state, 20, 31, 41, 46–50
nationalism, 5, 20, 48
Nepal, 151
   Nepali, 145
New Macedonia, 19–21
New Testament, 9, 20, 36, 88, 90, 92, 103–04, 121, 124, 132, 245, 259–60, 268
New York City, 4, 6–11, 43, 110, 155, 161–62, 210, 220–21, 258
New Zealand, 125
Nigeria, 151, 206
   Nigerian, 154, 170
Nimrod, 81, 87
Nineveh, 36–37, 82, 87–88, 90, 258
Non-governmental organization (NGO), 7, 50
North Africa, 69, 258
North America, 6, 38, 54, 73, 98–102, 109–11, 114–15, 119, 124, 140–41, 146, 154–56, 181, 184, 186, 197–99, 204, 247, 255
Nyack College (Missionary Training Institute), 126

O

Old Testament, 9, 36, 80–81, 88, 90, 103–04, 123, 258, 268
Operation World, 141
oppression, 86, 91–92
Ortiz, Manuel, 39, 54
outreach, 92–93, 165, 193, 195, 201–03, 211–13, 243–44, 255, 258, 260, 263–67, 269
Outreach Canada, 142–43

P

paganus, 37
Pakistan, 151, 170, 253–54, 257, 261–62, 264, 268
   Pakistani, 161, 254, 262–63, 268
Paris, 11, 50, 98
participatory rural appraisal (PRA), 105
Paul (Saul), 5, 21, 36, 92–93, 132, 164, 166–68, 260

Peace Corps, 20
penes, 63
Pentecost, 199–201, 207–13, 221–23, 228, 260, 269
people groups, 6, 20–23, 28, 113, 145–46, 154–55, 199–200, 248
    least reached, 145–46
    unreached, 19, 21, 23, 30–31, 113, 140, 145, 149, 152–56, 199, 255
Persia, 61, 259
Pew Forum on Religion and Public Life, 141
Philippines, 106, 203
    Filipino, 106, 169
Pisidian, 36
pluralism, 7, 13
Poland, 203, 237
Pontus, 60–61
poor, 13, 25, 29, 51, 60, 63–74, 86, 91–92, 103, 105–09, 160, 181
pornography, 133
Portugal, 124
postmodernism, 79–80, 97, 109, 240, 245
poverty, 1, 12, 29, 63, 65–67, 71–72, 91–92, 97, 103, 220
premillennialist, 135
prostitution, 120, 126, 129, 135, 235
ptochoi, 63, 66

Q

Quebec, 141, 148
    Quebecois, 140
Qur'an, 256, 268

R

race, 93, 165–67, 205, 256
racism, 38, 226–27
Reagan, Ronald, 20
Reformation, 38, 233, 251
refugee, 9, 44, 49–50, 151–52, 181
Rehoboam, 81
religion, 14, 42, 51, 143, 166, 203, 213, 256–57, 263–64
Renaissance, 38
Resen, 81
Roberts, Samuel, 183
Robertson, Roland, 45

Roman Catholic, 202–03, 236
Rome, 11, 36–37, 62, 259–60
    Roman, 61, 67–68, 259–60
        army, 61
        church, 21
        Empire, 36–37, 62, 73
        government, 61
        province, 61
Roschke, Volker, 241
rural, 1, 6, 12–14, 19, 24–27, 29–30, 37, 40, 86, 101, 105–06, 112, 119, 121–22, 124, 128, 130, 134–35, 170, 172, 181, 204, 258–60
Russia, 6, 151, 237, 263
    Russian, 170, 262
Rwanda, 44

S

salvation, 67, 82, 125–26, 135, 142, 187, 221, 223, 230, 270
Salvation Army, 24
Sassen, Saskia, 49, 52
Satan. *See* Devil.
Schaller, Lyle, 176
Schwarz, Christian, 241
Schwarz, Fritz, 241
Scribner, Dan, 154
Seoul, 11, 201
Serenianus, 62
sex, 128, 225, 229–30
    sexual
        addictions, 127
        intercourse, 133
        irresponsible, 226
        promiscuity, 120
    sexuality, 128, 133, 226
Simpson, A. B., 13, 126–27
Singapore, 11
Sioux Falls, 110
slavery, 59, 67, 81, 122
Slovakia, 237
    Slovakian
        literature, 3
Smith, Steve, 30
social
    barriers, 13
    contract, 3
    justice. *See* justice.

mobility, 11
networks, 8–9, 155
patterns, 3
services, 12–13, 111, 209
welfare, 12
Sodom, 86, 91, 121
Solomon, 81
Somalia, 152, 207
  Somalis, 140
South Africa, 125
South Asian Friendship Center (SAFC), 253–54, 261–69
South Dakota, 110
Southern Baptist Convention, 154
Soviet Union, 20, 203
Sozomen, 62, 70
Spain, 21, 150, 257
Spanish, 20, 161, 181, 196
spiritual, 5, 22, 29, 36, 60, 65, 68, 71–72, 83, 89, 93, 130, 132, 135, 166–69, 172, 176, 211, 213, 222–23, 233, 248, 256
  warfare, 89, 94
Sterk, A., 68, 70, 72
Stott, John, 53
Strachan, Kenneth, 30
suburban, 1, 13, 126, 128, 169–70, 253, 256
  suburbia, 120
sustainability, 12, 41
Sweden, 255
Switzerland, 235, 242
Sydney, 11
Syria, 61, 71

T

Tanakh, 36
Taylor, Hudson, 22
Thaumaturgus, Gregory, 59, 62, 64
The Christian and Missionary Alliance Weekly, 126
theological, 60–62, 72, 77, 80, 99, 102–03, 113–14, 163, 176, 200, 242, 245, 247, 249–51, 253, 258, 260
theology, 1, 9, 13, 59–60, 62, 72, 77, 80, 84, 87, 90–94, 98–100, 103–04, 106, 107, 112, 114, 132, 161, 165, 240–41, 247, 251, 260
  evangelical. *See* evangelical.
  Trinitarian, 59
Tilton, Jennifer, 226

Tira, Joy, 201
Tokyo, 11, 50
Toronto, 6, 148, 155
Tower of Babel, 36–37, 81, 87, 121, 258
traditional training program, 98, 100
traditionalism, 4
transitional neighborhoods, 181–84
  congregations engaging, 181–82
transnationalism, 44, 47, 49–52, 97, 109, 112, 155–56, 213
Trinity Evangelical Divinity School, 254
Trinity University, 254

U

Ulfilas, 67
unemployment, 59, 120, 207
United Nations, 6, 39, 41, 101, 150
  2007 report, 40
  Population Division, 6, 22
United States of America, 6, 10, 26, 40, 98, 110, 124, 139–42, 144, 146, 149–54, 156, 162, 166, 170, 199–200, 202–14, 226, 253–56, 258, 261, 263–67, 269–70
  American, 73, 98, 110, 197, 210, 213–14, 255, 263–65
United States Religious Landscape Survey of 2008, 141
unreached people groups. *See* people groups.
urban
  church planting, 106, 233–34, 238–40, 246–49
  complexities, 14
  compression, 3, 7
  context, 2–3, 5–6, 13, 30, 59, 64, 73–74, 98, 101–04, 106, 114, 116, 142, 156, 161, 201, 213, 220, 226–28, 230
  development. *See* development.
  dwellers, 24, 28, 30, 40, 42, 131, 135
  ministry, 1, 15, 28, 54, 59–60, 97–98, 100–03, 105–07, 109, 114–15, 120, 126–27, 134, 200, 204–05, 247, 259, 261
    training, 97–98, 100–02, 114
      relevant, 97–98, 100–02, 104, 109, 114–15
  missions, 19, 113, 159

population, 2–3, 25, 27–28, 40, 43, 101, 103, 236
renewal, 121
research, 139–41, 155–56
training models, 97
workers, 97–98, 100, 103–04, 114–15
youth ministry, 219–21, 223–24, 226, 228–30
  in immigrant churches, 219–20
urbanization, 2, 5, 12, 19, 24–29, 32, 35, 37–42, 45, 78, 94, 97, 101, 110, 120–21, 159–62, 170, 234, 236
  global, 19, 27, 101
urbanized training model, 97–98, 101
  twenty-first century, 97–98, 101–02, 109
URBANUS, 44
Utah, 146–47

V

Valens, 62, 67, 69
Van Engen, Charles, 183–84
Vicedom, Georg, 241
Vietnam, 150, 152, 203
  Vietnamese, 202
violence, 1, 63, 119, 130, 228

W

Wagner, C. Peter, 184
Währisch-Oblau, Claudia, 207
war, 93, 110, 121, 237
  Cold War, 20
  World War II, 1, 39
    post, 1
Warner, Stephen, 202
wealth, 8, 27, 29, 38, 59, 63, 66–67, 69, 73, 110, 125, 142
Wesley, John, 13
West Africa, 7, 203, 210
Western, 20, 29, 38, 78–80, 101–04, 108, 126, 149–50, 170, 199–202, 209–10, 264–65, 267
  Europe, 6, 204, 233, 240
  nations, 6
  Westerner, 94, 102
White, Randy, 164, 176
Wichern, Johann Hinrich, 241
widows, 13

Winter, Ralph, 20–21
Wirth, Louis, 3, 10
Woo, Rodney, 160, 162, 171
Woodberry, Dudley, 269
World Bank, 199
World Christian Database, 139
worship, 67, 86, 89, 111, 167, 170, 188–90, 195–96, 208, 222, 224, 228–29, 242–43, 245, 247–48, 251, 257, 262

Y

Yale Divinity School, 99
YMCA, 24
youth ministry
  urban. *See* urban.

Z

Zambezi River, 22
Zimmerman, Johannes, 241
Zion, 36

Scripture Index

Genesis 1, 85, 128
Genesis 1:26, 85
Genesis 1:27, 85
Genesis 1:26–28, 85
Genesis 1:28, 128
Genesis 2, 128
Genesis 2:8, 258
Genesis 2:15, 129
Genesis 3:16–19, 129
Genesis 3:21, 129
Genesis 3:23–24, 129
Genesis 4:10–24, 121
Genesis 4:17, 36, 258
Genesis 5:1–2, 85
Genesis 10:12, 81
Genesis 11:1–9, 121, 258
Genesis 11:4, 36
Genesis 14:8–24, 121
Genesis 18:23–32, 37
Genesis 19:1–29, 121
Numbers 21:2, 122
Psalm 9; 51; 69; 122; 132, 36
Psalm 14, 65
Psalm 55:9–11, 119
Psalm 127:1, 87
Psalm 132:13–14, 37
Proverbs 19:2, 140
Isaiah 2; 56; 60, 36
Isaiah 35:3–4, 130
Isaiah 47:9–14, 82
Isaiah 65, 90
Jeremiah 21, 82
Jeremiah 29:4–7, 10, 82, 90
Jeremiah 29:7, 36–37, 91, 163

Jeremiah 32:28–32, 37
Jeremiah 51:8–9, 82
Ezekiel 16, 82, 89
Daniel 4:27, 36
Jonah 3:10, 37
Jonah 4:11, 37
Nahum 3:7, 37
Zephaniah 2:13, 37
Zephaniah 3:5, 37
Matthew 9:35–11:1, 259
Matthew 10, 82
Matthew 11:20, 82
Matthew 13:5–7, 126
Matthew 14:13, 123
Matthew 19, 66
Matthew 23:37, 121
Mark 6:6, 5:6, 259
Luke 5:37, 114
Luke 10, 82
Luke 13:34, 37
Luke 21:20, 83–84
Luke 21:20–22, 37
Luke 21:21, 135
John 1:14, 266
John 17:21, 169
Acts 1:4, 260
Acts 1:8, 255
Acts 9:6, 36
Acts 14:17, 85
Acts 17:26–27, 85, 261
Acts 18:10, 37
Acts 28:30, 260
Romans 1:18–3:20, 85
Romans 5:12–21, 85

Romans 10:14–15, 255, 261
Romans 13, 92
Romans 13:1–7, 164
Romans 14, 166
Romans 14:13–19, 165
Romans 15, 166
Romans 15:21, 21
1 Corinthians 9, 164
1 Corinthians 9:19–23, 164
1 Corinthians 12:27, 166
1 Corinthians 14, 167–68
1 Corinthians 14:24–25, 167
1 Corinthians 14:33, 128
2 Corinthians 5:14–18, 166
Ephesians 2:1–3, 85
1 Thessalonians 4:11, 131–32
1 Thessalonians 4:12, 132
2 Thessalonians 2:6–7, 85
Hebrews 4:7, 135
Hebrews 4:8, 136
Hebrews 6:4–6, 135
James 3:9, 85
1 Peter 2:13, 164
2 Peter 2:22, 120
2 Peter 3:9, 85
Revelation 2–3, 36
Revelation 3:14–22, 37
Revelation 18, 36
Revelation 18:1–24, 121
Revelation 18:14, 82
Revelation 21, 37
Revelation 21:2, 258
Revelation 21–22, 36
Revelation 22:3, 258

www.ingramcontent.com/pod-product-compliance
Lightning Source LLC
Chambersburg PA
CBHW071230070526
44583CB00017B/2126